the fifth trimester

the fifth trimester

THE WORKING MOM'S GUIDE
TO STYLE, SANITY, AND BIG SUCCESS
AFTER BABY

Lauren Smith Brody

DOUBLEDAY

New York   London   Toronto   Sydney   Auckland

All rights reserved. Published in the United States by Doubleday,
a division of Penguin Random House LLC, New York,
and distributed in Canada by Random House of Canada, a division of
Penguin Random House Canada Limited, Toronto.

www.doubleday.com

DOUBLEDAY and the portrayal of an anchor with a dolphin
are registered trademarks of Penguin Random House LLC.

Book design by Maria Carella
Jacket design by Matt Chase

Library of Congress Cataloging-in-Publication Data
Names: Brody, Lauren Smith, author.
Title: The fifth trimester : the working mom's guide to style, sanity, and big success
after baby / by Lauren Smith Brody.
Description: New York : Doubleday, [2016] | Includes bibliographical references
and index.
Identifiers: LCCN 2016019667 | ISBN 9780385541411 (hardcover) |
ISBN 9780385541428 (ebook)
Subjects: LCSH: Working mothers. | Work and family. | Work-life balance.
Classification: LCC HQ759.48 .B76 2016 | DDC 306.3/6—dc23
LC record available at https://lccn.loc.gov/2016019667

MANUFACTURED IN THE UNITED STATES OF AMERICA

1 3 5 7 9 10 8 6 4 2

First Edition

To Ben, whose love makes me brave

Nothing can be more absurd than the practice that prevails in our country of men and women not following the same pursuits with all of their strength and with one mind, for thus, the state instead of being whole is reduced to half.

—PLATO

[Kids] don't remember what you try to teach them. They remember what you are.

—JIM HENSON

Your going-back-tomorrow guide to this book

✺

In a perfect world, you'd read the whole thing at a leisurely pace while pregnant. But if it's too late for that, here's a quick skim de la skim of a bunch of the tips inside. Zip on over to whatever info you need most now:

Contents

Introduction

As soon as I heard my husband's shower running, I changed my mind.

I'd been up since 4:30 a.m., hanging out on the couch, having a much calmer early labor than I'd imagined. My water hadn't broken, and the pain wasn't anything I couldn't handle. I'd felt just not-right enough to get out of bed, proud of myself for resisting the urge to nudge my sleeping spouse awake. Ben, who was finishing up his first year of medical residency at a big hospital nearby, worked hard. We both did. And I wasn't about to pull the rookie move of waking him up just to watch me have one manageable contraction every twenty minutes. If these things even were contractions. Surely I'd have at least one round of false labor, I thought.

By the time Ben's alarm went off at 6:15, I was pacing the floor, as much as one could pace in our little apartment.

"Definitely shower and go to work," I told him breezily, as he gave me a hug and wrinkled his forehead, looking one part skeptical, two parts impressed. "I'm fine. It's going to be so many hours." I figured—if this was even real—I'd call him when things got interesting. I'd grab a cab, and he'd leave his department and meet me a couple of floors down at Labor and Delivery. Simple. Low-maintenance mother-to-be. That's me. Plus, it was a Monday. I'd finished up my last day of work on Friday, spent the weekend getting organized like a maniac (nesting . . . right . . . that must have been nesting), and wanted at least half a day to sit around and do nothing for the first time since college. Maybe I'd go to a movie or watch all the junk TV I'd never had time for. I didn't even know which channels were the junky ones.

My cervix had other plans. Over the course of Ben's four-minute shower, I had two contractions. And as I leaned over the desk chair in the living room swaying my hips—in a way I'd never been comfortable doing on a dance floor—I changed my mind. We were having a baby. Today. Now.

On our way out the door, Ben grabbed the bag I'd so lovingly packed a full two months earlier: a blanket, a first little "going-home" outfit, our good camera, nursing bras, maternity yoga pants. We looked at each other, wide awake and thrilled. Here we go.

"Oh my God, wait!" I said as we buzzed for the elevator. "I forgot my folder!"

"Your folder?" he asked. "Why do you need a folder?"

I ran back in toward the bedroom, stopping to have another contraction leaning over that same chair—sway, sway, sway, done—and grabbed a yellow folder that held everything I would not want to be doing during my time in the hospital: insurance paperwork; maternity leave disability information from my employer, a big media company; and, yes, some actual work that I took with me from the office before tearfully hugging my boss at *Glamour* magazine goodbye on Friday. I'd do it in labor, I thought. Ha! There was a famous story inside my industry about a particularly She-Ra–like editor-in-chief who'd faxed back edited copy to the office minutes before pushing out her fifth child. My own boss's boss had taken a quick two-week leave with her first child, and was photographed and interviewed by *The New York Times* (dressed in Miu Miu, in her beautiful Soho loft) just days after having her second baby. This was what women did, I thought. They balanced!

You know how the rest of this story goes. I did not do any actual work at the hospital.

What I did do was: have a pain freak-out, then an immediate epidural (I'd arrived at four centimeters dilated—still proud of that). From the hospital bed, I did a little bit of texting, a lot of moaning, and made a couple of elated high-on-the-epidural phone calls to friends and family—not the office—and then, finally, I gave birth. Easily, thankfully, with my awesome husband cheering for me harder than he's ever even cheered for his beloved Pittsburgh Steelers. Our son was born. And with eyes nearly swollen shut and a face full of baby acne, he was the most gorgeous thing I'd ever seen. That work folder? It sat.

I brought the folder home from the hospital, and it sat some more. On a table right next to the bassinet, actually (like I said, small apartment). Eventually, it was covered up by piles of baby detritus: gifts, half-written thank-you notes, an unused Boppy. Still, it haunted me a bit every day. I knew it was there, a little time bomb, just ticking off the minutes until my twelve-week maternity leave would be over. Worried about money, I filled out the disability paperwork, then shoved everything else right back under that pile.

Our baby, Will, was six pounds of wonderful, but over those three months, I had what is kindly referred to as "a hard time." He wouldn't nurse well or soothe easily. He seemed so tiny; that "going-home" outfit I'd packed for him was miles too big. My body was torn up from top to bottom for weeks. I worried and had crazy, frightening thoughts. Young for parenthood—by NYC standards, anyway—I had no close friends who'd been through this yet. It took all I had just to stroll the carriage one block to the drugstore for diapers. A perfectly capable person, I'd made it through college, moved to New York City, broken into publishing, and was on leave from an executive-level position at one of the biggest magazines in the world. In my real life, my work life, I led an award-winning team of editors. I negotiated with celebrities (or, rather, with their "people," which is harder). I won awards and got promoted and edited stories urging the women of America to live full lives and demand what they deserved at work, and to do it all in fabulous shoes, damn it.

And now, suddenly, simply crossing the street with my newborn baby gave me heart palpitations.

After a few days, Ben went back to work, and his life resumed some semblance of normalcy, except for the crazy wife who now greeted him desperately at the door when he arrived home. Used to be, I was the one who worked late.

I told everyone that Will was an easy baby, assuming the problem in this equation was me. When he was fussy I relied, appreciatively, on the bible of baby soothing, Dr. Harvey Karp's *The Happiest Baby on the Block*. Dr. Karp advised swaddling, shushing, swinging, and a whole bunch of other *S* verbs meant to replicate the feeling of being in the womb. The first three months of a full-term baby's life, he explained, were actually premature. Because of the size of our brains and heads, human babies are born three months early and essentially have a "fourth trimester" outside of the womb. By around week twelve, the good doctor reassured me, my baby would start to wake up to the world. He'd laugh, hold his own head up, and look me in the eye and connect. He would be slightly less fragile and fussy, and maybe even start to sleep six hours in a row and nap at the same times every day. I just had to soldier on to week twelve.

Week twelve? The irony slapped me hard. That was exactly when I'd be going back to work.

And thus, the idea for this book was born right alongside my son. Sure enough, Dr. Karp was right. By about week eleven, the hormone clouds started to part over my head. I had loved my child from the beginning, but now he was giving something back. I experienced pure baby joy for the first time. And also, suddenly, work dread. I'd never disliked work, always loved the ladder climb and even the late nights. I adored the people I worked with: mostly women, a handful of cool, creative men. All so smart and funny. Incandescent personalities. These were people who preached the gospel of feminism and also gathered round the conference room TV together to watch the world debut of J. Lo's twins.

But the thought of leaving my baby—who now, newsflash, loved me back—killed me. How could I trust this nanny I'd just hired? How could I possibly pump enough milk to feed my child? How would I not make an idiot of myself on the job running on only four hours of sleep a night? This going-back-to-work thing was going to be hard. Maybe even harder than what I'd just gotten through.

And if I—a person with a stellar partner, a decent-paying job, a fair boss, and a supportive work environment—felt this ambivalent about looming working motherhood, surely millions of other women did, too.

What I needed was what's in this book.

(What I really needed, let's be honest, was three more months at home with my baby. But that wasn't an option because as the primary breadwinner back then, I also needed an income, and a career that didn't move on without me.)

So instead: I needed camaraderie. I needed new ideas and solutions. I needed the actual words to have the conversations that were going to make this transitional period surmountable.

I needed to know that it really was *just* a transitional period, simply a Fifth Trimester.

As predicted, reentry was rough at first. I hardly recognized myself. I sat in the same office as before, with that same yellow folder of work poking out of the pocket of my breast-pump bag on my commute, but I was a changed person with new priorities, and a new identity. I saw myself differently now that I was a mother. I could tell that my colleagues saw me differently, too. I'd never, ever, ever been the kind of worker to "just get by," and now that's what I felt like on a good day. At the office, I mostly kept it together. But at home, I picked fights with my husband over little things that were really about one big thing: He didn't feel as completely at the end of his rope as I did 24/7. I resented friends who made us all reservations for 9:00 p.m. dinners. On the phone, I worried my poor mother endlessly and only took her good advice after rejecting it, tearfully, first.

Thank God, it was all temporary. Just like my baby, this working mom had been simply thrown in over her head about three months too early. Maybe you've seen the pie charts friends post on Facebook about the United States' maternity leave policies compared with the other nations in the world. It's abysmal. In Croatia, women get more than thirteen months of paid leave. In the U.K., it's fifty weeks, also largely paid, that you split up with your spouse. In France, workers are paid for at least sixteen weeks at 100 percent of their salaries. Even Japan—a country that employs people with sticks to smush commuters onto the crowded subways so they get to work on time—grants mothers fourteen weeks at 60 percent pay.

Here in the United States, the Family and Medical Leave Act requires employers to hold a job for you for twelve weeks (*if* you've been there longer than a year, and work full-time, and your company employs more than fifty people)—unpaid. Zero dollars. The only countries with lousier stats than America are Papua New Guinea and Suriname. (Oman, which used to be on this naughty list, recently got with the program.)

The reality is that stronger parental leave policies do not negatively impact the economy at all. Of the seventeen countries in the world with the highest consistent economic performance, the United States is the only one that doesn't guarantee paid leave for new mothers. And the United States and Switzerland are the only ones of the bunch that don't also have guaranteed paid paternity leave.

Why? Why do American parents get so little when 182 other countries around the world prioritize paid leave? We're a young country, and we were founded on the American Dream: Work hard and move up fast so one generation laps the next. Don't look back, don't press pause. It's not that different from how I felt working in magazines in my twenties. I worked insane hours, often until 2:00 a.m. at one start-up. As a twenty-two-year-old editorial assistant in 2001, my annual salary was $30,000, but I took home nearly double that thanks to overtime. It was an investment in my future, I thought, and I got a lot of experience very quickly and moved up and out to bigger jobs at bigger magazines. I didn't realize back then that things actually would get less flexible as I advanced in my career.

The problem with U.S. maternity leave policies has become front-page news and talk show fodder as the situation gets more and more obviously wrong. More than half of mothers of infants under one year old are currently in the U.S. workforce. And as HBO's John Oliver so perfectly put it in his 2015 Mother's Day episode of *Last Week Tonight,* there's "nothing we wouldn't do for moms, apart from [this] one major thing." In late 2013, and again in 2015, the Family Act, a bill led by New York senator Kirsten Gillibrand and Connecticut congresswoman Rosa DeLauro, proposed twelve weeks off at two-thirds pay, financed by a minuscule 0.2 percent salary contribution to Social Security by all workers (to give you an idea, that would have been $60.00 of my editorial-assistant base salary annually). Sounds sensible, but it hasn't passed yet. Representative Carolyn Maloney from New York has been proposing some form of a similar bill on the federal stage, regularly, doggedly, since 2000. And in the 2016 primaries, the issue burned bright. Bernie Sanders cosponsored the Family Act, Hillary Clinton called for paid leave and affordable childcare as key components of her campaign, and Marco Rubio proposed tax credits for companies that offer paid leave. The plans were debated, but the general consensus on both sides of the aisle was that something must be done . . . or, at least, as Donald Trump put it, "Certainly there are a lot of people discussing it." But no dice, yet.

Meanwhile, that leaves the private companies out there to

decide to do better than required for new moms; perhaps you work at one of them like I did. Even still, only 11 percent of American workers in the private sector are eligible for paid family leave.

A few companies, blessedly, bravely, are sticking their necks out extra far to redefine the norm by offering much more. The tech and big finance industries in particular—booming, competitive, healthy companies fighting to woo and keep the best and the brightest workers—have made enormous strides recently. And guess who runs those companies? Parents. Sons and daughters. People who get the importance of supporting the next generation of workers and thinkers—and the mothers who turned their bodies inside out to give them life. When Richard Branson announced in June 2015 that Virgin Management, a division of his Virgin empire, would extend the new shared parental leave, nearly every news outlet showed pictures of him with his own three grandbabies, all born within the previous year. "As a father and now a grandfather," Branson blogged, "I know how magical the first year of a child's life is, but also how much work it takes." Hopefully soon that magic will be offered to the tens of thousands of Virgin employees who aren't top executives, too.

In March 2015, Vodafone, a massive telecom conglomerate in thirty countries, changed its policy globally to grant a minimum of sixteen weeks paid maternity leave to women who would then return to thirty-hour workweeks (at 100 percent pay) for the first six months they're back. This isn't just goodwill. Vodafone commissioned a report from auditing firm KPMG that showed that the money saved by retaining talent—by not losing good workers and having to search for and train new ones—would far outpace the cost of this new benefit. Globally, the report claims, businesses could actually save $19 billion per year by offering sixteen weeks of paid leave.

And for those economists who argue that these kinds of "accommodations" ultimately harm women's earning power and seniority—because businesses will be less likely to burden their budgets by hiring women—I offer up these two rebuttals:

1) Paid paternity leave. For every month of parental leave a
   father takes, a mother's future earnings increase by almost
   7 percent. And . . .
2) the sunny state of California, which began offering paid
   family leave in 2004. By 2010, 91 percent of businesses
   said that paid leave had a positive effect on profitability or
   no effect at all. And get this: Between 2007 and 2015 the
   percentage of women in director and highest-paid executive positions for companies based in California increased
   by 40 percent. To be clear, the percentage of women
   in those highest-level positions is still crap, at just over
   12 percent (just under the national average), but the graph
   is headed northward, and fast. (It's also worth noting here
   that longer maternity leave has been shown to increase
   job satisfaction.)

Changes in federal and state policies around new parenthood
absolutely can and should happen. But in my experience—having
worked for sixteen years with countless new mothers at all levels of
seniority—the most effective cultural changes come from within.
That headline-making policy at Vodafone? It was approved by a
male CEO, but the idea was pitched and championed by a woman,
Sharon Doherty, the company's Global Organisation and People
Development Director. Doherty had noticed that employee reten-
tion rates were higher in countries where the company was required
to offer a transitional period for women returning to work after
maternity leave. So here was one person, noticing one nuance in
her work environment, who acted on it and changed things not
just for her own company's employees but raised the bar a bit for
everyone, globally.

When I attended a small roundtable discussion with Chelsea
Clinton at the height of her mother's 2016 presidential campaign,
she told me that when she was born in 1979, Hillary's law firm—
the oldest west of the Mississippi—had no maternity-leave policy at all. "No one who had worked there and become a mother

had come back to work full-time," she shared. So Hillary wrote one, for both the lawyers and the support staff. "Parental leave is an important issue to my mom's heart because of her own story with me," Chelsea said, gesturing at her own then-nine-months-pregnant belly. "This is very much an issue she's been working on on a policy level but also literally on a personal level my whole life. We've come a long way, but we have a long way to go."

Call it Leaning In, call it Not Opting Out, but in order to achieve change—whether on a corporate policy level, or just at the water cooler—women have to stay in the game. And in order to stay in successfully, during those first few months back at work after a baby, you need some basic tools. You need to know how to have difficult conversations that mix personal and professional topics in ways you may not always find comfortable. You need to know how to do your job well and still feed your baby. You need to know how to trust someone else to care for your child while you're away from him, and to actually want your baby to adore that caregiver, without resenting the whole situation.

It took me a few years and a second baby to have the perspective to dive into this project. *The Fifth Trimester* started as a conversation with my downstairs neighbor and dear friend, Allison, while she was on leave from her job at a financial firm to care for her very premature twins (and to recover physically—she'd had a complicated delivery). Allison's experience was as hard as it gets, but she went back to work nine weeks after her boys were able to come home from the NICU, and then she got promoted, within eighteen months. I wanted to know how she did it, how we all did it. I kept talking, to friends, to coworkers, to any new mom in line at Starbucks, bleary-eyed, with a baby carriage and the telltale two iPhones (one for work, one for life).

Eventually, I got official about it and wrote a fifty-question survey and posted it online, asking American mothers to share all the intimate details of what worked and what didn't during their first three months back in the job after maternity leave. Hoping for one hundred answers, I ended up with 732 respondents from all over the country, hundreds of whom offered up their cell phone numbers and email addresses saying they'd love to talk. Just taking the survey, I heard again and again, was cathartic. I interviewed more than one hundred professionals of every background and talent: Fortune 500 executives, minimum wage earners, middle managers, business owners, freelancers, and independent contractors. I talked to single moms and primary breadwinners, women who worked because they had to or because they wanted to, or both.

Their answers and stories were eye-opening and quite validated the experience I'd had myself. Unsurprisingly, 75 percent of the women I surveyed wished that they had been able to take a longer maternity leave, but given the option of how much extra time they'd want, the most common response was that "a few more months" would have made all the difference (many had been able to cobble together about twelve weeks, using disability pay, some paid leave, and vacation time). That wish made sense, given that it took the average respondent five and a half months after having a baby to feel physically back to normal, and almost six months to feel normal again emotionally.

The majority of women I polled—71 percent—said that in the first three months back at work, they fought more with their partners at home than they had before. For some, that was the beginning of the end of their marriages. For others, the hard times actually brought them closer to their partners.

Their babies' milestones synced up in an incredibly ironic and challenging way with their work schedules. First real smiles happened at just shy of two months old. Naps solidified and became more regular at almost five months, on average. The typical baby started sleeping through the night (which I decided to define as seven hours straight with no feedings) at just over seven months old. These numbers agreed, roughly, with the studies out there in academia, too.

"At twelve weeks old, they're still what I call an alien baby," said Michelle, an advertising exec and single mother who I interviewed. "All they do is eat, poop, sleep, and do nothing." Nothing, that is, except require a tremendous amount of care. On workdays, mothers reported spending two hours and thirty-three minutes total with their babies during the daytime. The babies were so young—unable to sit up and hold a toy, still eating eight times a day—that the average working mom spent only *six minutes* each morning simply enjoying her baby and not doing basic baby care. And forget enjoying time to herself; 79 percent of the women I polled spent one hour or less per week doing something just for themselves in their first three months back.

In short, it's a mess. The typical professional mother in the United States goes back to work very, very sleep deprived. She's just started getting positive emotions back from her baby, and she's about to experience the rockiest period ever in her relationship. She has no free time. Every three hours her body makes milk that leaks onto her lovely work clothes if she doesn't do something about it. And baby and body aside, she's about to come back to a job that other people have been covering for her with various degrees of happiness and resentment about that fact.

"I was surprised by the expectation that I was one hundred percent back, or close to it, particularly given how gentle everyone was when I was visibly pregnant," Laura (not her real name), a tenured professor at one of the top business schools in the country, told me. "But of course, it was far easier to have a typical pregnancy than to care for a newborn while working, so the irony was a shock." She made it through, negotiating with her superiors and educating a whole slew of colleagues about the challenges of new-working-parenthood along the way.

Often—because of fear or finances—women don't take advantage of those opportunities that we do have to redefine the company norm. "When I was hired, I was newly pregnant with my first child," says Lila (also not her real name), who now runs human capital for a global finance company, approving things like benefits and leaves. "And I remember when I told the woman I reported to, she was so supportive and said to me, 'Look, if I can't make this work in human capital, then I'm a failure.'" Still, when it came time to take her own maternity leave, Lila didn't push the envelope. A few women at her company had taken six months (but they were all in-house lawyers, who seemed to have their own little subset of cultural expectations). "I never would have asked for all that time," she says. "Personally, I thought it would set me back. In the finance world, a significant part of compensation is bonus, and I didn't want to be perceived as asking for more time off than I'd earned. I'd already been out longer than I'd imagined because my baby was born a week late. It's a long time to be out." As we see around the world, three months is actually not a long time to be out—we just perceive it as such because it's what we're used to.

Michelle (of the alien-baby comment) has learned, out of necessity, how to break new ground. "There aren't many working moms in my field of advertising, which makes it really hard. The hours are terrible," Michelle says. "I learned pretty early on that there weren't any role models for how to do it, that *I* was the role model for younger people, and that really scared me. I was like, 'Oh, you people need better! This is not good!'"

Actually, we don't need better than Michelle—she's fantastic already—but we do need more women like her. And that's my goal here. I don't have all the answers, but collectively, we sure do. The hundreds of women who contributed to this book—to this Fifth Trimester movement—have learned through trial and error about how to make those first three months back more than just an exercise in treading water. That complicated, challenging time can lay the groundwork for a whole career of working-parent balance and success. And together we can foster a more compassionate working culture. We can change the rules. We can make things fair and right. And we can show our children how to lead and live. "I want to demonstrate to my daughter, Sydney, that she can both contribute to the world and enjoy what it has to offer her," Michelle told me. "When I ask her what she wants to do when she's older, the actual occupation changes quite frequently, but the promise that she can do it all is just automatic. She's got a whole list. This *and* that *and* the other. It's the 'and' that I love. There's no 'or' in my daughter's mind."

I laughed when she told me that, because both of my own sons, now ages four and seven, have those long lists, too. I flipped through Will's baby book recently, and as you could probably guess, it's a bit of a joke as far as baby books go. (And Teddy, baby number two, doesn't even have one, poor guy.) It starts out with a few painful, sleep-deprived entries about how much we loved him but also how surprised I was that everything was just so hard. By mid-September, when I went back to work, the entries stop abruptly and permanently. In fact, the only other thing in the book is a printout of an essay that my husband and I wrote about Will years later, when he was four years old and we were applying to kindergarten for him. "Until recently, our son Will was pretty set in his decision to be a fireman when he grows up," we wrote. "Then a few weeks ago, he amended that: 'Actually, I will be a fireman, and a doctor, and a Ghostbuster, and a daddy,' he told us. 'I think I can do the balance of that.'"

He thinks he can do the balance of that. I think you can do the balance of that, and that your babies can one day, too. Let's cheer one another on and get there.

the fifth trimester

CHAPTER ONE

❧

Who's taking care of your little person?

"And what would you say is the hardest part of caring for small children?" I asked hopefully, meeting the kind eyes of the stranger sitting two feet away from me on our navy blue couch. She had been all polite smiles until now, and suddenly she grimaced a bit, pursing her lips. I waited, as I had learned to do in interviews at work, forcing her to fill the silence. Near her knee, I spied a milk stain on the couch between us, and realized that Ben and I were about to make a financial commitment that would keep us from being able to replace the sofa for quite some time.

"That's easy," Jean said quietly. "It's saying goodbye to them when you love them so much." Apologizing, she began to cry a little, telling us about how hard it was to leave her previous family. The mother's job and hours had changed, and so here she sat on our couch, for the eighth and final—and only good—in-person interview in our search for a nanny for our ten-week-old son. This was after twenty-two phone interviews and many months of agonizing about this moment.

Did Jean smoke? No, of course not. Did she have twenty years' worth of glowing references? Absolutely. Could she describe how she'd spend a rainy day with our baby, now at three months, and later at nine months, or eighteen? Yes, yes, and yes. (Could we afford her? Barely.) But that basic list of interview questions, all check marks and lots of check-plusses, hadn't prepared me for this moment. With that tearful response, so pure and honest and loving that it embarrassed her and then didn't, Ben and I knew she was the one.

A week later, as I got ready to return to work, we spent two days in sync, the three of us: Me, Jean, Will. In retrospect, we should have had much more than two days to transition, as it was a bit of a crash course (for me, let's be clear, not her). But selfishly, I wanted every bit of alone time with my baby that I could get. I'd only just started to emerge from a shaky postpartum period.

On the first day together, we strolled to the park, slowly, at the pace of a nanny enjoying an outing with her charge, not a mother trying to get someplace. A bird pooped on Jean's head. An auspicious sign if ever there was one. I reached for a burp cloth; she hesitated to use it, first making sure there was a spare for her new little prince.

On the second day, we strolled to another park (also slowly). This time, she pushed the stroller and I walked alongside, feeling useless and a bit usurped. At the park's entrance she stopped. "It's okay," she said, "you know, if you have things you need to do? Errands to run or anything?" I wasn't sure whether to go. She urged again, "He's safe with me. You can trust me." And just like that, I turned around and cried my way to the drugstore to go buy toothpaste.

I'm glad Jean forced me to take that practice run, because on the third day, my first back at work, I handed Will over to her and then cried some more as she embraced me in an awkward group hug. In the arms of a woman whose perfume I didn't know yet, I dried my tears and took a deep, shuddering breath and went to work.

Thus began seven years of Jean, who got our boys through teething, sleep training, and potty training while Ben and I got through the daily and yearly triumphs and challenges of our jobs.

My one mistake, looking back, was in hiring someone so much like myself. I'm a bit (okay, a lot) messy, and while Jean was tidy, maybe if I'd employed a total neat freak our little apartment would have been cleaner. I'm no disciplinarian either, and perhaps if she'd been tougher, my boys would eat carrots like every other organic baby in Manhattan. But Jean snuggled my babies with endless delight and love. And she taught my boundary-pushing toddlers the meaning of no, spoken calmly, firmly, gently, eye to eye, while holding their hands in hers. I was comfortable with her style right from the beginning because it was my own, even if I didn't know what that meant yet. We'd made the right choice.

We actually had a few good choices, more than we realized at the time. We ruled out daycare because of our work hours and Ben's inability, during residency training, to miss a day of work due to a sick kid. We ruled out a nanny share mostly because we didn't know anyone else with a baby Will's age. Our parents lived out of state so family care wasn't a possibility. But in retrospect, we actually could have made any of those options work—we could have moved, could have hired a second-shift babysitter to do day-care pickup, could have used a nanny-share agency to hook up with another family—*if* that had been what felt right.

The options and work-arounds are actually pretty easy to weed through from a practical standpoint, and I'll happily help you do that in a moment.

Much more challenging is the emotional transition of peeling your baby out of your own arms—where she's been leeching on you cozily for several days or weeks or months—and leaving her in someone else's care. That's what most of this chapter will be about. *Because finding good childcare for your baby is as much about making peace with the model you've chosen as it is about finding the right model.*

Back in 2006, the National Institute of Child Health and Human Development (NICHD) released a massive report, the cul-mination of hundreds of studies on how "differences in child care experiences relate to children's social, emotional, intellectual, and language development, and to their physical growth and health." Good stuff. The NICHD had been cooking it up for years, following more than one thousand children from diverse socioeconomic backgrounds, in childcare centers, childcare homes, and in-home care (meaning, the child's own home, but with a non-mom relative or a nanny) across the United States, from infancy into their teenage years. Predictably, the media and the mommy bloggers went nuts searching the fine print for a definitive answer about just how bad or good it is for women to go back to work.

The upshot (kind of) is that daycare can be:

a) potentially better for small children's cognitive and language development than other forms of childcare,
b) potentially bad for their behavior as they get older, and
c) potentially better academically if kids start there as toddlers and not as infants.

I say "kind of" and "potentially" because the researchers found two enormously compelling mitigating factors: the individual child, and the individual parent. Yes, really.

The individual child, of course, at the point you're returning to work, is sort of a blob (or a tabula rasa, a blank slate, if you want to be fancy about it). Who knows what kind of kid you've got on your hands, beyond the info that a good look in the mirror at your own temperamental DNA (and your partner's) can provide.

What you do know—and what you can act on—as you make the decision about what kind of childcare situation is best for your family, is what *feels right to you:* what's going to make you happiest and least stressed out. Because that's what ultimately matters, both according to the mothers I interviewed and—surprise—to the NICHD. I've incorporated many of the NICHD's findings throughout this chapter, as noted, but the thing that impressed me the most about its excellent report was this sentence: "Parent and family characteristics were more strongly linked to child development than were child care features." Yep, fifteen years of painstaking analysis generated a lot of useful ways to evaluate your childcare options, but the most important predictor for how well your child will thrive in someone else's care is *you*.

So calm down about finding childcare.
(Easier said than done, but, really, here's how.)

"Finding childcare was the most stressful thing I hurdled with both of my children, and I realize it was my own stress over the situation; nothing to do with the kids," says Jen Lucky, a project director at a Bay Area nonprofit who spoke to me just after returning to work following the birth of her second baby. Maternal stress, unshockingly, is bad for babies, another strong predictor of "externalizing behaviors" (kids acting out and having bad impulse control). Let's fix that: To make a good decision for your own baby, first do what you can to reduce your stress around the childcare search. These strategies can help:

EXTEND YOUR LEAVE... This one's obvious, but let's keep beating this drum until things change: Longer maternity leave is associated with better postpartum mental health. That's been proven time and again, so for goodness sake, if you're lucky enough to be able to add on some weeks, do. With her second daughter, Jen negotiated and took eighteen weeks of leave, even though much of the time was unpaid. "At twelve weeks she just looked too tiny to me to leave," says Jen. "My body wasn't ready. I wasn't ready. That extra month and a half was so pivotal for me in terms of feeling confident and ready to return. And the childcare all fell into place in that time."

...**OR, "EXTEND" YOUR LEAVE.** Most women don't have workplaces that are as flexible as Jen's was. If that extra leave time isn't an option for you, consider finding a way to faux "extend" your leave setup for the baby, keeping him, temporarily, in the care of someone you already trust before you hand him over to daycare or a paid caregiver. I spoke to several women whose parents and in-laws provided that interim care. Even better: Many moms told me that their partners deferred some or all of their own parental leave for just this purpose.

Eileen Yam's husband, Elliot, took a month at home when she went back so that their son, Everett, wouldn't be quite so small when they left him at daycare. "We get sixteen weeks of unpaid leave here in D.C.," says Eileen, a researcher with an international development NGO/nonprofit. "But the visual of dropping off a baby who can't even sit up yet—who doesn't really have a personality yet, and isn't yet responsive—in an institution, made me pretty uncomfortable." That extra time with Dad at home also meant they were all closer to sleeping through the night—very stress quelling—before Everett went to daycare.

In Boston, Renée Farster-Degenhardt took a week off from her job so that her wife, Nathalie, who had given birth to their daughter, wouldn't have to make two major adjustments at once. "She could transition to work, and then we could transition Zaila to daycare a week later," says Renée. "Plus, that week at home caring for my daughter transformed my relationship with her. It was daunting and hard and incredibly special."

CONSIDER YOUR EMOTIONAL NEEDS, NOT JUST YOUR LOGISTICAL ONES. Ideally, what you're looking for is a childcare plan that helps reignite, or at least maintains, your identity as a working woman, says Laura Morgan Roberts, PhD, professor, executive coach, and CEO of RPAQ Solutions in Atlanta. "For me, childcare arrangements weren't simply about what would work with my lifestyle and schedule but also for my identity," Roberts says. "I needed a plan that gave me the comfort and security I needed to become re-immersed and reengaged in my work."

So you might *think* that your childcare choices look like this:

DAYCARE IS BEST IF . . .

- your work hours are predictable
- you want your baby to be on a schedule

- you want your baby to be socialized with lots of other kids
- you prefer an environment with lots of resources and toys
- you can afford a predictable "all-inclusive" bill each month

A NANNY IS BEST IF . . .
- your work hours are less predictable, especially in the evenings
- you travel for work
- you want one-on-one attention for your child
- you want your baby in a home environment
- you are flexible with money, able to spend a bit more some weeks, a bit less others

Makes sense. All those logistical bullet points are valid. But I talked to dozens of women who'd used daycare or nannies or both and uncovered a whole treasure trove of additional less tangible benefits and drawbacks. Ask yourself about more gut-check emotional desires as well. Perhaps your list would look more like this:

DAYCARE IS BEST IF . . .
- you don't want to have to "manage" anyone in your personal life
- you anticipate being jealous of the bond your baby might have with a nanny
- you want to make new friends with other parents
- you like the idea of splitting drop-off/pickup duties with your spouse
- you don't like the idea of having someone in your house all day
- you feel most comfortable with the "safety in numbers" that a whole center full of staff gives you
- you need to be able to compartmentalize at work, without interruptions from a caregiver
- you enjoy organizing and stocking your home yourself (or have a partner who does)

A NANNY IS BEST IF . . .

- you want a close, family-like relationship with your baby's caregiver
- you want your baby deeply bonded with someone in your absence
- you don't want to have to socialize with a crowd of parents at pickup at the end of the workday
- daily packing/unpacking stresses you out
- you're wary of resenting your spouse for not doing more around the house
- you want to be able to check in all day long, receiving texts and pictures of your baby
- you trust your instincts about people and know that you hire well
- you are good at delegating little household tasks, like keeping the pump parts organized and the onesies washed

These are the more emotional needs and desires that came up in my interviews. Surely you'll think of others, but *do* take the time to consider them as you make your decisions.

THINK OUTSIDE OF THE BOUNCY SEAT. In my survey of those more than seven hundred moms, 33 percent opted for daycare, and 32 percent used an in-home caregiver (who was not a family member or spouse). The remaining 34 percent had either a partner home with the baby (10 percent), another family member stepping in (20 percent), or a nanny share (4 percent). Seems pretty straightforward, right? Well, I proved myself wrong on that once I started doing my longer-form interviews.

Turns out, many, many women made themselves more of a pupu platter of childcare options that suited the life and careers they wanted to have. I spoke to one woman who had a seventy-hour-a-week nanny every other week. Her work was one week on and one week off, with days that ranged from zero to eighteen hours. Another new mom had arranged to work a four-day week, as had her husband. So they each covered one day of childcare, and then had Grandma babysit one day a week, so the baby only needed to be in daycare two days a week. The mom, who had been very emotional about returning to work sooner than she liked, took great comfort in knowing that her son was being cared for by family most of the week.

Later on in this chapter I'll give advice from women who found several nontraditional ways to arrange their childcare. Maybe one day the United States will catch up with the rest of the world, and we will have high-quality universal childcare (dream it with me). But until then, it's reassuring to know there are so many options.

AND, MOVE UP YOUR SEARCH SO YOU CAN DO A TRIAL RUN. If at all possible, many new moms I talked to suggested touring daycares during your pregnancy—both to have the best chance at grabbing a spot at the most popular centers and to avoid the drama of hauling your newborn around on your search. Do a revisit once the baby has arrived, and schedule a start date at least a week in advance of your first day back at work so you can practice the morning and evening transitions. Marion Campbell Kammer, a talent agent in Los Angeles, actually started her baby, Charlie, in daycare a couple of weeks early and found herself so at a loss for what to do with her time at home alone that she returned to work early. "For peace of mind, I just needed to rip off the Band-Aid and go back," she says. Since her office wasn't expecting her anyway, she worked half-days, picking Charlie up after lunch, and had a true phase-in period, both for herself and the baby.

Nannies tend to be available with less lead time—they don't want to sit around, unpaid, waiting for you to give birth. Still, start your search about six to eight weeks before you're set to go back to work—for those with shorter leaves, that might mean looking before you give birth. Then do a one- or two-day tryout, with you present the whole time. "I recommend families do trials of two different candidates," says psychologist Lindsay Heller, otherwise known as The Nanny Doctor, who provides consulting services for families and nannies. "You might be surprised that the person you thought was your second favorite quickly becomes the front runner." At a minimum, have them work for four hours—paid, of course—which covers about one newborn cycle of eat, play, nap.

Once you've found your match, budget in as much time with all three or four of you at home as you can afford. Sarah Davis, founder of the nanny placement agency Olive.You.Nanny (cutest name, right?), based in Austin, Texas, says a month of overlap is ideal. I know that was more than I could afford back then. Still, "if that's out of budget for this particular nanny, or if she isn't okay working part-time until you go back, then it's not the right fit," says Sarah, who worked as a nanny herself before starting her business, which has placed childcare for more than three thousand families in five cities. "Most nannies, when they find a family they love, will work to make it fit because they know that this is potentially a long-term, five-year relationship."

Stephanie, a director and sales team leader at a major (like, really major) tech company, says that pre-kids, she would have assumed that she needed only a couple of days of overlap with a caregiver before going back to work, but circumstances dictated otherwise: Stephanie was diagnosed with breast cancer while she was pregnant and spent the last part of her maternity leave recovering from a mastectomy. (She shares more of her incredible story and insights in later chapters.) "Having Carla there for a whole month with us was one of the real silver linings of my situation," says Stephanie. "I couldn't lift my baby for two weeks, which was super heartbreaking, but it also required me to take the time to really walk Carla through all of the little tasks of a day at home. Before I even went back to work, she knew things like exactly what to get at the grocery store. At work now, I have two women out on leave on my team, and I've encouraged them to do a one-month overlap. Long-term, it pays off exponentially for everyone."

If your nanny is going to be buying supplies for the house, or making other financial decisions—even just how many diapers to buy online to get free shipping!—it will save you money in the long run to show her firsthand how to manage those costs. And with fewer questions to answer during your workday, you will be freed up to, you know, earn more money.

HAVE A PLAN A *AND* A PLAN B. No matter what choice you make for plan A, you will sleep better knowing you've got backup for when the babysitter's sick or the daycare center loses power: a relative, a stay-at-home-mom neighbor, an underemployed friend who's happy to take a day's work, or a backup daycare center (call around—some keep a few spots open daily). Of course you or your partner could always take the day off, but what if this special form of new parent hell happens on the day of your annual review or your spouse's work trip? You need a plan.

Katie Fiamingo, a senior brand manager in charge of innovation at Nestlé Purina PetCare in St. Louis, pays an annual fee to a backup babysitting service. But her first line of defense for these little emergencies is her Sunday-night planning with her husband. "It's arduous, and I hate it, but it alleviates the most stressful part of being a working parent—the idea that at any moment I could get a phone call from daycare that my kid has a fever, and my whole day is destroyed, eight meetings. So, Steve and I open up our calendars every Sunday night and make a plan for who's covering which days and nights if something goes wrong. These conversations are quick, we don't linger on them, but we have to do them. These are the things you have to do to keep life from feeling fragile."

Right away, let's talk about the jealousy issue

"I'll admit, one of the main reasons we chose daycare over a nanny was that I did not ever want to feel like I was competing with one other person in the role of mothering my children," says Hayley Williams, a lawyer and mother of three in Cleveland. "I didn't want to feel like somebody was at home, at my house, doing my job—or what society says is my job, or what I feel like what should be my job. I was never even able to contemplate a nanny."

I personally disagree. But I think it's great that Hayley knew herself and her stressors well enough to make the decision that would give her the most peace. She made the right choice for her family. And if you feel as strongly as she did, that's A-okay by me. But I want to make a case here for why having your child bonded to another person—a nanny, or a special caregiver at daycare—can be beneficial all around.

Hayley's feelings were heightened, she realizes, because she's an adoptive mom. "I didn't have the bonding time of pregnancy," she tells me. With her first son, she felt, in the beginning, like she was already his replacement mom. She didn't want someone else replacing her. But when I heard the same sentiment from several other mothers over the course of my interviews, I started asking everyone I talked to: Did you feel jealous of the person taking care of your child? And if so, how did you deal with that? I remember being jealous of the time our nanny had with my son. I didn't love it, at first, when I came home from work, and he was dressed in an outfit I wouldn't have picked out. Petty, but honest. But very quickly, I became comfortable with how much Will loved Jean, which felt like a much more crucial issue. Whenever a pang struck, I remembered: I've chosen well; I've made sure he's loved and feels love when I'm away from him. That helped.

"I remember the first time my baby called our sitter Mama," says Jen, the nonprofit project director, who was surprised at how little this very common slip bothered her. It's the classic movie scene about the guilt-wracked working mom; cue the dramatic Rachmaninoff. And yet, in reality, it's not that big of a deal. "It doesn't take away from their love for you," Jen explains. "Why wouldn't you be happy that your child was with someone all day long who is like a parent to them, rather than their feeling 'I wish I was with my mommy' all the time? *That* would give me mommy guilt." Robin Fredriksz, a film and TV makeup artist based in Pennsylvania, told me that she was reassured by this quote that a friend shared with her: "From the moment your child is born, you are saying goodbye to your child, so don't forget yourself in all of this." Robin found that especially true going back to work. She explains, "One of the first times you say goodbye to your child is when you let someone else care for him, and allow him to have that emotional closeness."

And this bond is not at all limited to nannies. There are more staff members at a larger daycare center, of course, but babies tend to be assigned, in small groups, to the same couple of caregivers. Babies between the ages of six and thirty months have an "attachment-seeking response" that can be soothed by "a lasting secondary attachment bond with one caregiver who is consistently accessible to them," research has found. These babies are able to avoid stress and anxiety. Who wouldn't want that?

Still not convinced? Sarah Serafin, a medical transcriptionist in Chagrin Falls, Ohio, had to work from home for many years because she couldn't afford a nanny and couldn't find appropriate daycare for her daughter, who has special needs. To pay the bills, Sarah started her own in-home daycare, taking in other children. As a caregiver for other toddlers, and as a mom who finally, finally got to hand her own daughter over to schoolteachers after several years, Sarah says she's learned this: "You don't own your child or their affections. I was so eager for other adults to become important to my children. I wanted them to learn to respect, enjoy, and grow with people other than me, because Lord knows, I absolutely don't know everything, nor can I give them everything."

Your feelings are your feelings. I can't argue with that; only you know what's right for you. But your baby's feelings are your baby's as well. Let him have them.

Is managing your childcare provider
the same as managing at work?

Answer: Yes. (But it sure doesn't feel like it.)

Nanny Doctor Lindsay Heller has a private but star-studded

roster of clients, people who employ management teams and answer to corporate boards and the stock market. "And yet I can't tell you how many high-powered women run into trouble managing their childcare and wonder, 'What's wrong with me? I do this every day at work!'" Heller says. The stakes are just so high.

Most of the women I talked to who had nannies—and several who used smaller in-home daycares—said that they wanted their caregivers to be "like family." There's an intimacy that goes deeper than just being seen in your bathrobe and buying her birthday presents. Your nanny is with you at your most vulnerable working-mom transitions: coming home at night after a bad meeting, saying goodbye to your baby in the morning when she's sick.

That makes it awfully hard to give negative feedback. And awfully easy to become passive-aggressive. And no, I'm not just speculating. I'm guilty.

Compounding the issue is the fact that "your caregiver knows significantly more than you do about your newest and most-prized possession, so you are learning from an employee," says Andrea Olshan, mom of three and CEO of her family's real estate business, Olshan Properties. Andrea learned to deal with this imbalance by thinking of how she'd handle a similar situation at work. "In business, you have to manage people who have a specific knowledge of something that you might not—but that doesn't make you unqualified. For instance, I manage construction people. If they tell me we need to use a certain kind of more expensive concrete because the soil quality is poor, my instinct is to ask, 'Well, did everything else built there need this same kind of concrete?' You have to always remember, 'I have common sense.'"

So memorize her Starbucks order, let her borrow your rain boots when a storm pops up midday, text her with emojis in a way you never would with a colleague. But remember to trust your managerial gut. If you're clear and fair, she'll do better in her job. Here are some of the best ways to do just that:

WRITE UP A JOB DESCRIPTION. Just like at work, you may deviate from it for the perfect candidate, but you've got to start somewhere—and this document gives you a template for a contract eventually, if you want one. "Have your expectations written out," instructs Davis, founder of Olive.You.Nanny. "What sort of family are you, what are your philosophies? What do you expect this person to do around the house? What do you expect them to do with the baby? Going through the list makes it a lot easier to communicate exactly what you want without feeling awkward. You can say, 'I'm not really a morning person, so let's plan for you to stay ten minutes later at the end of the day so we can chat about the next day then.' Put it all out there, so the nanny will know exactly what she is signing up for."

INTERVIEW LIKE A PRO. Every candidate search at work starts with that job description. But let me ask you this: Have you ever chosen to hire someone you didn't feel a click with? I'm guessing not. Your goal is to hear one loud-ass click with this person. So, while of course you should ask nuts-and-bolts questions about her past experience, her likes and dislikes, and how she manages her commute (key for a timely arrival), slip in some more soulful questions, too—things that reveal her values and her heart, things that get you to that click. "I always ask, 'What's your dream job?'" says Andrea, the real estate CEO. "And I can't tell you how many women say, 'I want to be an interior designer,' or, 'I want to be in fashion.' And I say, thank you so much, it was nice to meet you, and that's that, because being my nanny isn't going to fulfill them. I want to hear 'I want to go back to school to be a teacher' or 'I've been babysitting since I was ten years old,' something that involves kids and caring for them." Some more great examples from the experts and moms I interviewed:

- "What are your favorite things to do when you're not working?"
- "Growing up, what were you like? What made you first want to care for children?"
- "What's your relationship like now with the families you've worked for previously?"

- "Tell me about some kind of adversity you faced in the past and how you got through it."

TAKE CARE OF YOUR LEGAL OBLIGATIONS. "Taxes are the rockiest part of the nanny business," says Davis. "It could be six months down the road and the nanny says, 'You're giving me a W-2, right?' and the family says, 'No, you're an independent contractor.' So it is *so* important to figure that out right from the beginning. Are you going to pay cash, or are you going to withhold taxes?" I'll add: You should look up the employment laws in your state so you can make sure you're compliant in terms of payroll taxes, unemployment, and disability insurance. The fines are no joke. "And remember taxes when you negotiate salary," says Davis. "If you work for a corporation, no one talks in net. But a lot of nannies do." If she says she wants to make $16 an hour, make sure you know if she means pre- or post-taxes.

BE SUPER CLEAR ABOUT THE BENEFITS. "I don't think any good nanny would ever take out her frustrations regarding her work situation on the children, but you do feel scared of that," says Jen. "So you have to spell out everything. Don't leave anything vague. Put holidays and vacation days and your sick-day policy in writing." (Check your local and state government to find out what your legal obligations are here as well.) Who pays her cell-phone bill? What about her bus or train pass? Or health insurance? Will you leave her petty cash for errands? After a false start with her first nanny, Monica, an institutional investor for a retirement plan, put together a much more thorough "roles and responsibilities" sheet for the second woman they hired. "It even included things like, Do we pay for a cab home or dinner if we ask you to work past a certain hour? I know it sounds restrictive and formal, but if people freaked out about it we knew it wasn't going to work out." Once you've made the hire, says Jen, "anything that isn't spelled out, you will probably end up bending on as the employer. And you could feel taken advantage of."

KEEP A PERSONNEL FILE. You'll need a place to keep your contract if you have one, as well as a copy of your caregiver's ID, résumé, contact info, etc. "That's something that sometimes gets lost in the shuffle, and in hindsight it can be terrifying not to have it," warns Heller.

PLEASE DON'T FORGET TO SAY THANK YOU. At work, you thank your boss for a plum assignment, your junior associate for a job well done, and the package dude for a J.Crew order promptly delivered, right? Same goes for daycare staff, family caregivers, nannies, everyone! Notice and praise when people go above and beyond, but also show gratitude for doing the work that's simply the job. "All it needs to be is words," says Davis. "Short and sweet is fine, just be genuine. Things like, 'I'm running out the door, but it's so much easier because I know you're here for my child.' Or, 'Knowing she was with you today, I felt reassured and was able to focus on work.'"

PAY THE RIGHT AMOUNT FOR WHAT YOU NEED. Some moms say to pay for the most expensive childcare you can afford. But if that leaves you strapped for money in every other area of your life, it may not be necessary. A less expensive daycare in a more convenient location is worth a *lot*. And for a nanny of a newborn, says Davis, "you don't necessarily need someone with thirty-five years of experience or a master's degree in education. You need someone to love the baby and keep the baby safe. There are really two chapters with nannies, the baby phase and the school-age phase. It's unusual to find someone who can transition, so it's okay to go into hiring a nanny knowing that you probably won't employ this person for more than five years."

Different story, however, if you have an older child, if you travel a lot for work, or if you want someone who is also managing your household. Kimberly Jaime, an entertainment lawyer in Los Angeles, purposefully decided to stretch her budget a bit. "The woman we hired was more expensive, but we have prioritized our lives in a way that incurs a tremendous cost of childcare but gives me the ability to do my job well. It's a sacrifice, but it's worth it to my family," she says.

"Do your research locally to figure out what pay rate is standard where you live. It varies a lot," says Davis. "Even if you're searching on your own, you can call a local agency and ask for general information like that."

COURSE CORRECT WITH SENSITIVITY. One hidden benefit of managing a caregiver is that it can make you a better manager at work. At her restaurant, Chef & the Farmer, in Kinston, North Carolina, Vivian Howard used to find herself being a little too abrupt with her kitchen staff (it's all laid bare on her PBS series *A Chef's Life*). At home, Vivian has learned to be clear but gentle with the woman who takes care of her twins. "Rather than pointing out what she isn't doing right, I'll try to establish a new habit, to ask for what I want rather than scolding her for what she isn't doing. And it works," says Vivian. "At the restaurant, it's pretty much the same now."

RECOGNIZE THAT YOUR CAREGIVER HAS A LIFE OUTSIDE OF YOURS. "It's hard sometimes, but you have to remember that a nanny has a personal life," says Lila, who runs human capital for a global financial firm in New York. "There are always health issues, or personal issues that come up."

About a year after hiring an awesome caregiver for her twin boys, Monica, the institutional investor, faced the most poetic personal issue of all: Her nanny announced she was pregnant. "I had a mix of emotions," says Monica. "As soon as she went home, I cried for an hour because I was afraid she wouldn't want to come back. And my kids love her so much." That response told her all she needed to know: She and her husband did everything they could to convince her to stay. "Our boys require so much energy. We told her: You nap when they nap. Don't worry about getting stuff done around the house. Crank the air conditioning if you need to." During her twelve-week maternity leave, they hired a fill-in. And then—here's where the pay-it-forward compassion really comes in—when she was back, they were sensitive to her Fifth Trimester. "She was so tired, and she would get really guarded at first if I asked if the baby had started sleeping through the night, things like that," says Monica, who could tell that she needed reassurance that her job was safe. "I also really didn't want to ask her to stay late at all anymore, so I told her to let us know if and when she wanted those hours. And in the meantime we hired sitters as needed, and it all worked out."

There will be other more short-term issues that come up: dentist appointments, family funerals. You name it. You have to see your caregiver as a whole person with a whole complicated life, just like your own. Honor the sick- and personal-day clause of your agreement and lean on your backup-care plan.

ESTABLISH A FEEDBACK SYSTEM. This one is just like managing at the office. And yet . . . even human resources executives have a hard time with it! "This is what I do at work. This is my job, giving feedback, firing people," says Lila. "But it's really really hard when they're taking care of your children." The key is having a system in place: both a constant trickle of communication, as well as a formal review process. That looks like this:

- Daily praise/feedback
- Weekly check-ins
- Annual or biannual reviews

The daily praise and feedback Allison Beer gives her nanny has actually helped her be a better manager in her job in travel partnerships at a major financial firm. "At work you have these really brief interactions with people," she says. "With Colleen, if I say something that wasn't as carefully constructed or as sensitive as it should have been, we're all in the same house. I can see how that feedback looks on her face an hour later. I've learned to really ask myself: What is this feedback meant to do? Am I trying to change a behavior, or just unhappy and expressing a feeling? The latter is simply not useful."

Allison relies on a weekly schedule check-in every Thursday

for the following week—to touch base about out-of-town visitors or work trips. "If I'm going to be traveling, I'll probably come home the afternoon before I leave to spend extra time with the boys, but if I don't let Colleen know that, it's not her fault if they're out at a playdate and I'm home disappointed."

And the review process: "We do it twice a year—I pay her to stay late—and I bring written feedback, and I ask her to come with written feedback for me," says Allison. "Mostly it's an opportunity to talk about the kids' changing needs. And then we have a glass of wine."

Doing daycare? Here's how to master the tour circuit.

At the first daycare Karen Lesh visited in Connecticut with her husband when she was pregnant, the director handed her a tissue as she walked in the door. "I was like, 'Oh, what's this for?' and when she explained that I would almost certainly cry, I was like, 'Nah, I'm good,'" recalls Karen. Sure enough, by the end of the tour, Karen was bawling her eyes out, but she was glad to know it was totally normal. That's the joy of daycare: There's a reassuring standard; you're not on your own just guessing what's okay.

But how do you know that a center is going beyond the minimum required for licensing and accreditation (which of course you should check)? The NICHD produced an amazingly thorough report to educate prospective daycare parents, in conjunction with its fifteen years of studies (see Resources on page 287 to access the whole thing). So the list of basic attributes you're looking for as you tour is clear. These are the qualities—not always met—that make a measurably positive impact on young children:

- For children ages six to eighteen months, the child-to-adult ratio should be no more than three babies per staff person, with no more than six babies in a group.

- Staff training should be beyond high school level, including certification or college degree in child development, early childhood education, or a related field.
- Caregivers should practice "positive caregiving." Sounds subjective, but the researchers really drilled down to define what this means: showing an optimistic attitude, having fun and reassuring physical contact, singing and reading to the children, asking questions, responding to babies' coos and cries, and praising good behavior with positive words.

And these qualities are all linked, of course. In general, the report says, "The more standards a childcare setting meets, the more positive the caregiving. The more positive the caregiving, the higher the quality of care and the children's outcomes."

Still, the basics listed above only tell you so much. Once you've done your touring and narrowed your options down (or narrowed your waitlists down, depending on the market), ask to come back on your own to visit again and observe for an hour or two. "All of the centers I called said yes when I asked if I could come back in and be a fly on the wall," says Hilary Herrmann, an educational coordinator in Fort Collins, Colorado. "It made it a lot easier to make a decision." What are you looking for? Comfort, ease, security. How will you find it? By noticing these six things:

THE EMPLOYEE CULTURE. "It's not necessarily the administration you deal with on a daily basis, it's the teachers and the classroom," says Hayley, the lawyer. So while you may fall in love with the lady giving the tour, pay attention to the women sitting criss-cross-applesauce on the floor with the kiddos when you come back. They're the ones who are going to determine the kind of experience your baby has day to day.

As an educator herself, Hilary was particularly interested in seeing how the teachers taught and modeled the behavior she wanted to see in her son one day. "Just the tone of voice that the adults use with the kids is really important," she says. "Are they being sarcastic or dismissive? Can you tell they are annoyed? How do they conduct themselves in stressful situations? Can they remain calm and fair? I want someone who can help my child navigate his emotions as he gets older."

THE PARENT COMMUNITY. No, you don't necessarily need or want to see that all the moms are carrying the same brand of work bag (in fact, I would find that a deterrent), but do check out the parents at drop-off or pickup time and ask yourself: Are these people I want to be friends with? This is especially important at smaller daycares like in-home facilities, which may only serve six families at a time. "All the moms at our daycare are friends," says Marion. "It was a big selling point to me when I toured and saw two other babies my son's age. They are all three best friends now—which really helps when they're all sharing runny noses, too."

THE COMMUNICATION STYLE. This is a good one to ask other parents about: How often do they hear from the caregivers? When they've gotten a call at work, was it for a good reason? How are new hires, policy changes, or just special themed dress-up days communicated? And—so important, says Sarah M., a museum curriculum manager who works about forty-five minutes away from her daycare—how does the staff share information among themselves? Sarah drops her baby off around 8:00 a.m., and the teachers have changed shifts by the time she picks up at the end of the workday. "If I ask, 'How did the carrots go over?' or 'Did he do tummy time?' they'll go, 'Oh, I don't know . . . I wasn't here then.'" Sarah has learned to call and check in during her midafternoon pumping session so she can talk to the woman who cares for her son the majority of the day. She's also gotten used to writing "a short novel" of instructions on his intake sheet. She doesn't mind. (She's probably a Virgo, like me, come to think of it.) But it's nice to know before you sign up if that's something you're going to need to find time for each night.

THE COMMUTE. This one has nothing to do with the facility but everything to do with your quality of life. Generally, the moms I interviewed recommended looking for centers that are close to your office or your partner's workplace (as opposed to close to home), no more than ten or fifteen minutes out of the way—very helpful on evenings when you're running late leaving, or when your baby gets a random fever midday. And, yes, that means commuting with your babe in tow, but that can actually grow into a nice ritual of time together, says Aliza, a nurse manager in Philadelphia. Aliza's husband commutes an hour each way, taking their daughter with him to a childcare center onsite at his workplace. "I think having that time in the car and having total responsibility for her has been really helpful in establishing him as a true co-parent," she says. "Those two are best friends. They listen to music, they talk, they play. It's really so sweet."

WHAT YOU *DON'T* LIKE. Karen offered great advice here. Most places you tour will be law compliant. They may have some of the same toys, the same cribs, and a similarly credentialed staff. So instead, look for the little things that pop out at you. "No place is going to be completely ideal so find out what those flaws are and then decide whether or not you can live with them," says Karen. Perfect example: Hayley was bothered by a slight sterility at her children's daycare. She noticed, for instance, that the caregivers have to wear gloves while feeding the children. But that's just a rule, nothing she can change, and she realized that if that was the biggest thing that was bothering her, the place must be pretty excellent.

WHAT THE OLDER KIDS ARE UP TO. Those little baby cribs and Bumbo seats can be distracting. Don't forget to check out the toddler area, too, if you're looking for a long-term fit. "I loved the school environment aspect of our daycare when I visited," says Hayley. "The coloring projects, the dress-up days, the multicultural aspects. Finley was only ten weeks old when he started, but even then I called it school. In my mind we were taking him to a place where he would play and learn and grow." Meanwhile, Karen, who now has three kids (all boys), has made life simpler by moving their youngest to a smaller home daycare. "What I miss out on is that they don't do the arts and crafts just because the woman who runs it is not so craftsy. But I love that it's a middle ground with the personal approach of a nanny with the socialization of a group of kids, including older ones he can look up to."

And now, the "what about"s . . .

WHAT ABOUT FAMILY CARE?

Are there downsides to the fortunate situation of having your parents or in-laws as the primary caregivers for your baby? Oh, sure. "What I didn't pay in childcare, I paid in guilt," one mom told me about how stressed out she would feel anytime she or her husband had to work late. And it can be a real challenge to have grandparents that up close and personal in your space. "It creates a different kind of tension," another new mom told me. "You can feel like you're being scrutinized about the choices you're making with your child, whether or not that's the case."

Consensus among the moms and experts I talked to is that there are two keys to making this lucky but tricky situation work:

1) Trust
2) Gratitude

"A lot of trust has to do with guilt," explains Carolyn Pirak, LCSW, founding director of the Bringing Baby Home program at The Gottman Institute for relationship research in Seattle. Pirak asks the mothers she works with if they feel a responsibility to keep a log of the baby's activities and report back when they care for them. "They all say, 'Of course not, I'm perfectly capable.' And I remind them that that's exactly the same feeling a grandparent has when you leave your baby with them. They're an equal partner and you have to let go."

As for gratitude, Wendy Shanker, a single mom by choice in Miami, shared this perspective, and I kind of think everyone who's got parents watching their baby could benefit from hearing it: "With my parents, the first choice that I made was to be very grateful for their help as opposed to assuming that just because it was their grandchild they were going to step up. I see a lot of my peers making this mistake, thinking their parents are going to be so ecstatic to have a grandkid that they're going to be in the trenches with you. And that's not always the case. So I chose to see their help as a gift. As a single mother, I'm so appreciative that my daughter can see that our family is bigger than just the two of us. The secondary joy to my being her mom is watching her relationship develop with her grandparents."

WHAT ABOUT STAY-AT-HOME DADS?

What about them? They're great! Ten percent of my survey takers say their partners stayed home with the baby when they went back to work. And nationally, the estimate is higher: Dads now account for 16 percent of stay-at-home parents. Neurologists have even studied and shown (thank goodness) that the male brain adapts to respond similarly to mothers' brains when in charge of childcare. "I think we're just living in a time now where more men realize the kind of impact they can have on their kids by staying at home," says Lance Somerfeld, cofounder with his buddy Matt Schneider of City Dads Group, a national network of meetup groups for stay-at-home dads in nineteen U.S. cities. The stereotype, clearly, of a bumbling Mr. Mom is being tossed out the door on the seat of its pleated chinos. The moms and dads I talked to offered this advice:

REMEMBER, YOU ARE NOT HIS BOSS. All the trust advice about grandparents, above, applies here, too, even more strongly. Your job is to go to work and do your job, not dictate his, says Cristyn Zett, a Pittsburgh police lieutenant whose husband, Rick, takes care of their children during her shifts (and then they switch—he's a cop, too). "You just have to resist the urge to micromanage and know that they have the kids' best interest at heart." says Cristyn.

THERE WILL BE A LEARNING CURVE. "Honestly, my husband probably does a better job taking care of our son than I would," says Amy Kawa, who works at a talent management company in Los Angeles. "But those first few weeks when I went back to work, he was like, 'Whoa, this is nuts.' He was exhausted and overwhelmed." The phone call Amy got at work when the baby pooped at Whole Foods and the diaper leaked in the store, the parking lot, and the car? Yeah, she's not forgetting that anytime soon. One gay mom I talked to who stayed home with her daughter for a while recalled feeling similarly at sea but even worse about it because, after all, she's a mom, too! (All of this partner-at-home advice applies to same-sex couples, as well, of course.)

HE WILL NEED TO FIND HIS PEOPLE. "There are so many mommy-and-me groups," says Amy. "It's hard to find the daddy-and-me things. I could tell he was very isolated." After researching several activities, she finally realized she needed to let her husband take the lead for himself. And as soon as she backed off, he did. "He looked into something this week, and I was so happy about that," she says, laughing. "It'll be good socialization for him *and* our son."

HIS BABY BOND WILL BE DIFFERENT FROM YOURS. One father—who asked to remain anonymous so that he would have a better shot at reclaiming his career once his family is out of the baby years (see? stigma's still there)—told me he relished the opportunity to make his daughter tough and confident in all their playground time together. "It wasn't conscious, exactly," he told me. "But to this day, when she falls down she never cries, and I'm proud of that."

PEOPLE WILL MAKE CRAZY ASSUMPTIONS ABOUT YOU. That dad, above? His wife tells me she's constantly getting people asking if he "sold a company" or if she "has family money" and that's why they can afford for him not to work. "Can you imagine?" she asks me, outraged. "People jump to all kinds of conclusions when the dad is home."

WHAT ABOUT AU PAIRS?

I'll admit, I always assumed au pairs were best for families with three school-aged kids all on different schedules. Turns out, they can be a wonderful, cost-efficient option for newborns, too: A young caregiver from another country comes and lives in your home, working up to forty-five hours a week for a year or two.

For Laurie Sandell, a freelance writer in Los Angeles, it was the best of everything: "My work schedule is incredibly erratic—if Jennifer Aniston is available to be interviewed, I don't want to have to scramble to find childcare," says Laurie. "And, as a single mom, once my son was about nine months old, I wanted to be able to go on dates sometimes in the evenings. I loved the idea of having someone who would be a kind of family member whom my son would feel completely comfortable with from the start." I spoke to Laurie (and her toddler—he was in the car seat on speakerphone) about a week after they had said goodbye to their beloved Cami after two wonderful years. Her best tips:

LOOK FOR A GREAT PERSONALITY MATCH. With au pairs, you interview them over the phone or Skype in their home country because it takes several weeks for them to get a visa once hired. So those conversations are vital. "I asked all of the usual questions, like, 'What would you do in an emergency?' and 'What are your thoughts on discipline?'" says Laurie. "But mainly I wanted to know if we had a chemistry, and if she was someone I wouldn't mind living with. Cami came across as calm, friendly, creative, and sweet."

THE ADJUSTMENT PERIOD IS MUTUAL. "I liked Cami right away, but I hadn't had a roommate in fifteen years," says Laurie. "And I was also adjusting to the fact that everything was brand new for her; the culture was new, she was away from her family for the first time. Luckily, she'd traveled previously and wasn't very homesick, but I've heard of that happening."

EVEN ROOMMATES NEED BOUNDARIES. "A good, happy au pair has a life," says Laurie. "They want to go out with friends, and they want their own space and time, just like anyone else. She was very open and sweet, but we never talked about her dating life or dramas with friends. There were things she simply didn't share with me, and I was grateful for that because it helped keep our roles as employer and employee defined."

WHAT ABOUT NANNY SHARES?

This option, though used by only 4 percent of the moms I surveyed, was particularly popular among my interviewees in larger cities like New York, Chicago, and San Francisco, where the cost of living is high, and neighbors are just steps away from one another. In a typical nanny share, two families with similar-age children share one nanny in one family's home. The cost is much less per family than you'd pay on your own, but overall, the caregiver may earn a bit more. Anecdotally, the moms I talked to who did nanny shares loved them but had much more transient experiences. There are simply more variables—two families, four parents with four jobs, two home locations, more kids—so the relationships were rarely long term. Interested in trying a share? Here's what I learned from moms and experts:

CHOOSE THE OTHER FAMILY AND THEN SELECT THE NANNY. "It's harder to find the other family than it is to find a nanny," says Davis, whose agency also handles making matches for nanny shares. "That relationship is so important, and it falls apart when families haven't truly researched their compatibility. For instance, say it's sixty degrees outside. One family could be like, Great, it's sixty degrees, go out and play. And the other could be like, Sixty degrees? That's too chilly to take the baby outside." Davis recommends going out to dinner together, having each other over, and really talking about your family philosophies before committing.

HASH OUT ALL THE WHAT-IFS. "You have to be able to have difficult conversations with the other parents if needed, about money and everything," says Koty Sharp, PhD, a marine biologist and professor in Rhode Island who's done a successful share. "So work out as many of those conversations as possible before the issues come up: What do we do if the nanny is sick? Or if one of the kids is sick? How much do we care about sticking to naptime?"

MAKE ONE PARENT THE COMMUNICATOR. "Sometimes it's hard to find a nanny who will do a share, but it's not the babies that drive the nanny away, it's having four bosses," says Davis. "Of course everyone should feel free to be in touch with the nanny about little things. But for any big issues that come up, there should be one designated parent who talks to the nanny after speaking with the other parents."

BE PREPARED, IT'S INTIMATE. "It felt like a co-op in a lot of ways," says Heather Ladov, a social worker in Oakland, California, who loved sharing a nanny with her friend Katie, who's a pediatrician, for a few years. "We were essentially living in each other's houses. We were close to their marriage, their home, their bathroom, their everything." But that closeness was reassuring, too. "Katie and I grew up together as parents," says Heather. "I have such fond memories of every little thing: the first teeth, when they both walked at the same time, supporting each other through breastfeeding. It was all so *lovely*."

Lovely and comfortable. Which is probably exactly how you'll feel about your own childcare decision—however hard that may be to believe on your first day back—eventually. Bottom line: Just make the choice that gives you the most peace and your child the most love. Because those two are probably one and the same.

CHAPTER TWO

✧⇛

The second cutting of the cord (this one you feel)

A couple of weeks before I was scheduled to go back to work after my second baby, Teddy, was born, I called my work wife, Wendy, to check in. She caught me up on the usual office gossip—who'd quit, who was pregnant, who'd gotten engaged, who'd worked late the night before. It was a little taste of a world I'd slipped away from almost entirely for a while. It felt both meaningless (who cares what celebrity had demanded almond milk at her photo shoot! I was keeping a helpless baby alive with human milk!) and also refreshingly adult and real.

"How are you doing with coming back?" Wendy asked. "Are you feeling more excited or more sad?" Both, actually. And then also guilty for feeling excited, and lame for feeling sad, and additionally a bit paranoid, come to think of it, wondering why Wendy was asking. Had they all moved on without me? Did they even need me anymore? And would I find meaning again in the work I loved deeply just three months ago?

"Can I give you some advice that someone gave me?" Wendy offered, knowing me well enough to fill my silence. "Whatever you do, do *not* spend these precious last couple of weeks feeling sad about leaving the baby. That's such a waste of time." I was going to be a little heartbroken upon my return no matter what, she explained, accurately. And I likely wouldn't have another week "off" (I use the term loosely) until Christmas. (So much for my paranoia . . . they needed me, it was clear.) So I might as well fill up my remaining free days with things that made me happy and fulfilled, or things that made my baby smile. And at ten weeks, Teddy did actually smile now, a lot!

I thought back to the tail end of my first leave, with my older son, and knew that Wendy was right. I had spent much of that time distraught but had exactly one happy flashbulb memory of a picnic I'd forced myself to take Will on in Central Park, basically for the sole purpose of saying I'd done so. I'd brought along a blue-and-yellow blanket that had his name knitted into it over and over in rows and columns: *WILLWILLWILLWILLWILLWILL. Will* I be okay? I'm *willing* myself to be okay. I ate an overpriced sandwich and tickled his tummy—he was finally getting one after eleven weeks of my worrying about how skinny he was—and he smiled a lopsided, gummy grin that showed off the dimple he and I had in common. I caught it perfectly on my camera phone. It was a manufactured moment, but it was truly happy.

This second time around, I wanted more of those moments, lots of those moments, with both kids. And I didn't want to waste my precious days worrying. Wendy's advice was a gift I've since passed along to many other friends.

Here, in no particular order, are some things I did that made me happy in those last couple of weeks of Teddy's maternity leave:

I bought new bras. They were nursing bras, but they were maybe even a little bit pretty, and they fit better than the ones I'd worn right after giving birth. (I also bought new pants, a lesson I'd learned the hard way the first time around—more on that indignity in Chapter 5.)

I took my three-year-old on a bunch of adventures, including his very first (very mini–) roller-coaster ride. And I sure as hell spent $8 on the souvenir photo they took of us coming down the hill. (My arms looked good. Kidding . . . but only kind of.)

I cooked a massive batch of my favorite Mario Batali Bolognese sauce and portioned it out in freezer bags for future dinners (because apparently I actually am my mother, circa 1983). I'd made the recipe countless times, but this time I got crazy and doctored it a bit. Now I always add a big spoonful of cinnamon to the pot (trust me).

I pumped a little extra milk for the freezer. I think I only became an honest-to-God "mother" when I started caring this much about my freezer.

I saw a movie with my husband. Actually, I can't remember if I saw a movie, but I'm going to say that I did because either way I certainly should have.

I napped. Probably only once. But, damn, it was good.

I got a pedicure and a haircut. Last ones for a while.

That was my list. Steal it, add to it, make your own. But no matter the details, use the couple of weeks before you go back to set yourself up for success. And then actually *have* that success. This chapter will tell you how, with advice to help you . . .

> . . . prepare for the work/life storm to come (with more than just deep breaths),
> . . . deal with whatever drama happened at work while you were away,
> . . . learn to embrace your new-mom identity professionally, and
> . . . do your job and still get the eff out of there on time.

To do before your last day of leave

Do not stress if you are reading this after already having arrived back at work. It still applies. But if you do have even a couple of days of leave left, here's the prep work worth doing.

You want to focus on two things right before reentry, says Sarah Best, LCSW, a psychotherapist specializing in reproductive and maternal mental health (and a mother of two): (1) taking care of logistics and (2) taking care of your feelings. "It's helpful, of course, to attend to any nuts and bolts that you can ahead of time," says Best. "But what I've seen helps my patients the most is really managing their expectations for that immediate transition back. When moms have a sense that they need to feel great on day two or day three in the office, disappointment runs really high, a sense of failure runs really high."

So the easy part first, the logistical brass-tacks stuff: If you're going to be dropping your baby at daycare, Best recommends doing a practice run packing the diaper bag first. Do you have everything you need? Will it all fit? Dress rehearse your whole morning if you can. In the first three months back at work, 48 percent of the women I surveyed said that they worried more about getting out the door in the morning than they did about their baby's development. (Not that I'm advocating spending your mornings stressing about milestones instead!) For inspiration, think back to your hyper-organized state right before you had the baby. The experts call that hormonal instinct nesting, but at work it's more like you were getting the nest ready to be abandoned. Starting around thirty-six weeks, you even might have had a hand-off memo, or some equivalent, ready to go in case you didn't show up to work the next day. Same applies here. Think about how much milk you'd like to have in the freezer; prepare a memo of contacts for the babysitter. If you're breastfeeding, go ahead and schedule your pumping into your work calendar if you can access it remotely. Try out your commute if it's changed in the time you've been away (my survey respondents said that their commute was 49 percent more stressful after having a baby—let's fix that).

To be fair, much of this logistical prep work requires child-care and—ding, ding, ding, emotional prep-work alert—leaving the baby. With my first son, I tried to do it all with him in tow. By baby number two, we had our nanny at home anyway, so I got to fly solo at the nail salon and the bra store. Having done it both ways, I recommend getting a sitter, if only for a couple of hours, to let you do some of these "I'm human again" tasks and also to have a little practice run before you have to officially cut the cord and untether yourself for the whole workday.

Now for part two, the "managing expectations" part of the prep work. My advice: Don't have many. Assume your first day back is going to be a running-mascara, bra-pads-soaked, pants-too-tight, insensitive-coworker-comments kind of day. And you'll be pleasantly surprised when it's not all that bad. Best suggests a more meditative-sounding approach. I am very bad at that kind of thing—I roll my eyes the whole way through yoga—but I've met this woman, and she's normal and not from some galaxy where women don't worry about their pants still being too tight, so I listened and appreciated her take: "Really do your best to *be with* whatever your experience is," Best instructs. "To not judge yourself no matter what your feel-ings are about going back, and take those expectations off the table and be okay with the experience." Be okay? I know. I was skeptical, too. But listen: "Being okay with it doesn't mean that you're giving it some big thumbs-up," she explains. "It's saying, this is where we are today and this is just what it's like today." It's finite. Tomorrow (or tomorrow's tomorrow) will be better.

But even if you're reading this while sitting in the parking lot at 8:55 a.m. on your first day back, with no preparation at all other than the tossing and turning you did on your pillow the night before, I'm here to tell you: You will be fine. "Once the adjustment phase is over, most women find it good and gratifying and excit-ing to go back to work," says Elizabeth Auchincloss, MD, a psy-chotherapist, mother, grandmother, and Vice Chair of Education for psychiatry at Weill Cornell (she's helped see dozens of female doctors through this transition). "Even if it's logistically hard, it's psychologically good."

Look around that parking lot: All the other parents getting out of their cars and heading in? They went through this, too. Go get 'em, champ. Here's how.

And, we're back. First, let's deal with
what happened while you were gone.

Throughout maternity leave, day in and day out, you sweated the small stuff: You timed your infant's naps on an app, you moved a safety pin from one side of your bra to the other to remember which breast you nursed from last (or, like me, you forgot to move it and frequently, quizzically fondled your own breasts in public to solve this mystery), you planned your hair-washes around the timing of the Mozart ditty played by the vibrating bouncy chair. You were on high alert *all the time.* So it's only natural that, when you think about what went on back at work during your leave, you might imagine countless "important" details of conference calls missed and memos unseen.

There were hundreds of things that had happened during my leave—like the hiring of an assistant not in my department, or a presentation by a guest speaker everyone had enjoyed, or a new design strategy that had been tried and discarded—that really didn't matter. Well, it's not that they didn't matter. They just didn't require rehashing, or analysis, or anyone else's additional time.

When you're on leave, life may feel like it's standing still in babyland. But at work, it's moving on, temporarily without you. No matter how important your role, the company continues to function. In my case, the magazine still hit newsstands on time. There it was, staring right at me at the CVS checkout, with a cover with words on it that, for the first time in years, I hadn't written. It's humbling—and confusing, especially when you think back on your pre-kid life and remember all those nights you "had" to work late, or the vacation hike through the Redwoods that was so rudely interrupted by emails. But there's a huge plus here: You'll remember this reality when you need to leave a meeting early to pump. Or head home at a reasonable hour to get to daycare in time.

So the minor stuff: Forget about it. Instead, focus on the small handful of VIMTs (Very Important Missed Things), and you'll be back up to speed in a matter of days.

What's a VIMT?

A new colleague at your level or above

A major new client—or one that's being wooed

A game-changing, new HR policy (like the glorious pumping room they installed, hopefully!) or a shift in the way your workplace conducts its annual reviews

A scandal big enough that it made industry news outside of your actual workplace (Debbie's husband's affair doesn't count; your biggest competitor's CFO's tax fraud does.)

The rescheduling of a major deadline

A recalibration of resources (people, or money) that changes a project you're responsible for

The emergence of a new competitor in your industry

You can think of more, I'm sure, that make sense for your workplace. Jot down the list before you go back—and then give yourself permission to ignore most everything else.

One thing I found really challenging is that people assume you come back knowing the VIMTs already. So treat the first few days back like a listening tour; it's the advice you'd give any new hire, and that's kind of what you are. Hopefully, you have the benefit—temporarily—of not having a backlog of long-term projects, and your calendar is, for a brief moment, mostly white, not chockablock blue with meetings. Use that time to schedule a quick catch-up with your boss(es), immediate colleagues, any important underlings, and anyone who's new to the staff, too. Here's how many of those meetings will go:

THEM: Oh, welcome back! We missed you! How are you feeling? How is the baby? Can I see pictures? Wow, do you miss her soooooooooo much?

YOU: Of course . . . um, hang on, wait, trying to find some pictures on my phone where we are both appropriately clothed.

THEM: Coo, coo, coo, etc., etc., etc.

YOU: So, can you fill me in on what happened with the Peterson trial while I was out?

THEM: Oh, sure!

And then you get the fill-in. Every time they ask a baby question, you ask a help-me-not-look-clueless question, and all will be right with the world. It's a dance. An exhausting but informative tango. You certainly don't have to entertain any lines of questioning that are uncomfortable, but embracing a slightly more personal relationship with your colleagues can truly help in this moment. One study of new working moms found that two things stand out as "the most significant facilitators of women's return to work" after leave: (1) satisfactory child care and (2) supportive relationships in the workplace. Translation: Who's taking care of you matters just as much as who's taking care of your baby. (Thank you, Work Wife Wendy!)

Generally speaking, people feel very generous on your first day back. You're relieving them of the work they'd taken over for you, and many colleagues are just glad you didn't quit entirely. "People tend to offer help. Take it all," says Ellen, an editor and writer, who returned to work fourteen weeks after her son Max, who has cerebral palsy, was born. Ellen's circumstances were special, but the takeaway here applies to everyone: "Remember that people usually aren't sure what to say or what to do for you. So when they ask go ahead and tell them how to help," she says. You want help finding your special ergonomic desk chair that went missing while you were gone? Ask for help with that. You need to claim a chunk of the intern's time every day? Ask. It's a quick honeymoon, and then it's business as usual.

"Very quickly," says entertainment lawyer Jennifer Justice (she goes by JJ) who is the president of corporate development for Superfly and was EVP of Jay Z's company Roc Nation when she had her twins, "there was a line out my door. A line! The junior associate, the CFO, the head of the company." Jay Z himself? "No, he was not waiting in line there," she says, laughing. "But I do remember him needing something from me very soon after coming back to work. And while it's great, it's super all-business, and sometimes you want it to be a bit more fuzzy. When I was pregnant, people were more careful, but then it was like, Okay, she's back? Here we go."

What if some huge shift happened while you were out? What if another colleague ended up claiming something far bigger than your Aeron chair? "A very weird thing happened during my leave," says Emma (not her real name), a financial analyst. "Every single man that had come into my group at the same time I did got promoted within two weeks of me leaving on maternity leave. They promoted all of them. I wondered: Did I just get punished for being a mommy?" In fact, before she went on leave, Emma had restructured one of her company's portfolios, essentially growing her job and doing all the work of her maternity leave ahead of time. Then she went on leave and everyone else got promoted due, at least in part, she believes, to her efforts. Emma had handled pre-eclampsia and a near-fatal infection. She could handle this. Still, it took a year, and she was sheepish about telling me how she went about it. "I threw a bit of a protest; I protested until I got promoted and I did that by slowing down my work. This is probably a horrible message to send young, ambitious mothers . . ."

Nah. Go on.

Back from leave, Emma initiated a series of "very challenging, very hard" conversations with her supervisor. What he was paying her for, she calmly explained, was the job she had been doing before she grew her job. If she was going to jump back into that bigger role she created, she wanted the title and salary bump that reflected her contributions to the company. At first, when that didn't work, she simply stopped doing the extra tasks she'd added before the baby. "In my case, 'underperforming' was actually doing the job. I did the job, did everything I was supposed to do. But nothing more," she says. It was a ballsy move, and one that Emma made knowing that she could find another job pretty easily if the plan backfired (a crucial detail if you want to try this, too!). "I figured, if I'm working harder than I need to and my efforts aren't being recognized, I might as well do the basic job and also focus on my very young kid," she says.

That worked. And—happy ending—the promotion came through just as her baby was getting into the groove of being a baby. She was ready to amp back up. And amp she did. Two years later, as I write this, Emma is being considered for another promotion.

Can we pause and talk about "mommy guilt" for a quick minute?

Have you seen those word clouds of language where the most common words used are made the biggest? If I created one of those graphics of all the things people said in my interview transcripts for this book, "guilt" would surely be in the largest font—*everyone* brought it up: the police lieutenant who had to return at exactly the six-week mark because that's when the annual promotions were being made; the interior designer who worked from home but tried to ignore her baby's cries from the other room, where the nanny was. But that word-cloud visual would hide the more interesting truth: "Guilt" meant wildly different things to different mothers. There were those who said they "felt guilty" because they ached to hold their babies and worried that they'd left them, unsoothed, in less capable hands. Then there were others who luxuriated in the freedom of the office—the air conditioning, the lovely bottled water, the intelligent conversations, the almost-forgotten bliss of being alone in their own skin. Those mothers also "felt guilty," they said. Why? For not missing their babies more! Guilt was an automatic. Like some unconscious tic.

By the way, both of those kinds of women made it through the Fifth Trimester.

My own experience with guilt was some kind of sick hybrid of the two. Like most of you reading this book, I had to work. My husband was still in his medical residency and I was, at that point, the breadwinner by a factor of three. So I didn't have to make a big guilt-inducing decision about whether or not to go back to work. Of course I was going back to work. I felt sad, sure, to leave my sweet baby. So sad, crying-on-the-sidewalk sad. But not really guilty. Still, when I said as much, people frowned at me, confused. Or they assumed I was in denial.

You know when someone coughs in your general direction and then you cough a minute later and are convinced it's the flu? It was like that. Very quickly, I started feeling guilty. Guilty for not feeling guilty. Then guilty that I was so susceptible to guilt. Some women, I suppose, take comfort in their guilt, a little self-flagellation. But heading down that path would have been the most distracting and destructive thing I could have done during my reentry at the magazine. I just didn't have time. I was swirling (and also exhausted).

I tossed in my bed by night and clicked my clicky pen at my desk by day, and after about a week, here's where I ended up on back-to-work guilt: It's stupid. It's a relic left over from a time when women had more of a "choice" about whether or not to work and those who didn't openly judged those who did. (Of course those mommy wars continue to a degree, but I think we've reached a point where it's no longer cool to call someone out publicly for their decision.) So what the hell? Let's be post-guilt. Doesn't that sound good?

"Guilt," by definition, implies a feeling of "should," a comparison between you and some other supposedly better parent or better worker or better decision you could have made. But if *all* of us working moms are feeling guilt in some form there is actually *nothing to compare* here. We're all in the muck of it. There is no other, better, less-guilty working mom to aspire to be. So what if we just cancel guilt out entirely, like some ugly common denominator? Banish guilt.

Or at least let's not *call* it guilt. Call it whatever it really is deep down: sadness, elation, confusion. The point of this book is not to help you squelch whatever feelings you may have about going back to work. It's meant to help you acknowledge them, see how common they are, and move forward, one day at a time, until you get through to the other side. No guilt.

Make "mom" part of your work identity
(because, yes, that's a good thing)

Congratulations. At work, you are officially now a Person with a Personal Life. Maybe you were always seen that way and everyone at work knew where you'd brunched on Sunday and how gel-formula toothpaste makes you get cracks in the corners of your mouth. Or maybe they didn't. Maybe they knew nothing about your life outside the office because that's what you were most comfortable with or because that's just the norm at your workplace.

But now? Everyone knows: You had sex. You made a baby. There's a good chance there's milk being made in your breasts right now and that you're wearing round little pads in your bra to keep it from leaking all over your clothes. Blushing yet? I'm not telling you this to make any part of the transition harder. (And adoptive moms, second moms, egg-donor-recipient moms, surrogate-using moms, forgive me for generalizing . . . the basic point here applies to you, too.) But I am telling you to embrace a new kind of transparency. Or roll with it, at least.

Over the years, I worked with women who had wildly different approaches to how much of their mom life they brought to work.

There was A., whose children's wide-eyed and gorgeous baby pictures wallpapered the side of her desk. She was all business, direct to the point that the young-uns at the office were intimidated by her as she offered up resolute work and parenting advice rat-a-tat to the rest of us brave enough to listen: "Do not go in there now if you're asking for something . . . the boss is in a bad mood." "Make sure your nanny actually holds the baby when you interview her." "Sit at the end of the conference table so you can look the meeting's leader in the eye." And, "Breastfeeding? Yeah, I didn't bother." If you complimented her earrings, she would likely tell you that she bought them to console herself on a work trip, shopping therapy for career stress and mommy conflictedness. (See how I didn't use the word "guilt" there?) I loved her.

Another executive rarely mentioned her children. Her office was full of framed awards, professional accolades, and photos of her with world leaders. Over by her computer were tiny, discreet family pictures that only she could really see.

An impossibly cool fashion editor surprised me one day when she marched into work wearing Balenciaga, Proenza Schouler, five-inch heels—and a rainbow-colored pipe cleaner bracelet her daughter had made.

There were editors who privately color-coded their personal calendars so their assistants could schedule meetings around pediatrician appointments and preschool interviews. And there was the new girl whom we'd *heard* had had a baby. But there was no evidence of him in sight for months, until a single, perfect professional photo showed up one day, positioned among her Lucite and leather desk accessories. He was beautiful. Dressed out of another era in white linen.

Do I sound like I'm judging the women who were more private about their motherhood? I don't mean to. Everyone does her best. If they're there, they're making it happen. And I'm glad I worked in a place where all these approaches were welcome. But the moms who were bravest about saying, "I am here at work, but I am also a mother" . . . they made things a lot more manageable and warm for new moms coming back from leave.

Many moms in less traditional circumstances find themselves saddled with the added pressure of redefining modern working motherhood for their colleagues. "Even though I wasn't the one nursing and up in the night, I was still going back to work sleep deprived and unsure of my new identity as a parent," says Renée, then a therapeutic spa co-owner, whose wife, Nathalie, gave birth to their baby. "Nat got much more bonding time before going back, and I didn't want to just fit into that societal expectation of 'the dad goes back to work sooner,' but there I was. I'm also a mother. I'm tearing up right now just thinking back on it. This is new emotional territory." For everyone.

"Be authentic! Bring your whole self to work," says Jennifer Dorian, General Manager of Turner Classic Movies, part of Turner Broadcasting in Atlanta. Jennifer consciously shares photos of her (now school-aged) daughters with colleagues to help foster a family-friendly environment as a manager. "I'll talk about the funny and heartbreaking things going on with them; I'm self-deprecating," she continues, explaining that this tactic does more than just make people comfortable—it makes them better at their jobs. "I believe that perfect is the enemy of good," says Jennifer. "If you're trying to be a perfectionist mom, or perfectionist employee, you're going to fail, because there is *no such thing* as perfection, and a lot—a lot—of the things we need to do in business are messy and creative and innovative. When I think of the great, charismatic, successful mavericks of industry who are men, they're not buttoned up and in control all the time. As female role models, we shouldn't be either."

Remember that, now that it's your turn.

If it's uncomfortable to march around the office toting your breast pump; if you have to excuse yourself from a meeting to answer an urgent text from the daycare, know this: You're making things easier for everyone who comes after you. And that next mini-generation of moms will stay and work *for* you one day and be loyal.

I acknowledge my workplace was a little looser than many others. No one was riding Segways around the halls, Google-style, but no one was wearing suits and (heaven forbid) pantyhose, either. You have to use your own best judgment about how much of your mommyhood to bring to work with you. A good rule of thumb is to try to balance (a) how distracting you might be to other people's work, with (b) how helpful you might be to the moms who come after you. Two examples:

> **Very distracting, not very helpful:** "Oh, wow, I have had the worst morning. I pumped all this milk and then spilled it all over my keyboard. Such a waste, and what's the IT guy going to say?!"

> **Only mildly distracting, actually helpful:** "Hey, would you mind if we bumped our lunch back fifteen minutes so I have time to pump?"

All that said, the number one most distracting thing you can do as a new mom is also one of the most effective ways to marry your two worlds, and I totally get behind it: Bring the baby in for a visit. Nitzia Logothetis, the founder and executive chairwoman of the Seleni Institute for maternal mental health, did it daily for a few weeks when she first transitioned back. Her caregiver would bring her baby to her at lunchtime. "I'm very lucky, I know, to be in a situation where I could do that," she says. "But it really helped to see her and nurse her. Just a little check-in every day." And then after a month, she was ready to be apart from the baby for longer stretches.

More typically, a lot of women—at least the ones who didn't work in dramatically male-dominated offices—told me that they brought their babies into the workplace just once to meet their colleagues while they were still on maternity leave. (Clear the visit with your coworkers so you don't bust in on a deadline day or arrive when your closest work friend is on vacation.) Sarah, a curriculum manager at a world-renowned museum, found that one baby visit vital to her ability to come back to work. With the days ticking away toward the end of her leave, she had "anxiety and depression, and just this feeling of my baby is so great, oh my God, and now he's going to be taken away from me," she recalls. The day before she was set to go back, she took him in with her for a visit (and a delayed office baby shower). "It was so sweet," she says. "And I know it's silly. He was eight weeks old and had no idea what was going on, but I walked around the museum with him, brought him to my desk, put out all my pictures of him and was like, 'Look, Mommy's got you right here and I'm going to be looking at your face all day.' And it was so lovely, after being away for so long, to have everyone get so excited about him." The very next day, she started work again, and felt like she'd already cleared an enormous hurdle. "I was like, Okay, I went this far already. I've got this." And she really did.

I've got to say, there's just something about seeing someone with a baby that makes you realize how capable they are. It always made me laugh when someone who previously couldn't change the toner cartridge in the printer could unswaddle a baby, collapse a stroller, and give me a hug at the same time.

Still, a lot of women worry that revealing their motherhood somehow makes them seem weak. If you're in a work environment where you couldn't dream of mentioning a sleepless night, let alone bring in your baby, I feel for you. I also respect you if you can grit your teeth and get through it with enough satisfaction. One mom who worked on a trading floor after the birth of her daughter anonymously told me, "Under no circumstances would I have brought my baby in—and I wouldn't have wanted to in that environment. I would have been fired. Or, well, really, I just would have gotten a smaller bonus." But if you're torn, listen to Corey McAveeney, founder of kulturenvy.com and an expert at Culture Amp, a software company that helps start-ups understand and define their workplace culture. I asked McAveeney, a new mom herself, to offer advice for exactly this dilemma: "I think it comes down to, can you be yourself at work and are you happy with your work identity?" she says. "Some people think that in order to be professional, they can't be themselves. But suppressing your feelings isn't going to help you be more productive. If you're in a work environment where you can't be yourself, you need to explore other options, even if it means getting out of your comfort zone."

What if you're the boss? What if you have the power, right now, to make motherhood a more open topic in your workplace? Do it! And stop—please, please stop—being afraid of looking vulnerable. JJ, at Superfly, is also the chairwoman of the advisory board of Women: Inspiration & Enterprise (WIE), but even she is learning as she goes. Back at Jay Z's empire Roc Nation, where she worked when she gave birth to her twins, she says, "All of the men that founded the company were raised by single moms, so they truly appreciate women, but they still don't know what it's like to be one." As the only executive-level woman at the company with children, she felt obligated to teach them. "One thing that was super helpful was at my first WIE panel, one tech executive talked about how she noticed that around two thirty or three o'clock many days, someone on staff would claim to have a 'doctor's appointment,'" she says, making little air quotes with her fingers. "She realized that many of her employees really just wanted to go pick up their kids from school and come back to work. So she started doing it herself, announcing, 'I'm going to pick up my kids . . . will be available after,'" to lift the taboo. JJ's twins were only two years old when we talked, but she's adopted that strategy bravely in other ways and refuses to hide her mom-related obligations. "I'm very vocal about them," she says. And she still gets the job done.

We do have a bit of a boss problem. In my survey, 22 percent of women said that their bosses "rarely or never" asked about their baby. And 23 percent said that their bosses with kids of their own rarely or never talked about them. Almost a third, 30 percent, of bosses with kids didn't acknowledge them with photos or artwork at the office. I'm sympathetic to the struggle. How do you lead a team with spit-up on your skirt, or negotiate a deal with a doily valentine on your desk? Or ask your boss for a raise the same day you have to leave early for your baby's six-month checkup? JJ's got the answer here, too: Admit what's hard and brag about getting through it.

That's worth repeating. In italics: *Admit what's hard and brag about getting through it.*

"I think taking credit is one of the biggest responsibilities we have, an *ultimate* responsibility," JJ says. "It's no different than Beyoncé calling herself Sasha Fierce. Women don't like to brag about themselves, to seem egotistical." She gets quiet a minute and thinks back on her own challenging childhood, about being proud of the success she's had since, as a top-top-top entertainment lawyer and a mother: "You think it's easy for me to tell my whole story? In high school I wouldn't let people come to my house because I was so embarrassed. It wasn't until I was a lawyer, well into my twenties that I would let people know where I was from. I know what government cheese tastes like. I know what food stamps and medical vouchers are. It's time for women to stop pretending to be men, and stop being scared to be women, to take on these roles *as* women."

Welcome back! Hey, look at how efficient you are!

I wonder how Winston Churchill would feel about being in this book? Good, I hope. Because Nitzia Logothetis says she thought of him often when she first went back to work, feeling blue and distracted. (Nitzia, by the way, grew up in England, so imagine her saying all this with clever authority, in a British accent.) "Churchill used to have moods—he went through terrible periods of darkness—and I've heard that's why he was very industrious," she says. "He would paint or read while he worked. But he was always doing *something* so that his thoughts wouldn't take over." The key to focus, she found, was simply staying busy.

Luckily, that's not hard to accomplish. You won't have to set up an easel to keep yourself occupied! Because you will be busy. More than busy. Maybe not your first day back, or even your third. But very quickly, you too, will end up with your version of JJ's line out the door of her office (perhaps minus the phone messages from Jay Z and Bey). And you'll have fewer hours to work with than ever before.

So how the hell do you get it all done?

Eh, you just do.

I'm not being a jerk, promise. It's a boring answer, but it's remarkably simple and true. That time at home with your newborn, when you were essentially responsible completely for keeping two human beings alive, fed, well, clean, and safe around the clock in three-hour intervals? It trained you well. Now it's your job to capitalize on your new abilities and use them. The moms in my older son's first preschool class, most of whom worked, taught me a ridiculous-sounding but accurate philosophy: If you want something done well and fast and reasonably, give it to the busiest mom to do. Sometimes, often, that was me.

In my life's millionth example of "everything interesting happens at once," our younger son, Teddy, turned three months old in September, and I headed back to work—just as our older son, Will, was starting his very first fall of nursery school. Pumping and working would have been more than enough to keep anyone busy, but with preschool came a whole new previously uncharted brainstream of tasks. When the class guinea pig needed exploratory surgery, and the parents wanted to collect funds for the vet bill, who sent the email? Me. When the teachers needed empty paper towel rolls and "translucent recyclables"? Me. When someone needed to sign up for an extra slot on the "healthy snack" calendar? Me. My husband thought I was out of my skull, but I knew that by raising my hand for a bunch of these little minutes-long tasks, I was getting out of the big stuff, things like months-long fund-raising efforts, or the weekly decorations committee meetings for library week (dear to my heart but not to my Outlook calendar). I'd order a bagel delivery (sliced in quarters for little mouths) and congratulate myself on my industriousness.

Here's the secret: Each of those little tasks took less than five minutes. And they gave me a whole lot of cred, even if it was largely in my own head.

That was my rule, at home with the baby, at work with my colleagues, and wherever betwixt the two worlds met. If something would take five minutes or less, I'd do it right then and there and avoid the heavy psychic weight of a longer to-do list. You needed a headline written? An old job candidate's résumé dug up? An intro made or someone "looped in" over email? Yes, sure, why not, right now! Maybe you're wondering if that was distracting, if it interrupted the task I was already deeply heads-down in and working on? Nah, in reality, the request had interrupted me already anyway. So no further harm done. Leigh Abramson, a lawyer and writer, uses the same strategy, especially when work interrupts mothering, or mothering interrupts work. "Look, in a perfect world, I would compartmentalize completely," says Leigh. "In reality, if I did that I would feel like I was constantly failing. Sometimes it's easier just to get the task done so you can move on and not keep thinking about it."

Evaluating requests for my five-minute rule also forced me to grade their importance, to prioritize the value of my time, and to say no more readily, too. One seemingly simple little rule did all that.

Ben and I have a running joke with our boys that there are only ever three given rules at any moment. At the beach: no throwing sand, no swimming without a grownup, no refusing sunscreen. In the car: no kicking the seat, no drinking milk (aka, future vomit), no complaining about Daddy's Grateful Dead music. We change the rules all the time, but there are only ever three to remember.

Same goes here. Pick any three of the following rules (or two if you want to steal my five-minute one). That's all you'll need to feel like the most turbo-charged, organized, efficient version of yourself. "The holy grail for working moms is to figure out how to optimize your schedule so that it is the most productive in the hours you've got," says Allison Beer, the travel partnerships exec. "It takes so much planning just to get *to* work in the first place, I want *all* of my work hours to be productive." Here's what helps:

DECIDE WHAT'S SACRED. The first holiday season after having Teddy, I had to cancel half of my planned Christmas vacation. No one forced me to, but it was pretty necessary, and I've got to tell you, I never really got over it. We were driving to my in-laws', not flying, so the dates were a little flexible in my mind, I suppose, and I just didn't give myself (or my boss) a firm cutoff. Lesson learned: Babies set new limits on your life. And you have to set new limits at work. No one else will set them for you. Wendy Shanker, who's a single mom, told me she refuses to travel more than three nights away from her daughter. It's one of the first things you should do when going back to work, says Jennifer Dorian. "Right away, you have to decide what is sacred. For me, it was really sacred to not miss the at-home rush hour of dinner, bath, and bedtime from six p.m. to eight p.m., even if it meant getting right back online at eight thirty to check in with work." And remember, she says, that your musts will change as your children grow. These days, Jennifer does work late occasionally. But she always makes it to her girls' weekly Suzuki violin lesson—right in the middle of Wednesday afternoon.

GO HOLLYWOOD ON 'EM. If all else fails, just fake like you know what you're doing. "I was in meetings all the time, presenting to executives but thinking about my baby," says Karen, a marketing executive in Connecticut. "I'd wonder, can they tell? One of my friends at work made me feel better by saying, 'Learn quickly that all working moms deserve Oscar awards for their ability to pull this off without anyone knowing what's going on in their minds.' That really helped. Your performance trumps everything else, and I've got to say, I've gotten some of my highest performance reviews since having kids."

DON'T EVEN TRY TO TOGGLE. This option is for anyone who completely balked at my five-minute rule. I get it: Everyone's brains are different. I once had a boss who confessed that anytime she was on vacation, she put her phone in the bedside table drawer and closed it, except for two specific times a day. She knew that was the only way she'd be able to focus entirely on her family. What about the flip side: ignoring the baby to focus on work? If you're one of those people who simply cannot focus on two things at once, set up a plan for emergencies (i.e., hand your cell to a colleague) and give yourself permission to *only focus on work at work.* "If you're doing exciting and challenging things," one mother of three told me, "you eventually learn that, yes, of course you love your children unconditionally, but it is okay to focus on the job and be one hundred percent immersed in it for set periods of time."

EAT A FROG FOR BREAKFAST. That is, do the hardest thing on your list first. This one's a personal favorite. (But do yourself a favor and don't actually try it until you've been back at work a few days— and skip it entirely if you're at all tempted to quit your job; see page 63.) So I was thrilled when Jennifer, the exec above, taught me the catchier froggy terminology. "Mark Twain said if you ever have to eat a live frog, eat the live frog in the morning—one of my favorite people at work told me that," cites Jennifer. "You want to get the most unappealing thing on your list out of the way so you don't have to feel a distracting sense of doom the rest of the day."

STOP OVERPRODUCING. This one's also from Jennifer, who calls herself a "time management ninja" (love that). "It's so important to develop a filter of what really matters," Jennifer says. "Before I had my children, if someone asked me to do something at work, I would just do it and do my best. Even if I knew I was chasing windmills or overproducing, I would do it. Now, after kids, before taking something on, I always ask myself: Is it business critical? Is it going to make a difference to my company or my career?" If the answer is no? "I either do the bare minimum or I don't do it at all."

Laura Morgan Roberts, PhD, a professor and executive coach, offers an example: When she started giving lectures again after the birth of her first child, she didn't have the bandwidth for all the fancy bells and whistles she might have previously included in her PowerPoint presentations. "But you know what my students needed, more than the perfect video or the most beautiful colors in the report? My presence," she recalls realizing. "What mattered most was simply that I was there and fully engaged when I was in that room with them. That was the best I could do, and it was enough."

DON'T WASTE TIME PRESOLVING PROBLEMS. "Before I had my daughter, I was very type A, I was a planner, I was twelve steps ahead of everything," says Katie Fiamingo, a top innovation strategist at Nestlé Purina PetCare in St. Louis. "I'm still a planner, but now I actually plan out the fact that I won't worry about something until next week. Before, I'd be worrying about everything all the time. Now, I say to myself, okay, I'm going to concentrate on this problem right now, and that one can wait until tomorrow."

DECIDE EXACTLY HOW MUCH YOU WANT TO KNOW ABOUT YOUR BABY'S DAY. I had a colleague whom I used to hear on the phone with her caregiver every time the baby ate: how many ounces, how many bites of mango. She found the interruptions predictable and reassuring—and then was able to go on with her day without worry. Another colleague told me that she knew she'd fully adjusted when she got to 5:00 p.m. and realized with relief that she hadn't checked in with daycare all day. I loved it when once or twice a week, our nanny texted me pictures of the boys. It was just infrequent enough to be special but not distracting. Figure out what level of communication works for you and ask for that explicitly.

PRIORITIZE FOOD. If you're breastfeeding, I'd totally make this one of your three rules. "Looking back, the advice I'd give myself and any new mom going back to work is that you need much more food than you think you do," says writer and comedian Emmy Laybourne, who started full-day grad school when her daughter was a couple of months old. "You need to eat like forty grams of protein at every meal. That's like two chicken breasts!" What do amino acids have to do with productivity and efficiency? You are not efficient if you are a wreck. "Before I figured this out I just kept falling apart," says Laybourne. "I was so tired and so hungry, I couldn't keep it together emotionally."

ALSO: PRIORITIZE FACE TIME . . . It's really important, especially after your colleagues have been missing your face for three months. And I'm not just saying that because I worked in an industry where you knew if you'd interacted with someone that day based on whether or not you could remember their outfit. In fact, 69 percent of my survey respondents ranked face time a seven or higher for importance on a scale of zero to ten. So get seen, but also: Don't waste your time *not* getting seen. "Before having my boys," says Monica, "I was in the office from 8:45 to 6:15, first one in, last one out. No one else would show up until 9:30, and it is dead on our floor by 5:45. And I just realized: I was the only one making myself stick around. As long as my work was done, it really didn't matter." That said, Monica's no slacker. Sometimes, after an afternoon meeting outside of the office, she'll come back to the building for a couple of hours just as everyone's leaving for the day. "I'm not doing it just to be noticed," she says. "But it's always nice to get those points."

And recognize the difference between face time and gossip time. Everyone wants something of a social life at work (good sign that you're working with people you like), but limit your nonwork-related chitchat. "I used to sit in colleagues' offices for forty-five minutes after a meeting just talking," says Lydia Fenet, a senior vice president at Christie's and a charity auctioneer (so you know she talks fast). "I just don't do that anymore. I focus entirely on the things that are really important to my job, so I can get home. It's better for me, and frankly, it's probably better for my coworkers, too!"

―――――

I realize I've put bold-type titles on these little rules and summed them up like they're easy-peasey-lemon-squeezy, as Will says. But make no mistake: Some of these shifts take major changes in the way you see yourself. Jennifer, the wonderfully insightful frog-eater above, says that learning to stop overproducing required more than just breaking a bad habit; she had to rethink her whole MO. "The biggest adjustment coming back to work for me was that before having children I never minded working late," she says. "My whole identity was: I'll do it, I'll get it done, you can count on me." But she quickly realized that wasn't sustainable with a baby at home. "I was like, How am I going to be me and stand out and do a good job—what's my new identity going to be?" Her background is in branding, so she turned her career skills on herself. "I decided that one of my other strengths is not being afraid to ask what everyone is thinking, not being afraid to be frank myself," she says. So frank she was: about the challenges of working motherhood and everything else. Now at her company, when you want your time to be well spent, when you want to be listened to, when you want an honest opinion, you go to Jennifer. Everyone relies on Jennifer. In dialing down her hours, Jennifer dialed herself up a reputation as a true leader. Naturally, she just got promoted— again.

✠

CHAPTER THREE

Getting through "I have to quit"

Your Five-Step Pain-Free Plan

As I was writing the previous chapter, heading out to the library to work, I ran into a neighbor in my apartment building's elevator. She had her tiny, new, two-week-old baby boy with her in the stroller, and was also managing two roller suitcases, two stuffed tote bags, and a leash, at the end of which was her adorable bulldog, all resting doggy bitch-face and the skeptical raised eyebrows (surely you know a bulldog like that, too). My neighbor looked tired, sure, but she looked good. I knew the hours of patience and just the sheer competence it had taken to get out the door hauling all of that, and the baby was two weeks? He was probably smack in the middle of a feeding frenzied growth spurt, too.

"He's so beautiful! How's it all going?" I asked, wide-eyed, in our twenty-two-second ride down to the lobby together.

"Oh, it's okay . . . It'll be okay, at least I hope it will," she replied. "I'm off to my parents' house for the night for a visit." The bulldog snorted.

"I'm writing a book for new moms, actually," I offered, "about going back to work . . ."

"Oh, God. Work. I'm gonna have to quit my job," she said as

the door opened and her dog pulled on his leash, and I tried to help with her suitcases. "There is just no . . . way."

And she was off. It was too quick for me to tell her: You're only two weeks in! And look what you're doing: You're traveling, and you packed, and it's 8:30 a.m. and you're on your way out of the house, good for you! If you can manage all that, you can definitely handle work.

Chances are, if you're reading this book, you know at your core that you need to work, that you want to work. You may even know that mothers who continue to work have been found to have more ambitious daughters and kinder sons. And that working mothers earn more relative to non-mothers than they ever have before. But the drumbeat of "I have to quit" can be loud in your ears: as you stare into space washing bottles, or get suddenly teary-eyed touching noses with your baby, or open up an email from HR about your expected return date. I have to quit, you may think. I have to quit, I have to quit, I have to quit, like some backward-running Little Engine That Could. I have to quit.

"The day I went back to work, it felt just like this biological wrong I was committing," Kim, a neuroscientist and pediatrician told me. "Like there was this little animal that was supposed to be with me and I was willfully ripping her away." Kim expected to be sad, and certainly her training had taught her about attachment and transitions. But this wasn't rational, this feeling. "I was like, We have to move, I have to quit my job. Oh my God, there's no way."

Heather Ladov, a social worker in Oakland, California, who helps immigrant families dealing with mental illness, says she never expected to feel so ambivalent about her job. "I felt very connected to it, with all of the time, energy, values, effort, and money I'd put into developing my career. When I was pregnant, I was all up on my soapbox saying of course I would work. I would never stay home." Then she had baby Caden, went back to work, and for several weeks, she says, "I don't think there was a minute that went by that I wasn't longing to be with him. I was so sad. I wanted to quit. Every time I pumped I was angry at the pump because I wanted it to be him instead."

Women in my survey reported that it took an average of almost six months after delivery to start feeling normal again emotionally. The vast majority were back at work months before that point, though. Your fuse is short, your nighttime sleep is shorter; it's only natural that the desire to quit can become a fixation and a distraction. Here are the five things I've found in my research that silence the drumbeat and get you through, sanity and career intact.

1) Remember that the discomfort is temporary

Years ago, pre-kids, when I was home in Atlanta for some wedding planning, I landed "a whopping case" (my mother's technical term) of appendicitis. It took the ER staff many hours to diagnose me, and in the meantime, I writhed pretty much nonstop in pain. In a tiny voice I asked my mom, "When I have a baby, will childbirth be this bad?" No, no, definitely not, she told me and then revealed something that I filed away for my future labor and deliveries, and lots of other painful occasions, too: "Contractions are temporary," Mom said. "You have them, and then they let up before you have another. And when you know pain is temporary, it just hurts less." (I should note that my mother had zero epidurals and three deliveries. I had two with two.)

Know that this transitional time is temporary, and it will hurt less. Every learning curve has an apex. "We all accept to varying degrees that there will be a learning curve with new motherhood," says psychotherapist Sarah Best. "That taking care of a baby is a new kind of job. But there's this assumption that returning to work is going to be the same as always, the same role, the same job, that it should feel easy. But the fact is, you've never *been* a working mom before. It's a totally new scenario." When you find yourself being self-critical, Best advises, "remind yourself: oh, yeah, this is only day four. I may be a pro at my job, but I'm an absolute beginner at being a working mom."

Occasionally, Best will have a patient who, after three months back at work, truly feels like she needs to make a major change. But much, much more often, the women who tell her at week two that they need to quit come back a month or two later with a different story entirely: "They say," notes Best, " 'I'm so glad I'm back at the office; I don't think I would have been able to stay home!' "

Heather, the social worker, made herself wait two months before making any decisions. "I remember I said I needed to get to Halloween," she says. And in that time she figured out very clearly that her limit was three and a half days a week of work. Any more than that was too much emotionally. Any less didn't feel like enough. When her request for a part-time week was denied, she moved to a different agency and found the hours she wanted— doing the work she loved.

2) Think about what you get out of work . . .

Simple but true: "Women's perception of their work as rewarding" is the single biggest predictor of whether they'll resume their employment. More than their occupation level. More than their education. More than their husband's paycheck! Carolyn Pirak, LCSW, founding director of the Bringing Baby Home program at The Gottman Institute, often works with couples who are having a tough transition into parenthood. She advises them to think back on why they first became a couple, to renew the root of their friendship. And the same thing applies, she says, with your career, especially if you're feeling resentful of your job. "Think, why did you choose to work in the first place?" Pirak instructs. "Did you choose to work only for money, or because you love the work and the people? You did at some point *choose* to work where you work.

So, now that you have a baby, are you getting just money from your job . . . or are you getting esteem and confidence, too?"

I'll add: Are you getting experience that will keep you moving upward so you can make cultural, institutional change for new parents from within?

Speaking of moving upward, a lot of what you get out of not quitting is that several years from now, you won't be an at-home mom who quit. Blunt, but there it is. Liisa Hunter, who works in marketing solutions on a global sales team for Facebook, says she found this idea really motivating and true coming back after the birth of her first son. "I remember a colleague saying to me—and this was so poignant—that this is the most difficult time in your life right now as a mom," Liisa says. "She said, 'but you need to understand that in five years your son will go to kindergarten and in that time you'll either have moved up in your career from here to here'—I still remember her gesturing with her hands—'or you will be calling me trying to get back into the workforce.' I decided then, okay, I'm going to be so grateful I didn't drop out. Those years really do matter at work."

Something else a lot of type A women (or type A-/B+ women, like moi) get out of work: a sense of control. Pirak tells me about one Microsoft executive who revealed that the thing that most drove her crazy about becoming a new parent was that nobody gave her feedback about how she was doing. (Side note: Do they not have nosy little old ladies out there in Seattle—because I got far more feedback in line at CVS than I ever wanted. But I digress . . .) "She said she was so used to sales statistics and employee ratings, and all of a sudden she went home and nobody was like, Okay, today you were a five out of ten, today you were a ten out of ten," says Pirak. "Her husband was like, She's making me crazy, but I'm not going to rate her parenting!" A lot of women, Pirak tells me, crave that kind of feedback while on maternity leave, and going back to the land of P&Ls and performance reviews can feel like a relief. You know how you're doing! (By the way, while Pirak cautions that "no baby fits perfectly into an app," she does admit that moms like this one can benefit from tracking things like sleep and diapers on their phones. "It helped her calculate the value of her role," she says, during this transitional period.)

It's ironic that such a chaotic time could give you a sense of calm, but that's a sentiment I heard repeatedly in my interviews. "The moment I went back to doing my work again, I just felt more like myself. I felt like more of an adult," says Hannah, an interior designer who has her own small firm. "I loved being at home with my baby, but I realized that I'd felt really adrift." Work gives you destination, goals, purpose.

3) . . . And realize what work gets out of you!

JJ, the entertainment lawyer, describes this as a tool she's used over the years to remember her own worth: "It's a negotiating thing," she says. "Once you're there at the company, once you're part of the deal, people aren't just going to get rid of you. It's *hard* to get rid of you. So know that you're just as important coming back from leave as you were when they first tried to get you to take the job." (More important, actually, because they've invested in your training.)

Everyone works harder and more happily when they feel valued. So make a list—yes, really, a bulleted list—of all the things your boss and colleagues and the greater industry get out of having you, ass flattened in that chair, doing your job. These three months, this whole lifetime, really, is riddled with compromises. No one's saying you won't have to compromise to stick with your career. But research has shown that if you are able to see the value you bring to your work—if you feel valued by your managers and coworkers—you'll feel more confident in those compromises. So make the list. Go on.

4) Consider phasing back in for better focus

Focus is an enormous issue when you first go back; phasing back in really helps, according to numerous studies—and many of the mothers I spoke with. Unsurprisingly, women who experience those distracting "daily reentry regrets" are most likely to intend to leave their jobs. Also unsurprising—but so important—is the fact that women with shorter leaves have more of those regrets. If you can extend your leave, even only part-time, you increase your chances of staying at work long term. "It helped me not feel overwhelmed. It helped my heart feel less crushed," says Aliza, a nurse manager at the Hospital of the University of Pennsylvania, who negotiated at the last minute to work two eight-hour shifts a week (instead of three) for her first couple of weeks back.

Marcy Axelrad, a lawyer and human resources expert in Boston, worked two days a week when she first came back to work, then three days, "and that's when I realized, yeah, my baby's fine," she says. "I've got a great, great caregiver at home and he's happy. So then I came back full-time." Now the Global Senior Director of Talent Operations at the online furniture retailer Wayfair, Axelrad is the brains behind the company's family-friendly policies. She's seen it time and time again: "That flexibility is one of the reasons why our working moms come back after their leave. And most do eventually come back full-time."

There are all kinds of scheduling scenarios you can propose to stretch your maternity leave and ease back into work life: After her first child, my work wife, Wendy, took one week less leave and then applied those five days to five Fridays in a row so she worked four-day weeks for a while. Monica, the institutional investor, took some extra unpaid leave to work two three-day weeks, and then two four-day weeks before going back full-time. "I look back now and see my texts to our nanny. I used to send like five messages a day all about poop. Did they poop yet? Was it a big poop or a small poop? I can't believe that I managed their poop like that," Monica says, laughing. "I mean, it was crazy, but that's where my focus was." By the time her reentry weeks had passed and she was back up to speed full-time, she'd chilled and redirected her focus on work (pretty sure her nanny appreciated it, too).

Do not underestimate your rights to do a phase-in and the positive impact it can have on workplace culture. Many companies have an established written policy (one study showed that only 50 percent of workers were aware of it when such a policy existed at their firm). And even those that don't might have had a precedent set by other new moms. FMLA allows you to take your twelve weeks *over the course of the year* (if your company is cool with this kind of intermittent leave). Do your research! When we ask for something for ourselves, we're really asking for all the moms who follow us, too. So if you can, please do.

Some motivation for you to be the change maker in your workplace: One study out of Germany looked into why workers in a competitive environment (in this case a hospital) weren't taking all the parental leave they were entitled to (German mothers receive fourteen paid weeks—six before the birth, eight after). It turned out that the employees felt like full leave-taking workers were "effectively demoted" in their jobs since the environment was so intense. Researchers investigated what kind of institutional framework would need to exist for workers to feel like their status was protected and came up with four requirements, one of which was the "redirection of funds to facilitate part-time work schemes temporarily upon return." The workers knew, in other words (this is my interpretation) that they wouldn't be at full-throttle upon return. If the management acknowledged that fact by budgeting for it, their ambivalence would dissolve, allowing them to take better advantage of the time allowed. Let's change some policies, people!

5) Enjoy a bit of success (it sustains you)

Generally speaking, I'm a big believer in doing the hard thing first, eating that Mark Twain frog. Once you get through that task, everything else in the day feels easier. Well, permission to cheat, if you are in the "I have to quit" doldrums. This is the time to do the *easiest* thing on your list first. Hell, write things on your to-do list that you've already done just so you can scratch through them. Success is extremely motivating. So whatever it takes for you to feel like you're doing a good job—clocking in at 8:58 instead of 9:00, or meeting with that college sophomore who wants to hear about your career path, or introducing your boss to an impressive new contact (really, just a five-minute email)—do it. You'll be happier coming to work tomorrow. Because you are coming back tomorrow!

CHAPTER FOUR

✎

On looking human again (a noble goal)

Part 1: Beauty

A s I opened up my laptop one morning to prepare for an interview, I glanced at Twitter and tumbled down the rabbit hole
into my new favorite account: @ManWhoHasItAll (bio: "Top tips
for men juggling a successful career and fatherhood"). His—or
possibly her?—tweets are tongue-in-cheek bits of advice for busy
men that call attention to just how silly we sound offering the
same kinds of tips to women. I laughed out loud in the library's
silence-only room at quips like: *"ALL MEN! Learn to take credit for
your accomplishments. It's okay to be good at something!"* And: *"I have
absolutely no problem with male conference speakers, as long as we can hear
them at the back."*

Totally brilliant. But scrolling through, the gems that made me
laugh hardest also made me—I must admit—a little uncomfortable writing this chapter of the book, which is all about looking
good coming back to work postbaby. *"Working husband?"* Man-
WhoHasItAll opined in his 140 characters, *"How do you juggle kids,
housework, job & combination skin? . . . 'I lean in.'"* Hmm. So, funny
thing, I had actually just done an amazing interview with a world-

class dermatologist and mother of two about, yes, going back to work with postpregnancy hormonal skin.

And this one made me cringe, too: *"Working husband & father? Feeling overwhelmed? YOUR FAULT. Drink more water, get up earlier & dress in your 'wow' colours."* I giggled uncomfortably. See, I'd also just interviewed a fantastic image consultant (she's close enough with Bill Gates and Mark Zuckerberg that she refers to them as "Gates and Zuck"), and she had . . . advised wearing brighter colors. And two other experts had extolled the benefits of drinking a lot of water! Oh, boy.

In my old job at the magazine, where we covered beauty and health, fashion and politics, with equal passion and expertise, I was pretty comfortable explaining that these are all things that add up to the whole experience of being a woman. You can love Prada *and* public policy. You shouldn't have to hide the curves of your body just to be taken seriously while giving a PowerPoint presentation. Wearing lipstick really can make you feel more confident. Etc. Etc. Etc.

But during the Fifth Trimester? It would be really disingenuous of me to simply tell you to Flaunt What You've Got and Feel Great Doing It, Exclamation Point!

If you're up for flaunting, fantastic, good for you. But if you're going back to work before you feel back to yourself physically—and in my survey, there was a two-month-plus overlap there for most women—it's okay to not just happily accept that this is the new you. It's *also* okay not to diet and Botox yourself into an oblivion trying to get back to the old you. *You're* the only one who should decide how much you care. I'm just here to put the advice in your back pocket for if and when you want it.

In truth, I think we all feel this conflict, this push/pull of wanting to look good, look professional, look confident, but also embrace the changes, external and internal, that having a baby forces upon you. Yes, your body is different now, and yes, you may need a different hair and makeup routine to get out the door in the morning, but inside you feel different, too. You may find yourself—as I did—simply caring less about all that superficial crap. In part, I think, it's a defense mechanism (I don't look good because I'm *choosing* not to look good, thank you very much), but it's also a genuine perspective shift: You've just poured your lifeblood into creating another human; and now you're supposed to prioritize curling your eyelashes?

I struggled going back to work. I really struggled.

Before kids, I commuted in heels. A seven-minute walk and two subway rides, each way. Afterward: no way. I needed shoes that got me home fast enough for the 6:30 nursing session. Before kids, my power outfit, the one I felt amazing in, was a twirly, black A-line Club Monaco skirt and a thin gray cotton V-neck T-shirt belted with my mom's vintage black satin bow belt from her cocktail-party getups from the eighties. (Think: Chanel inspired.) For meetings I'd throw on a blazer, too. Postbaby, the skirt was too small, I didn't have enough of a waist to feel good in a belt, and the shirt was stretched out from being slept in while nursing. Oops.

My instinct was to go back to work and dazzle everyone with my *work*—the good editing and leadership that I'd hoped they'd missed while I was out—so that my colleagues would hopefully ignore the fact that I still looked a few months pregnant. And actually everyone very kindly did ignore my visible nursing-bra straps, the totally clichéd spit-up on my sweater, and the fact that several of my pairs of pants were of the pull-on variety. They told me I looked great (I didn't) and that they missed me (thank God). And after about two weeks of this personal appearance disaster, I realized something: I was getting my work done, I was getting home on time, I was pumping enough milk and making enough money to help pay our nanny. I actually had it together-ish.

Except when I looked in the mirror.

I wish every one of you had a little sister as wonderful as Blair Smith, mine. She staged the world's kindest intervention, whisking me away on a two-hour shopping excursion that made me feel better than I had in months.

I protested the whole way: I couldn't spend the money. This was my precious weekend time with baby Will. I hadn't seen Ben during daylight hours all week. Anything I'd buy now wouldn't fit in a couple of months anyway.

Blair ignored me and pushed me through the revolving door at Zara with all of the no-bullshit attitude of my own personal Joan Rivers (may she rest in peace).

I have to pause here and acknowledge how ridiculous my stubbornness must sound, given my profession. For years, I had edited all the fashion and beauty pages of the magazine. We had teams of fashion market editors who sat front row at fashion shows, and beauty editors whose desks were covered with an avalanche of pastel-colored bags from cosmetics companies, stuffed with samples. My job was to help those editors distill the trends and expert advice on the pages of the magazine every month for millions of readers, making the deluge of information usable and inspiring. Much of it, blessedly, sunk in. If I'd had a friend coming back to work from maternity leave, I would have known just the correct under-eye concealer to recommend. I would have marched her right off to the stores in search of her perfect, body-flattering silhouette. Isn't it funny how much better we are, sometimes, at dishing out advice than we are at taking it ourselves?

Thank God for Blair.

While I stood naked in the dressing room, trying to look everywhere but in the mirror, she flew around the store bringing me options.

"You need a new uniform," she instructed, thrusting an armful of hangers through the curtain. "Your boobs are huge but your legs are thin. And I know you don't like your stomach. So here's the deal: Short skirts with black tights, plus loose tops. Jackets on top for structure and shape."

She was right: That's exactly what looked good.

More important, that's exactly what felt good, walking back into the office on Monday morning. Stella had gotten her groove back.

In this chapter, you will, too, whatever level of groove you want. I talked to some of the world's leading dermatologists, style advisers, hair care experts, beauty editors, fashion industry bigwigs (you know they have to look good), and more, to give you this personal appearance playbook for a time in your life when, as one Ralph Lauren exec told me, "a simple but great beauty and fashion routine is *the* key to being a working mom." Cherry-pick the advice you need and want for your life and your job. Skip the rest. And definitely leave time to retweet ManWhoHasItAll on your commute.

But first, I want to show you (a) how doable it is to look decent even when you feel like crap, and (b) why—no matter how modern your thinking (or how casual-Friday-every-day your workplace may be)—it's worth the effort.

Find your new generous minimum

There were days—of course there were days—when I relied on dry shampoo or a quick strategic donning of the black cardigan I kept in my desk drawer for shirt-covering emergencies. Still, for the most part, thanks to Blair, I established a new bar for myself. Mind you, I wasn't re-creating Chanel runway looks with vintage accessories pilfered from my mother—those days were on pause— but I was wearing clothes that looked good on my in-between body, and I wasn't avoiding looking at my face in the mirror when my under-eye circles had a rough night. (Tell me: Is a baby's sleep regression even a regression if the *progression* lasted only a week?)

In the end, I found a very happy medium. I looked like I cared, but deep inside I knew that I didn't care *so* much that I was neglecting my new sense of grand life priorities as a mother. It all added up to what I called my New Generous Minimum. It wasn't "good enough"—it was just one notch above that. Because if doing something good enough makes you feel like you're simply checking off a box, going even one tiny step beyond that makes you turn that check into a check-plus, and then you feel great.

In a perfect world, you would identify your actual barrel-scraping minimum only theoretically. But lots of women find theirs accidentally and then swear they'll never dip that low again. It happens. Monica, an institutional investor for a retirement plan, laughs when she recalls a morning during her first week back at work after having her twins: "There was one day I texted my sister and was like, 'I didn't have time to shower yesterday or today, and the boys threw up on me last night and it's all over my hair.' And she's like, 'You're at work?!' And I'm like, 'Yeah, I'm mortified, but hey, I just found my rock bottom!'"

Wendy Shanker, a freelance writer and single mom by choice, thanks a NICU nurse for snapping her back to her sense of self, in the most harrowing circumstances. Wendy's baby, Sunny, was born at twenty-nine weeks. Obviously, her baby's health was the most important thing, but as an independent contractor, Wendy also had to tend to her clients so she could focus on (and afford) Sunny's care. "I remember one of those first nights, going into the NICU in my hospital gown and mesh underpants, and I just started weeping," Wendy recalls. "And the nurse said to me, 'Uh-uh, not in here. Your baby wants to see you happy and strong and smiling. You can feel however you want to feel, but you're not going to do it in here.'" Wendy decided then and there to pull it together, at least superficially. "I knew for my peace of mind, I needed lipstick and a manicure. That's always been a signal that my life is in control, and when I didn't have those things it wasn't," she says. That was her Generous Minimum. "You know that classic photo of the mother's hand in the incubator?" Wendy says. "My hand always had gorgeous red nails. Somehow I found the thirty-five minutes, and I'm still a good mother." I remember that picture. Wendy is a friend, but she's also a freelancer I'd hired annually to script *Glamour*'s Women of the Year awards when I was at the magazine. After Sunny was born, she sent her clients a picture: red lipstick, red nails, tired eyes, gorgeous tiny baby. Now, at four years old, Sunny is healthy and hilarious and, "really critical if I have a hole in my nightgown or something," says Wendy.

"Yep, I get it one hundred percent," my friend Rekha, an endocrinologist with two kids said when I ran the Generous Minimum idea by her. "Mine is earrings and blush. Every day. Otherwise I look jaundiced!" Our friend Emily, a pediatrician with two little ones, concurred: "My Generous Minimum is tinted moisturizer, deodorant, and a necklace if I'm feeling fancy but am actually a mess. I find this concept both inspiring and reassuring—a great combo."

Meeting (and then exceeding) your minimum lets you prove to the world and yourself that you're doing better than just getting by. You're succeeding. "My grandmother's rule was that as long as the chrome was polished on all of the fixtures in her home, it didn't matter what the rest of the house looked like," says start-up culture expert Corey McAveeney. "You create your own rules," and they help you feel in control, she says, citing her own. Corey, who has one baby, works almost entirely virtually, with her company's offices all over the world, so her colleagues would have no idea if she worked in sweatpants. Still, she doesn't. "When it comes to playing the part in your job, it's psychological," she says. "I started doing this thing where on Mondays and Fridays I will put in a little more effort. Just psychologically, it helps me start and end the week on a positive note, and that makes a huge difference for me."

Tough-love warning: if you look like an impostor
at work, you may feel like one, too

If you've ever taken a Social Psych class or read Sheryl Sandberg's *Lean In,* you've probably heard of something called Impostor Syndrome. It's a term that was coined back in the 1970s by researchers to describe the mind-set of seemingly successful people who go through life feeling like frauds, unable to internalize their achieve-ments or believe praise. The phenomenon has been documented, quite notably, in high-achieving women. And I think a lot of us get a temporary case of it during the Fifth Trimester.

We come back to work changed (for the better, in my opin-ion). We see ourselves differently; we are seen differently. We actu-ally *look* somewhat different. And yet, often, we're stepping back into our old jobs—jobs our former selves were great at. Will our new selves be, too, we wonder?

Most of the women I talked to and surveyed came back to work two to three months after their babies were born. When I asked women at what point they started to feel physically normal again postbirth—not when they'd necessarily lost every pound of the baby weight, just when they started feeling like themselves, in their own skin again—the average response was 5.6 months. That means for two or three long months (pretty much the whole Fifth Trimester) they were back at their jobs, but not back to themselves physically. I also asked women how important appearance is in their chosen fields. The majority, 53 percent, ranked it a six or higher on a scale of zero to ten. (That may not sound so intense, but think of it this way: If job performance were measured *only* by the quality of the work done, without appearance factoring in at all, that would rank a zero. So six is significant.) We know, like it or not, that the way we look impacts our work. So what happens when we don't like the way we look? Or when we don't see some-one we recognize in the mirror? We might wonder—painfully—if we deserve the same success we used to enjoy.

Tia Williams felt like a drastically different person when she went back to work after the birth of her daughter, and, almost like learning to walk again, she had to reteach herself confidence. Her story is wild and inspiring.

A well-known beauty editor and expert, Tia had left the cor-porate world to work for herself and write novels, intending to start a family. She settled happily into freelance life, and finally, partway through her second book, the fertility treatments she and her husband had done worked and she got pregnant with baby Lena. "It was actually kind of liberating after I had Lena to just let it all go and sit home and play with her in pajamas and maternity sweatpants," she recalls. "Somehow I found time to write while she was sleeping."

But this wasn't a simple happy ending: Eight months after the birth, she and her husband made the painful decision to divorce. Tia quickly and gratefully took a new job, a big, visible one, as the beauty director of essence.com. "I needed a steady salary. I was on my own and it was terrifying. So all within the same year, I had a baby, got divorced, and went back to work," Tia says. "But I was definitely not ready. I didn't have the clothes, the attitude. I felt insecure. I didn't feel like myself at all. I felt like an impostor, like I was pretending to be someone I wasn't anymore." Every Friday, Tia remembers, she had to do a video for a YouTube series, reporting backstage from fashion week, or giving beauty advice. "I look back on those videos—I'm fluffing my hair awkwardly, and not looking directly into the camera—and I want to give whoever that person was a hug. It was awful."

The actual happy ending, the real one, is that Tia made it through one day at a time (much of her hair and makeup advice appears later in this chapter), and she's still mothering and working (now as a novelist and as Bumble and bumble's copy director) in a much happier balance.

What helped? The solution to this temporary postpregnancy Impostor Syndrome is a two-parter:

TREAT YOURSELF WITH THE SAME EMPATHY YOU WOULD GIVE A FRIEND. Recent research shows that self-compassion helps mitigate the impact of "body-related threats" (gotta imagine postpregnancy pooch qualifies as one) on your self-worth. In other words, if you're nurturing toward yourself, you'll feel more confident. In a moment of desperation, Tia actually taped a mini–pep talk up on her bathroom mirror (yes, it came to that). "I would read it while I was brushing my teeth," she says. "Mostly, I just absorbed it through osmosis. I knew it was part of the fabric of me and started believing it. Also, I had a really spicy affair at that time, so that helped, too!"

AND PULL YOURSELF UP BY YOUR DROOPY BLACK TIGHTS AND MAKE A BIT OF AN EFFORT. "I really recommend dressing for how you *want* to feel," says psychotherapist Nitzia Logothetis, mother of three and founder of the Seleni Institute for maternal mental health. "If you look in the mirror and see your reflection, and you see somebody who's put together, it makes you feel more put together." Simple as that.

There's a third solution, too, of course: just letting time tick on. Get through the transition, physically and emotionally, and know that things will get better. Along the way, use these beauty shortcuts and strategies for better postbaby skin, makeup, and hair. And body and closet advice are in the next chapter, too.

Let's start with your skin

More than hair (which can be cut or colored), more than your clothes (which can be changed), skin is uniquely personal. It's private, and yet it's public—everyone sees your face—and the hormones and shape-shifting of childbirth put it through the wringer. By the time you're back at work, your stretchmarks or C-section scars are likely hidden away under your clothes, but other gifts of pregnancy, like acne and skin discoloration? Yeah, they can be visible and they suck. ("After I had Lena, I got face *and* back acne," says Tia. "It was like going to junior high school all over again.") So, I'm going to spend several pages on skin here. Great skin is highly confidence inducing.

"We see a ton of new moms in our practice," says Jessica Weiser, MD, a dermatologist at the celebrity-beloved New York Dermatology Group, founded by skin-care guru David Colbert, MD. "A lot of those women had great skin for nine months, and they're saying, 'Now look at me!' or they weren't allowed to use their regular products and routine during pregnancy, so they come in to get back on a new plan."

Why is skin such a particular point of sensitivity for those going back to work? "It's the first thing people see when they look at you. Whether they're judging you for it or not, they're still seeing it," says Dr. Weiser. "If it's good, you feel confident. But the opposite is true, too. Skin can be really challenging in that regard." One depressing survey conducted by the skin-care company Cetaphil found that 38 percent of women ages twenty-two to forty-five have had a day when their skin was so embarrassing that they didn't leave the house. Clearly, *that's* not an option, so instead here's some good advice, issue by issue.

ISSUE: "PLEASE, I'VE GOT NO TIME FOR ANYONE'S SKIN EXCEPT MY BABY'S." "The ideal with skin care is that you can walk out of the house with nothing on your skin and feel good about it," says Dr. Weiser. That's the goal, and if it sounds easier said than done, she swears that's not the case. "It takes less time to commit to a good skin-care regimen than it does to try to cover everything and make sure your face is 'on' for the day."

What's that routine look like? Dr. Weiser says to focus on nighttime care so that your mornings can essentially be splash and go. "Night is when everything penetrates into the skin, so even if you're not sleeping well, your skin can look good. It's also a time when you're not running out the door."

   At night . . .
1) **Wash off the day:** "You just *have* to," says Dr. Weiser. "It's the most important thing I tell everyone. Cleanser at night is essential."
2) **Enhance cell turnover:** Built-up dead skin cells can make you look ashy and dull. Solution: exfoliate. "Pick a treatment to help the skin turn over so you look more rested and more fresh faced," Dr. Weiser instructs. "If you're

breastfeeding, you need to avoid retinoids and vitamin-A products, but glycolic acids or other fruit acids are generally considered safe. They're also antibacterial and can help with breakouts." Alternatively, you can use vitamin C– or vitamin E–based products for antioxidant skin renewal.

3) **Lock in moisture:** You need moisturizer whether you have dry, normal, or even oily skin (just use a lightweight lotion). "This final layer traps moisture into the skin, repairs the skin barrier function, and plumps cells overnight to make skin appear refreshed in the morning." Keyword: appear!

In the morning . . .

1) **Moisturize:** "You don't have to do a big wash routine," says Dr. Weiser. Just mist your face with water (or splash from the tap), and then apply a face oil to your face, neck, and chest. "Even if you have acne, it is okay to put oil on your skin, I promise," she says. The oil locks in the moisture and "gives skin back a little bit of life and radiance, so you don't look as tired."

2) **Protect with SPF:** Use whatever you like: a moisturizer with SPF added, plain old sunscreen, or the pros' favorite, a BB or CC cream (all-in-one products that incorporate a bit of color, too).

ISSUE: "I HAVEN'T SEEN ZITS LIKE THIS SINCE MIDDLE-EFFING-SCHOOL." "Hormones have a major impact on your skin while your cycle is trying to normalize itself," says Dr. Weiser. "So you're either going to be that woman who has the fabulous glowing skin—or the one who doesn't typically break out but suddenly has terrible acne." Dr. Weiser herself was in the latter camp, dealing with breakouts when she was just back from leave with her first son—during her dermatology residency, no less. "I was a mess. I was the dermatologist with the bad skin," she recalls quietly, still upset.

There's no need to get all fancy about treatments. One special cleanser (as opposed to a whole line) from your dermatologist, who can also keep in mind which ingredients are safest, can do wonders.

If you're breastfeeding, you'll need to become a label reader; the same rules apply as during pregnancy. Safe treatments, according to Dr. W., include fruit acids (look for AHAs like glycolic acid) and sulfur. "Anything with sulfur is a wonder," she says. The salicylic acid and/or benzoyl peroxide in many common products is a little trickier. "Salicylic acid is pregnancy category C, meaning not adequately studied to say if it's safe or not, but most derms will agree that in the form of a short-contact cleanser—not a leave-on product—it is typically acceptable," says Dr. W. "And it's always best to check with your own doctor to be sure."

ISSUE: "I'M NOW FAMILIAR WITH THE TERM 'BACK-NE.'" All the above advice for your face applies to your back—and your chest—as well. A couple of additional insights from my time deep in the pages of women's magazines:

1) When you put conditioner in your hair, lean way back so that it doesn't leave a film on your skin. If it does, be sure to wash your skin afterward.
2) Dirty sports bras are the devil for causing body zits, and the same absolutely applies to nursing bras. Wash them constantly to avoid irritation and clogged pores.

ISSUE: "GOOGLE JUST TOLD ME THAT THIS THING ON MY FACE IS MELASMA—YIKES." Never heard of melasma? Thank your DNA! Women who do get the so-called mask of pregnancy—a patchy pigmentation that darkens the skin over the focal points of your face (cheekbones, jawline, brow-bone)—tend to have a genetic predisposition, says Dr. Weiser. Still, that's little comfort when pregnancy ends but you're left with a very visible souvenir that can last for months, or even forever. Things to know:

- Melasma can occur in all skin types and colors.
- Sun protection is vital, especially during pregnancy and nursing, because estrogen triggers the pigmentation.
- Many women find that it fades over time.
- If it doesn't fade, a derm can help. "For women who know that they're going to have more children, I recommend a simple chemical peel," says Dr. W. And for those who are closing up shop in the uterus department? "There are laser procedures, more intense peels, and prescription lightening agents, but we advise waiting until your hormones are settled, usually when your regular cycle is back."

ISSUE: "THE STRETCH-MARK-PREVENTING CREAM WAS AN EPIC FAIL." The good news: Most of the places you can get stretch marks don't show on the job (at least not in most jobs, but if you are a Hooters server or an Olympic volleyball player, I salute you even more passionately at this moment!).

The less-good news: Stretch marks are not 100 percent curable by modern medicine. "I don't advise going out and spending a ton of money on treatments," says Dr. W. Her best advice: "The key with skin is that the more you hydrate it, so cells are plump, the better you look." So (a) drink copious amounts of water, and (b) try a bio oil, an allover body oil, followed by a moisturizer to "trap the active nutrients and ingredients into the skin that help improve the appearance of stretch marks," she says.

ISSUE: "WHY VISIT THE GRAND CANYON WHEN I CAN SEE TWO OF THEM UNDER MY EYES EVERY DAY?" If you have horrible under-eye circles—and really, who doesn't?—hydration is genuinely helpful, says Dr. W. (Again with the water! See, ManWhoHasItAll, we are not ashamed!) "Water makes fine lines look better and under-eye circles less intense." Other good options here (besides concealer, of course, more on that in a sec), which she says are safe if you're breastfeeding:

- Eye creams with caffeine. "It constricts the appearance of blood vessels" underneath that thin skin, she explains, keeping the area from looking quite so shadowy.
- Eye creams with algae. Another great ingredient, "it activates an enzyme that breaks down blood products to diminish the purple hue under your eyes," says Dr. W.
- Good old-fashioned cold compresses. Dr. W. is a big advocate of chilled tea bags and cucumber slices. They work!

And now, for what to do with the degree of darkness that remains? Concealer, a product that I don't think I ever used on anything but a zit until I had babies.

A concealer tutorial for under-slept women (practice it before your first day back) . . .

1) Get the right kind: You want a thick, creamy formula that comes in a pot, not the thinner, watery kind with a wand.
2) Get the right color: Don't try to match your skin. You want something with peach or yellow undertones (relative to your own skin tone) to counteract the purple/ blue of the circles. This is universally true. I have pale Irish/Jewish skin and use a peachy color. Tia has medium-brown skin and also uses a shade that is peachier than her complexion. "It's got to have some yellow in it," Tia says. "If you go too pink, you look like you have the flu." Also (highly controversial), I like to go one shade lighter than I probably should because I then blend my blush up and over my cheekbones a bit. So it all gets a bit mixed.
3) Prep your skin (optional): Tia always uses an eye cream (to counteract crepeyness) and translucent powder before applying concealer. I do not. But I am lazy like that.
4) Apply it the pro way: That means tapping it on with your middle finger, says Tia. If you rub it instead, it'll settle into the creases and make things worse. And dab it not just

under your eyes, instructs Rachel Hayes, Executive Director of Editorial for Clinique and founder of the working-mom beauty website Pretty Impressed, "but also put it in the inner corner of your eyes and over the eyelid, anywhere that's dark or red."

A few words about makeup
(whether you do, or don't, like to wear it)

Speaking to you as someone who spends about five minutes on my makeup every morning (and has edited approximately two thousand magazine pages of makeup advice), here's what I love about "putting your face on" for work, specifically: It's not about looking sexy. It's not about looking pretty. It's not even about looking particularly stylish. It's about looking like the most confident, together version of yourself.

When you're pregnant, people at work like to remark upon your glow. And it's real: You've got a lot of extra blood coursing around your body, you're taking all those delicious prenatal vitamins with fish oil, you're eating well. And then you have the baby. Most likely, people start saying you look "happy." And you probably do! But I always found that to be code for: *Woman, you look drained and tired and like your life is full.* Pass the blush and lipstick and mascara. It all helps. And it doesn't have to take long. (Responders to my survey said that they spent, on average, thirty-three more minutes getting ready in the morning postbaby—but seventeen fewer minutes on themselves. The advice below works within that time crunch.)

If you gaze in the mirror before going back to work and suddenly feel like you look older, you'll find this (scientific!) study interesting: Makeup makes you look four years younger. If you look in that mirror and worry at all about what your coworkers are going to think when they see you again for the first time, know this, too: Makeup has been shown to improve the first impression you make on people by 37 percent. (I'm not saying that's fair. But apparently it's true.)

Another study out of Canada specifically examined how wearing lipstick makes women feel over their lifetimes. Looking back, women reported feeling a higher sense of peer acceptance when wearing the stuff when they were younger. Older now, they reported they felt prettier in lipstick. As a new mom returning to work, you're in the sweet spot right in the middle. As Tia puts it, "Lipstick is my armor." Tia once saw a picture of her former grandmother-in-law washing dishes in her 1950s kitchen, wearing red lipstick. "I asked her, 'Why would you have red lipstick on?' And she was like, 'Because you never know who is coming over. I'm ready for anything.'"

Most likely, you already know what products you like and what looks good on you. Makeup is so personal. One woman's desert island product may be cream blush, while another can't live without eyeliner. That said, here's a handful of efficient expert advice to add to your repertoire—so you can spend less time primping and not set your alarm clock one second earlier than necessary.

AIM FOR MORE DEFINITION, NOT MORE STEPS. "You don't need an arsenal of twenty makeup products to look great," says Rachel Hayes, the Clinique exec. "It's just about giving your face natural definition so you look polished. That means dark lashes, a pretty lip color, and groomed eyebrows—I had mine dyed recently and it's amazing how little makeup I need now."

IGNORE THE BIG BEAUTY TRENDS. Generally speaking, I believe in defensive driving. The thing we are defending against at this moment is purple lipstick on your teeth. This is not a time to break out your swerviest beauty moves. I actually enjoy an occasional beauty dare, like a swipe of aqua eyeliner in the summer. But here's the thing. Right now, you are The New Mom Who Just Came Back to Work. Don't be TNMWJCBTWWAE (The New Mom Who Just Came Back to Work with Aqua Eyeliner). You're interesting enough right now as is, and this kind of beauty daredevilry requires precision and time to get right. Two things not likely to be in your wheelhouse at the moment. Don't risk it.

HAVE A ONE-MINUTE ESCAPE PLAN. There will be a morning when your baby decides to nurse twice, or poops on your clothes, or just needs to be held during the exact time that you usually reserve for getting ready. Under normal circumstances, makeup only needs to take a few minutes, but sometimes, you need a sub-sixty-second plan. Here it is:

Seconds 1–10: Pat concealer under eyes.

Seconds 11–20: Dot tinted moisturizer (or CC cream, or BB cream) on your nose, cheeks, forehead and chin, blending with your fingers from the center out.

Seconds 21–40: While that sinks in and dries a bit, do your eyes. Skip liner and just apply two quick coats of mascara, top lashes only.

Seconds 41–50: Rub cream blush onto the apples of your cheeks.

Seconds 51–60: Put a big dot of lip gloss on your bottom lip and smush it around while you look at the rest of your handiwork and fix any blending issues with your fingers.

DO THIS ONE HIGH-MAINTENANCE THING. This one's not on the sixty-second plan, but every makeup artist I've ever interviewed swears by it: Curl your lashes. "Everybody skips this, but it truly opens your eyes like nothing else and then your mascara goes on perfectly," says Hayes.

BUY TRIPLES OF YOUR PRODUCTS. When you're carting around baby board books and a WubbaNub in your work bag, you don't want to have to remember to pack your makeup bag, too. Just get duplicates of everything and keep them in there (or in a drawer at work). If you travel more than once a month, get a third set and keep it in your suitcase, too. Buy cheaper versions of the same colors to save money.

Now, about your hair!

I could fill pages and pages here proving that hair, more than anything, affects the way that women see themselves—and are seen—in the workplace. Instead, let me sum up the (annoying and not very scientific) "data" like this: Straight hair is taken seriously; curlier hair is seen as more casual; short hair connotes confidence; blondes are more energetic; brunettes are more driven. And on and on. Every hair stereotype you can imagine seems to have some "study" to back it up.

It's all such a bunch of B.S., isn't it? Your hair is your hair! And right now you have less time than ever to fight its natural inclinations. You can change its texture and color if you'd like, of course (advice on all that is below), but I like to think, instead, of long-haired retired Pittsburgh Steelers strong safety Troy Polamalu. A football player? Yes. Listen to this wise man: *"When I let my hair down, I just let it down. It's more comfortable in my helmet,"* he once said. Polamalu's hair—wild, long, thick, leonine—isn't the least bit typical for his profession. But it became his signature. Fans could always spot him on the field easily. He has a huge endorsement deal with Head & Shoulders shampoo. Perhaps most endearingly, Polamalu's hair is a tribute to his mother's Samoan background, which more people know about because he hasn't cut it off.

That's the goal: Be Polamalu. Have hair that works for work, and expresses who you are, and doesn't require time-consuming upkeep. "You're looking for the most gratification with the lowest maintenance," says celebrity hair colorist Sharon Dorram, whose clients have included The Kates (you know, Hudson and Winslet). Her number one bit of advice (and mine): Get yourself into the chair of a professional right before you go back to work. "There are days when my salon is like a maternity ward; everyone wants to come in right before they deliver," she says, laughing. "But coming back in *afterward* is so important. You want to feel like yourself again. Maybe you still have weight to lose, or you're just not feeling on top of your game. Hair is the first place to start. It's pivotal." Spend the bit of money and the time and ask a pro to help you establish a template that's actually possible to replicate at home. No one is easier to bitch to about your life needs than a hairdresser, after all. Whether you have specific issues like the ones listed below, or just the holy grail wish of good hair, she'll set you on the right path.

Here's your hot toolbox of tips straight from the experts:

IF YOU ARE FREAKING OUT ABOUT POSTPREGNANCY SHEDDING: "Anyone can be confident with a full head of hair," crotchety comedian Larry David reportedly once said, "but a confident bald man—there's your diamond in the rough." So how about a balding *woman*? Particularly one with a newborn? Her self-assurance is way, way, way down deep in that diamond mine. Like where the canaries go to die. And yet: Losing hair after giving birth is really common. Conventional wisdom tells us that the hair loss isn't actually balding per se. It's a loss of all the extra hair that your body hung on to during your pregnancy. "We get women coming in asking us about it all the time," says Dr. Weiser. "It's crazy the amount of loss, usually three to six months after giving birth." Aka: prime Fifth Trimester timing.

Oren Lazanski, co-owner of Shaggy Hair Studio in New York City, says his new-mom customers often ask about this shedding. "When you see hair in the shower drain, it can be dramatic. But I tell them to calm down and that it's just that they were used to the exaggerated shine and thickness from their prenatal vitamins." Dr. Weiser has a heavenly sounding suggestion here that she recommends to her patients: scalp massage. "It increases blood flow to the area, which might help with regrowth. It certainly doesn't hurt!"

IF YOU HAVE "BABY HAIRS" AROUND YOUR FOREHEAD: After hair loss, of course, you'll also experience regrowth, often in the form of cute (I think they're cute) baby hairs right around the hairline. "It was so not cute," says Tia, who became an expert at hiding them at work. "At first I wore headbands to cover them. Then I learned to use a little brown eyeshadow to fill in my hairline to help it look denser." Eventually, Tia wised up and cut bangs. "I told myself I was the black Marianne Faithfull—a total 1960s long, mod bangs situation—and the hair that had broken off in the front grew and caught up with my bangs." Strategically placed face-framing highlights can help, too, suggests Sharon Dorram.

IF YOU WANT LOW-MAINTENANCE COLOR: First, if you've gone back to your roots, consider keeping your natural color! "I've had girls who didn't do any color their whole pregnancies," says Dorram. "And then they get back in my chair after having the baby, and we look in the mirror, and they have really amazing natural hair color and we decide not to do highlights anymore." And that is officially the lowest-maintenance tip in this whole chapter: Do nothing!

But if you are color dependent, know that hair color "gives you the biggest change for the longest time—you only need to do it every three months. So it doesn't cost as much as you might think," says Dorram. (If you're wary of color while nursing, Lazanski recommends Inoa color, which is ammonia-free. And Dr. Weiser concurs: "I would be comfortable using a low- or no-ammonia shorter duration product myself assuming there's no scalp contact," she says.) For the easiest grow-out process, Dorram recommends highlights as opposed to all-over color. "A few around your face adds color to the skin, and you might even find you end up needing less makeup," she says. Rachel Hayes, the Clinique exec and beauty blogger, suggests asking for highlights underneath the bottom layer of hair as well. "If you suspect you might be wearing your hair up a lot, it's a great trick, so that when you wear a bun, your hair isn't obviously darker underneath."

On a tighter, more DIY budget? "For at-home color, I think it's always best to be realistic and keep things very simple," says Hayes. "Get a color kit that either matches your hair or is within one or two shades lighter or darker, no more. And don't try anything crazy like at-home highlights with a toothbrush. It's not the moment for risks!"

IF YOU WANT TO FLATTER A ROUND FACE: Don't go on a diet! Just get the right haircut, says Hayes who went back to work before having lost much baby weight. "A side part with a swoop of layers or long bangs across helps a round face look a little more structured and elongated," she says. And get a few little face-framing pieces cut as well if you like to pull your hair back into a ponytail or bun. "Very flattering," she says.

Another point of information about cuts: Shorter hair is not necessarily easier. My grandma Dolores had beauty-queen gorgeous hair as a young newlywed. Two years later, along came my mother who spit up in it and inspired the haircut that Grandma instantly regretted. She spent years growing it back out. "I don't endorse the 'mom cut,'" says Tia. "It's actually easier to have long hair because you can put it up and still look chic." Lazanski has a firm talk with any of his new-mom clients who say they want to go short. "I tell them, cut your hair short when you really want to. Don't cut it off just because you're a mom," he says. Instead, Lazanski suggests a substantial trim of 1.5 to 2 inches so it lasts a good long while. And so you look like you got a haircut! "A cut makes such a first impression when you're back," says Hayes. "It shows that you took the time and you're in control, regardless of how you may feel inside. I tell my friends to book their back-to-work haircut before they even give birth."

IF YOU NEED TO GET OUT OF THE HOUSE FASTER: Countless mothers told me that they've switched their hair wash to night to reclaim some precious minutes in the morning. If you find that you wake up a bit greasy, Lazanski suggests switching out your shampoo for a clarifying formula twice a week and applying conditioner only to the ends of your hair. And every new mom with shoulder-length or longer hair should have a couple of dirty-day updos to fall back on, says Hayes, who recommends texturizing spray, clear hair elastics, and color-matching bobby pins to keep things looking professional.

If you have super-curly hair, like Tia's, that requires air drying, so sorry, but "You actually have to do it in the morning," Tia says. "It gets wonky if you sleep on it wet. It needs air and has to rise naturally, almost like baking bread!" Which leads us to . . .

IF YOU HAVE HIGH-MAINTENANCE CURLS: When she was first back at work, Tia used relaxers to give herself more flexibility and options with her hair. Typically, she'd go for a weekly blowout on Sunday, using hair powder in between, and sleep with her hair in a bun for beachy waves in the morning. These days, "I keep it natural but still get blowouts sometimes," she says. Since there's no relaxer in the mix, the straightening effect only lasts two or three days. Then she washes and scrunches with a hair primer (she likes Bumble and bumble's). "It reverts the curls back, moisturizes, and fluffs it up. It's awesome."

IF YOU WANT TO FAKE A BLOWOUT: Hot curlers are your answer, says Windsor Hanger Western, the cofounder of Her Campus, a new-media brand for college women, whose baby girl was only a few weeks old when we talked (Windsor had already been back to work—and walked an event red carpet—in that time). "I know, it's so funny, you're like, 'Oh, God, I'm one of those women in a bathrobe with hot rollers,' but they're amazing!" she says. "It takes three minutes to get 'em in, and then you can nurse while your hair's setting."

So, there you have it. Bouncing hair, blemish-free skin, and eyes that look like they've had a vacation's worth of sleep over-night. The instructions are here, and hopefully they make sense, but I also want to be very clear about this (and ManWhoHasItAll, I hope you're reading): It's all good. Seriously. As long as you feel okay, *you'll look fine.*

CHAPTER FIVE

※

On looking human again

Part 2: Your Body and Style

The day I announced my pregnancy at work (a mostly fun exercise when you work with mostly women), one particularly blunt-but-lovably-so colleague and I got to talking.

ME: Alison, guess what? I'm pregnant!

ALISON: That is awesome! How are you feeling?

ME: Tired, happy, relieved to be out of the closet. You know.

ALISON: I thought you looked different.

ME: Really?

ALISON: How much weight have you gained?

ME: God, like eight pounds already.

ALISON: That's nothing. I gained sixty with my first. [I should note here that Alison—after two kids—is as thin as an haricot vert.]

ME: [mic drop silence]

ALISON: Yeah, it wasn't pretty. But I didn't care. Just wait, you'll see.

ME: Well, I, uh, I actually lost thirty pounds a few years ago so I guess I'll get back up to about that number, at least, huh?

ALISON: Oooh. You used to be heavy? This is going to be hard for you. This whole transition and gaining weight and then losing it is going to be *really, really hard.*

In a way, she was right. My relationship with my body has always been complicated. Whose isn't? And my industry—with its constant influx of models on go-sees and a fashion closet full of borrowable goodies (but only if you're sample size)—didn't exactly help dial down the pressure in that department. I once had a 5' 10" boss who wore hot pants to work. Seriously, like Daisy Dukes, but pink. And leather.

But a funny thing happened when I gained (and then struggled to lose) the baby weight: I also gained perspective. My body was strong and capable. It did what it was supposed to do, and then it healed. It fed a baby and housed a brain that could both work *and* mother. For a girl who'd always been picked last for kickball, I felt, inside, like a champion. I also sometimes felt like a loser—usually around 7:20 a.m. as I searched through my hopeless closet for something that fit. But I knew deep down that my body could rally and win the season.

It was a giant sea change for me.

One recent synthesis of seventeen different scientific papers on postpartum body image found that women, overall, have unrealistic expectations—and, worse, that "the physical manifestations" of motherhood are "incongruent [with] their role as wife, or partner, or working woman." Or all of the above. Geez. The *Today* show did a 2013 project around body image and motherhood, and one of its polls showed that 31 percent of all mothers (not just new ones) hate their bodies. Their favorite body part? Their eyes. Are eyes even a body part?

Still, as I interviewed women and asked them how they felt about their bodies when they first went back to work, I noticed a trend: Those who had the hardest pregnancies or the most physically demanding jobs had made the same mental leap I had. They appreciated their bodies' strength, and that, in turn, actually made them stronger. You'll hear from some of those women in a minute. Here's what I suggest: Don't diet. Don't force yourself to exercise more than feels manageable. You'll do more good for your body by simply appreciating it. The more you notice its capabilities, the better you'll treat it. And the better you treat it, the healthier you'll be. Make this shift in mind-set for yourself, for your stamina at work, and for your family.

Three perspective-changing
and body-loving thoughts for right now

1) **In five short years, you will look back on pictures of this time and think you looked great.** "I probably have six to eight pounds that I didn't lose," says Monica, an institutional investor and mom of three-year-old twin boys. "I don't know if I'll ever lose them. But you know what it made me realize? Just how hard women are on themselves and how they probably looked great before and were blind to it. I'm like, 'Oh, I used to weigh six to eight pounds less and I didn't even appreciate it!'"

2) **Your body just made . . . another body.** That's crazy and amazing. And if part of the reason you're working is to set an example for your children, to show them that they can contribute to this world, then apply that same logic here: Respect your body, with all its strengths and flaws, and you will teach your child to respect hers, too. She's only four months old, you say? She doesn't speak English yet, or worry about her thighs? Practice now for when she's four. Or fourteen. Or twenty-four. (And by the way, having boys doesn't get you—or me—off the hook in this regard. If you treat your body respectfully, you're teaching your son to respect girls' bodies as much as he does his own.)

3) **If you like your body more, you'll like *every*body more.** Karen, a marketing executive, used to spend her days in

a vicious cycle of: wake up, get the baby ready for day-care, go to work, play with the baby, work more, go to bed. "For *years,* I didn't get one ounce of exercise," she says. "And what did that do? It made me feel not great about myself. My husband and I barely had a relationship." Recently, she started going to the gym for one hour once a week with her neighbors, and even that small dose of self-care has affected her whole family. "I feel better about myself and have more energy," she says. "But most of all, I'm just in a better mood with my boys and my husband."

Your *only* fifth trimester exercise mandate: Just don't do nothing

For me, it was purely a matter of biology: While nursing, I could not do any exercise that required a sports bra without getting mastitis. That eliminated virtually all traditional workout options. So I learned to rely on that whole Generous Minimum idea again. Guess what counts as exercise?

- Doing baby bath time in the big tub. That kneeling, duck feet thing you're doing right there? That's a squat, actually.
- Pushing a baby stroller with a jumbo bottle of fragrance-free Tide and four cans of formula in the bottom.
- Standing in the security line at the airport for more time than you'd like while holding the baby in the car seat. Hey, triceps.
- Staying upright for hours on end while wearing your baby, who can sleep only while physically on your body.
- Taking the stairs at work, or in the parking garage, or at home, or basically ever.
- Running frantically for the bus that you're about to miss because your nanny showed up late.

Add to this list. Come up with your own "exercises"—and recognize your strength.

What if your job requires actual physical strength?

Meet Kimberly, your new working-mom-body hero.

Kimberly Shannon Murphy has the kind of body other women might (ignorantly) be tempted to hate. She is tall and slim and strong in a long, lean, yoga-ed kind of way. And in fact she does rely on yoga and lots of strength training for her job as a Hollywood stunt double. Seriously, that's her job. She doubles Cameron Diaz and does lots of other film and TV work. She's a badass.

Kimberly found out that she was pregnant with her now eighteen-month-old daughter when she was in the middle of filming a movie and immediately had to quit for the duration of the pregnancy. "It was actually kind of nice," she says, "because I've spent my whole life having to work out and to look a certain way. I really didn't do anything except eat and watch TV for nine months. I gained sixty-eight pounds—even got cellulite on my arms!—but my doctor wasn't worried, so I just enjoyed it."

Then, three and a half months after her C-section and a very weepy postpartum period, an unmissable job came up. "I wasn't physically ready—I still had at least twenty pounds to lose and a lot of strength to regain—but I felt like I had to take it," she says. The job was intense, requiring her to jump into cars, fight, leap over fences, and be "ratcheted" through the air on pulleys. Some days she left the house at 7:00 a.m. and returned after 9:00 p.m. She was broken physically and emotionally—but as her Fifth Trimester ticked on, she was also healing. Within three more months Kimberly had lost the rest of the weight and was in better shape than ever, with new respect for her body's fluidity.

Few of us have jobs that require the strength and focus of Kimberly's, but plenty of women have to be on their feet all day (teachers, restaurant servers, physical trainers, surgeons), and that's especially challenging when your body isn't as strong as it once was, and when you're going home to a whole other kind of marathon at the end of the day. Kimberly's advice here is for anyone with a job like that—and for the rest of us mere desk-bound humans, too. I was expecting her to suggest planks and core strengthening. Instead, she preached the Tao of working-mom self-care:

GET STRONG *YOUR* BEST WAY. Punishing your body is never truly motivating. What is? "Realistically, it's all about doing something you love that makes you feel good about yourself, not bad," says Kimberly. "I think it's different for everyone. Maybe it's classes, or yoga, or running." Or maybe it's just being out in nature, walking instead of driving. "Everyone has their own goal, their own method," she says. "You can feel really gross and really out of shape, go take the class that you love, and then leave after a good sweat feeling thinner, and clearly you aren't thinner than you were one hour ago, but you *are* in a better place mentally. This is what exercise does for your brain," Kimberly says. And it's vital and good-habit–forming.

AS MUCH AS YOU CAN, MAKE PEACE WITH THE PHYSICAL MANDATES OF YOUR JOB. Kimberly's job requires more than just extreme physical fitness. She also knows that she has to look a certain way. "I don't love that aspect of it at all, but I accept that it's part of the reality of my career," she says. And that helps. Getting frustrated about it would be a waste of time.

When I interviewed Aliza, a nurse in Philadelphia who worked intense twelve-hour shifts on her feet when she first came back to work, she echoed this point: "I know it sounds funny, but I was actually grateful to have such a physical job," she says. "If I'd been sitting at a computer I definitely would have fallen asleep. Being mobile weirdly kept me going."

PACE YOURSELF. "Being a mother has changed my view; there are certain stunts that I simply won't do anymore because of the danger level," says Kimberly. (Aliza, similarly, has learned to avoid overdoing it, especially in her off-duty hours. At work, she has to be on her feet, but once she's home, she lets herself crash. "Especially in that first year, I knew I had to be easy on myself. I'd come home, shower, eat a slice of pizza, nurse the baby, and go right to bed." She kept up that whole "nap when the baby naps" habit for many months, not just the first few. "And I definitely did a lot of knitting that year," she says, laughing.)

JUST KEEP SHOWING UP. On her first day back, Kimberly tore two ligaments but chose to tape herself up and work through the injuries rather than have a false start. That might seem above and beyond, but not in her line of work. She'd committed to the shoot, after all. In her off hours, she relied on crutches and was grateful her daughter wasn't crawling yet. "And on set I just muscled through every day." This may seem like crazy advice: Work through the agony. But looking back on what she'd achieved each day, mentally and physically, prepared her for the next.

AND JUST BE PATIENT WITH YOUR BODY. Getting your strength and your body back "just takes time," Kimberly says. "Don't focus on the number of pounds. Just eat right, exercise faithfully, and be patient."

Important P.S.: Let's all promise not to comment on one another's bodies. Ever.

Getting back to your old self isn't always about losing the baby weight. When Cheryl Kramer Kaye, now the executive beauty director of *Shape* magazine, went back to work after the birth of her twins, she looked . . . well, to the untrained eye, she looked great. Cheryl was happy to be back on the job, and she was thinner than she'd ever been in her life—something a bunch of her well-meaning colleagues felt the need to compliment her on.

Only problem? Cheryl had had the worst pregnancy known to man: difficult-to-conceive twins, extreme nausea, gestational diabetes, fatigue so awful she had to sit down just to brush her teeth, and eventually bed rest—but only on her left side. Left-side-only bed rest. It was like the pregnancy equivalent of a really terrible country song! And it keeps going. She also had HELLP syndrome, a life-threatening form of preeclampsia, and her babies were born premature and wound up in the NICU for a month.

So when Cheryl came back to work in a size of clothing she'd previously only dreamed of wearing, she wasn't exactly celebrating. "The only thing I wanted was to be able to feel healthy," she says. "I'd always been a squishy person, so I'd look in the mirror getting dressed and think, I should appreciate this, but actually, I just couldn't wait to put the weight back on. So every time someone would say to me, 'Oh my gosh, you're so thin, you look great,' it would make me feel like, 'No, I don't look great. I am sick. I was sick.'" Here she laughs. "And don't you dare think less of me when I gain twenty pounds back, because it's going to happen!"

Cheryl, like Kimberly, learned to value strength above all else. These days, when she exercises, it's to feel functionally strong so she can care for her kids and lift them and their stuff (they are now healthy six-year-olds, with backpacks and sports gear). "If it happens to make my waist look smaller, so be it," Cheryl says. "But you really stop caring so much about appearance, and start focusing on capability."

Oh, right, and you need something to wear!

My mom has never seen *The Breakfast Club* or *The Blues Brothers*. If "Achy Breaky Heart" comes on the *'90s on 9* on SiriusXM, she is clueless. She's a huge bookworm, but she's never read Margaret Atwood's dystopian bestseller *The Handmaid's Tale* or Toni Morrison's classic *Song of Solomon*. Why? Those hits all happened in 1977, 1980, 1985, and 1992—the years my siblings and I were born. Mom makes no apologies for her ignorance. "Those are my cultural dark years!" she'll say, annoyed, when we torture her with Billy Ray Cyrus. "I was feeding you! I was working. I wasn't sleeping." She also wasn't shopping—at least not for up-to-the-minute trends. Still, my mom has always had enviable style.

Here's the key: When it comes to fashion trends right now, you get a pass. You do not need to buy the Pantone color of the year or the new skirt shape. But when it comes to style? Absolutely *yes,* you can have great style without spending your baby's fledgling college fund or mummifying your midsection in Spanx. It might even make you feel better at your job.

Like it or not, "style matters," says former Facebook exec Debra Bednar, "because **the way we dress affects the way we think, the way we feel, the way we act, and the way people react to us.**" I'm going to bold that sentence because it's just so true. Debra, who goes by DB, is the founder of DB+co., a female leadership coaching company with a focus on personal style. She's worked with and advised everyone from the Silicon Valley hoodie brigade to top fashion industry brass. She's seen the impact your clothing choices can make in the workplace.

Look, I know that getting advice about how to dress—especially at this transitional time—can be beneficial but also kind of vaguely insulting. Hear this: I do not believe in laws about fashion except for the handful that I enforce upon myself privately in my own head. What I've rounded up here are some helpful truths from experts, not commandments from the fashion gods. Just like putting together your look of the day, choose the items from this list that fit, flatter, and make you feel great.

Eight back-to-work style truths

STYLE TRUTH #1: YOU ARE THE BOSS OF YOUR CLOSET (NOT ITS OBEDI-ENT MINION). Here is your goal for the week before you go back to work: Create a mini-closet within your closet of pieces that fit and look good for work right now. There may not be many of them, but you'll have a core wardrobe to pull from every morning, and you'll get to add to it as you get back into your old clothes piece by piece. If you find that you're missing whole categories (e.g., you don't currently own a single pair of non-jeans pants that fit), you'll also be really clear in your shopping needs so you can keep that excursion quick and precise. "This is what I say to all new moms," instructs Eva Amurri Martino, actress and founder of mommy lifestyle blog Happily Eva After. "You need to try on every single piece of clothing you own, and if you do not feel in this present moment one hundred percent great about yourself, that item should not be an option right now."

On closet reckoning day, pump some breastmilk, then have a glass of wine, and settle in to try on everything and make some decisions, keeping in mind . . .

You might still want/need a handful of your maternity clothes. Blow out that match, and don't set them all on fire quite yet. I would recommend abolishing anything empire-waisted or with a maternity panel built into the waistline. But swingy tops and stretchy pencil skirts from your first or second trimester might fold in nicely with your transitional work wardrobe.

You shouldn't write off all your old clothes just yet: That silly old closet-cleaning rule of "if you haven't worn it in a year, give it away" doesn't apply to women in their prime child-bearing years. "After I had my twins, I donated all my clothes because I just could not envision getting back to normal size," says Jessie Randall, founder and creative director of (my favorite) shoe line Loeffler Randall, who is a mother of three, including twins. "This was a stupid mistake because eventually, after about a year, I did get back to my old size. So I would definitely hold onto the old clothes."

If you're pumping, you may need clothes that help: Page 140, over in Chapter 7, has a list of items to embrace and avoid while you're doing the lactating thing.

Your best closet is a closet that makes 7:00 a.m. decisions easy: Once you've established your mini-closet-within-a-closet of yesses, organize it for easiest dressing. "Chaos can be incredibly toxic, and the more you can minimize stress as a new mom, the better," says DB. "Organize by color, going from dark to light across your pieces, and then by length within each color palette (white dresses to white tops)." The upshot? "I'm a huge believer in dressing for your mood, and this strategy makes that easy. You'll feel so much better if you're in the right color for how you're feeling."

Every item in that mini-closet should be "my favorite _____": If you're wearing black pants, they should be your favorite (and maybe even your only) black pants, not your second-favorite black pants that kind of gap at the waist and only work with the pair of shoes that gave you a blister last Monday. I will be the first to admit to you that I am not humanly capable of full-on Marie Kondo–ing my apartment. I love options. I love stuff. I love options of stuff. But the easiest way to streamline your morning is for you to genuinely love, without reservation, every item in your clothing arsenal. "If you have a white button-down shirt that you feel like a million bucks in, and you can pair it with your favorite nice jeans—things you feel excellent-excellent in—you can get dressed decisively," says Eva.

STYLE TRUTH #2: YOU CAN DRESS FOR COMFORT AND STILL LOOK PROFESSIONAL. I think I might print out these words of DB's and tape them to my closet mirror: "When you feel more comfortable, you feel more confident. When you feel more confident, you push through fear. When you push through fear, you learn, grow, and evolve. When you evolve, you are on the right path to reach your greatest potential." Awesome, right? And a completely legitimate argument for not wearing the "correct" but uncomfortable thing.

But what do comfortable clothes that aren't yoga pants look like? "I love flowy pieces for comfort," says DB. "The key is proportion and juxtaposition. For example, if you want to wear a long maxi dress, pair it with a fitted denim jacket, sweater, or blazer. If you want to wear leggings, pair them with a longer cashmere sweater and riding boots or ballet flats. If you're wearing an uber-feminine top, pair it with a masculine blazer, trouser, or shoe. The pairing of opposites (loose/fitted, textured/soft, feminine/masculine) is what creates interest in an outfit; it's what makes style fun for you and inspiring for others."

STYLE TRUTH #3: SHOPPING IS A MIND GAME. Even the wealthiest and most body-accepting woman shouldn't go out and buy a whole new expensive wardrobe right now. All you really need to buy are things that fill in the holes—those missing categories within your mini-closet—as your body and lifestyle continue to shift and change.

As you shop, try to have a moment of Zen peace about the labels. "It's not about the size on the tag," says DB. "Respect your body and the amazing job it performed. Your shopping options really open up when you let the way something feels matter most."

And there is no need to spend a fortune! "For the price of a quality postnatal massage, you can score a temporary wardrobe from fast-fashion spots like Zara, ASOS, and H&M that can fill in the gaps in your wardrobe," says Ashley Baker Staats, executive editor of *The Daily Front Row* and fashionweekdaily.com. "At the bare minimum, buy pants in whatever size you're currently wearing, and then donate them to Dress for Success in a few months if they're too large." Still dying to put a dent in your Visa after a pregnancy of abstinence? Shop for accessories, because . . .

STYLE TRUTH #4: ACCESSORIES ARE EVERYTHING. Accessories scratch that fashiony itch that you may feel when your clothing options are temporarily limited. Sure, you may not want to wear your dangliest earrings (baby-grabbing bait) or carry your tiniest clutch (where's that Medela Symphony going to fit?), but you can have fun digging into your jewelry, bags, and scarves—or even buying new ones. If you're going to spend money on anything right now, by all means make it something that'll still fit next year! A killer luxe-looking bag also distracts from the fact that you may be wearing the same pair of pants three times this week.

DB loves statement pieces for impact. "Try a chic tote bag, a great pair of sunglasses, a power watch, bracelet, or ring," she suggests, to send the message that you care about how you look. Corey McAveeney, who spends much of her day on video conference calls away from her team, has a pearl necklace that she swears by: "It gives the illusion that I'm making an effort; otherwise I'd come across as lazy, because that's how I'd feel about myself."

STYLE TRUTH #5: YOUR SHOE GAME WILL CHANGE. IT JUST WILL. It's not that you'll never wear your highest heels again—you'll just learn to be strategic about them. With a new baby, heel-wearing requires an almost stupid level of forethought and logistical analysis. Some women skip the headache entirely.

I'm short and like the extra inches that heels give me, so I opted in for that headache, keeping a lineup of commute-unfriendly shoes under my desk to change into.

Other women (taller women, I'm guessing) make peace with shorter shoes and never look back. "The biggest thing that changed in terms of my style when I went back to work was that I had to accept the fact that four-inch heels were no longer an option," says Cheryl. Over her twin pregnancy and maternity leave, she says, "I had grown way too comfy in my army boots and flip-flops; putting on a stiletto felt moronic. I still have all of those shoes, by the way, but I now call them my 'bedroom shoes,' as in, 'Enjoy these for ten minutes, Honey, because they're never leaving the house.'"

"It was simple," says Tia. "I no longer wanted to be uncomfortable for fashion because life was hard enough. Everything shifts when you have a baby—you become this warrior woman with this baby you need to be able to protect." I felt the same way. Even in heels, I always, always had a flat option just in case I needed to get home urgently. September 11 happened long before I had my boys, but walking up Manhattan on that awful day early in my career brought out the Girl Scout in me permanently. I always wanted to be prepared.

So: flats. The good news is we are living in a veritable Renaissance age of gorgeous options. Even shoe designer Jessie Randall wears nothing but! "I am a flats girl," she says, offering this further comfort advice: "Get your feet measured after pregnancy using a Brannock Device at a shoe store—most people have two different-sized feet, and feet can change during pregnancy." No one's got time for blisters.

STYLE TRUTH #6: UNIFORMS AREN'T JUST FOR UPS EMPLOYEES. I resisted finding my "uniform" for the longest time prebaby, because I thought it would mean I was boring. Who wants to wear the same basic look to work every damn day, right? Wrong. Because let me tell you what is *actually* boring: The voice in your head scolding you for the umpteenth time this week for being late for work because you couldn't figure out what to wear. Or stopping by the office bathroom mirror for the fifth time in one day to adjust a dress that doesn't sit well on your body. That is boring. Not to mention defeating and distracting!

So, what is your uniform? A uniform is one big closet short-cut. If you know your collarbones look great in V-necks, buy only V-necks. If limiting your outfit palette to black, white, navy, and pink makes you feel positively Parisian, there you go. *Allez-y!* A uniform can be a style (preppy) or a silhouette (fitted tops, flared skirts) or a brand of shoes that faithfully makes you love your ankles.

A uniform doesn't have to be un-special at all, actually, because it lets you experiment, safely, within that theme. Eva's business meeting uniform is a fit-and-flare dress, often with a cool leather jacket or blazer on top. "When I've been heavier, or when I've not, I always feel great in that kind of dress," she says. If she's working on the blog or on mom duty, you'll find her in jeans and a white T-shirt—but that T-shirt "has got to be cut beautifully or have something special about it." (Undoubtedly you'd notice that something special because it's on such a basic canvas. See? Not boring.) A uniform also lets you cheat and find the single most flattering shapes for your body, and just press repeat every day. "Be really honest with yourself about what you feel great in," says Eva. "Maybe that's workout clothes. Okay, so then you find a way to wear a legging, like a really high-quality legging with boots. So you have the same secure feeling you get in workout clothes, but it's work appropriate."

STYLE TRUTH #7: YOUR BABY WILL PUKE ON YOU. You know who loves your baby almost as much as you do? Your dry cleaner. My friend told me once about a colleague's baby who popped in for an office visit with her caregiver. The mom was wearing something fluttery and silk and expensive. No basic burp cloth would have protected this thing from various baby biohazards. "The way she hugged her baby broke my heart a little," my friend told me. "It was like the way we all danced with the boys in the sixth grade, touching, but only at arms' distance apart." Let's not be that lady.

Obviously, your office clothes are not going to be made out of the same washable, wicking goodness as your athleisure-wear. But I tried to abide by this logic: If I was wearing it to work (which meant that I was also wearing it in the moments before leaving the house and in the moments upon arrival back at the house—prime baby-hugging times), it had to be either:

a. Wipeable (leather is surprisingly so), or
b. Washable (either in my own washing machine—which was running daily anyway—or by hand with the spot-treating miracle that is Forever New Fabric Care Wash), or
c. Tossable (not disposable, per se, but something that I would not weep over if it had to die a sudden and crappy death in the giveaway pile).

STYLE TRUTH #8: A JACKET SOLVES IT ALL. Blazer, knit, tuxedo, bomber, cropped, long, nipped, *whatever* shape works on you; jackets consistently save the day for postpregnancy work dressing. Here's why:

They give your body structure: "After wearing shapeless clothes during the last few months of pregnancy, there's nothing like a jacket," says Ashley, who pulled off the incredible hat trick of having two babies under two while working in a fashion-forward office. "I find that jackets remind me of my prepregnancy body image—that this crazy postpartum thing is temporary, after all."

They make every outfit more polished: "Going back to work, my old clothes actually still fit me, but they didn't look the same on," says Tia. "I was uncomfortable and had muffin top and back fat. So I wore blazers over anything—sundresses, rock T-shirts. They pulled me together and covered me up."

They help with the breast situation: And not just for the big-busted among us. "My boobs were really tender even though I wasn't breastfeeding," says Tia. "And since they're very small, I sometimes would wear these silicone pasties instead of a bra when a bra was too painful." A jacket kept her covered.

They're great for pumping: "When you spend half of your day with your blouse open or your T-shirt hiked up or down, a jacket keeps you warm and provides the illusion of being mostly dressed," says Ashley.

They make you feel strong: Maybe it's the shoulders, or the typically heavier fabric, but jackets act like armor, notes Ashley. "Psychologically, I always feel more in control when I'm dressed well."

And that's exactly what all this seemingly superficial stuff—the body pep talk, the makeup plan, the closet strategy—is about: putting *you* back in charge of your looks after that adorable, lovable parasitic creature temporarily took up residence in your womb. Because he's out now, and you're in your own skin again. Ahh.

CHAPTER SIX

⇝

On feeling human again

Your Most Essential Goal

One day, perhaps, my firstborn son will read this book, so I'll preface this chapter with this:

Sweet boy, I loved you from minute one. Actually before that. And the heart-swelling, eye-stinging shock of love I felt when nurse MaryAnn placed you, wet and naked, on my chest was better than anyone could have told me it would be. "Shock" is the word: An electrical pulse through my whole body (even the numbed parts) that instantly incinerated a gauze through which I'd viewed the world for the previous thirty years. Everything was sharper and clearer and significant and more meaningful and oh my God, how we loved you.

I was frozen with love. "Don't let him fall," MaryAnn instructed, genuinely worried, as she guided my hands up to hold your slippery body. I actually had to be told to put my hands on you, to hold you tight. This was nothing like what I'd anticipated. Where were my instincts? Why did I fumble with the snap on my bra? Why was your mouth so small? Where, I ask again, were my instincts?

Those next weeks were the most ecstatic and most disappointing of my life. Here was this baby that I had wanted desperately, and while I loved him, I hated myself. My ankles were so swollen from Pitocin that I could barely walk. They wouldn't even bend. Every painful trip to the bathroom was an exercise in personal negotiation: If you do this now, you won't have to do it again for a few hours. My breasts? Nursing was every unnatural hell I had never imagined. But the physical challenges were nothing compared with what was going on in my head. If I hated what I saw in the mirror, it was mostly because I hated what I saw in my own eyes: ineptitude, letdown; these were the eyes of a child, not of a woman who'd always declared herself a "baby person." I was a mess.

Five days in, nipples already scabbed and raw, I took some advice I'd Googled and walked around the apartment topless ridiculously for a couple of hours (not an easy feat when you're sporting two beach balls). "Sweetheart. It's time to snap out of emergency mode," my husband implored, unhelpfully. "Go take a shower. Life did not just become one big emergency." Reader, I lost it on him. Lost it. Because, actually, *yes it had*. I was crying constantly. Ten times a day. Emergencies, real emergencies, of the fire and tornado and terrorism variety, do two things to me. They freeze me physically, and they make me cry. This sure as hell felt just like that.

I need to pause here to mention two things.

One: My husband is a wonderful person. He is empathetic and so smart, and he has fantastic instincts.

The second thing I need to mention is that at this moment in our lives, when Will was born, Ben was starting his second year of residency in one of the best psychiatry programs in the world. And now I'll go on.

ME (CRYING, HYSTERICAL, NUMB): I think maybe I have postpartum depression. This is not how it's supposed to be!
HIM (RATIONAL, CALM): Nah. You just have the baby blues. It'll pass. Take a shower.

In Ben's defense, I didn't tell him a lot of the terrifying and ugly thoughts I had about myself and the baby. He had no way of knowing how bad it really was there in my brain. Years later, when I felt comfortable sharing some of that—and ribbing him for being so clueless—he was shocked and saddened. I wish I had let him in sooner. It wasn't fair to either of us that I hadn't.

It did pass, eventually, but not for many weeks. And it wasn't a life-or-death emergency. But it was real. Three years later, while pregnant with my second son, I saw an amazing therapist—Ben found her for me the minute I asked—to help quell my fears that my second time around the newborn block would resemble the first. When I told her about my experience, she said that I likely did have a postpartum mood disorder after Will. I felt amazingly validated to know that what I'd experienced looking in the mirror was common—but wasn't normal. In my case, the fog started to lift about six weeks after the baby was born, but I felt a bit like those crooked people in the old V8 TV commercials from my child-hood until almost exactly twelve weeks postpartum. Something (hormones, and going back to work, actually) set me straight, and I liked myself again, and I felt rational. I understood that my expec-tations had been totally out of whack.

So, long story long, I started feeling better basically right around my return to the office. But what if I hadn't? What if—like many women who have postpartum depression or anxiety—that proverbial fog hadn't lifted by the time I had to be a normal work-ing human person again?

This chapter is for anyone who needs help. Serious, holy-crap-I-can't-work-through-this help, or just help figuring out how to contribute meaningfully at the office when you're colossally sleep deprived. Help controlling an embarrassing outburst at work, or help recalibrating your expectations of yourself.

In other words: It's for all of us.

I talked to mothers who were positively gleeful about getting back to work after months adrift at home. They were relieved to return to their workplace and their formerly familiar lives. Chef and North Carolina restaurant owner Vivian Howard told me point-blank that her failure to live up to the "pink bathrobe-wearing, smiling, baby-holding mom" image was so traumatizing that she felt like "maybe I shouldn't even have had children." Only when she got back to work, in a restaurant kitchen, where she'd spent so much of her successful adult life, did she feel sane again.

More common, though, were the mothers who—and I don't exaggerate here; I have the audio files—groaned with the memory when I asked them to think back on their emotional state in their first few months back at work.

> "[Groan] God, I was depressed."
> "[Groan] I just didn't feel right yet."
> "[Groan] I had no idea how postpartum I was."
> "You come home each day to this magical baby. The baby is heaven on earth. And still, you cry. [Groan]"

The research itself could depress you: New mothers who have fewer than twelve weeks off of work are more likely to experience depressive symptoms, and those with fewer than eight paid weeks off are more likely to have a decrease in their overall health. (Another recent study pinpointed twenty-four weeks as the amount of time needed for mothers to be least likely to experience depression.) And this is not some fleeting issue to be muddled through and looked back upon wistfully: A more generous leave after the birth of a first child has been shown to benefit a mother's mental health decades later, in old age.

It's enough to make you throw a stapler across a work-share space. Or possibly cry.

Because in the real world, not some researched utopia, most American women have to return to work long before they feel emotionally ready. A couple of chapters ago, I mentioned that my survey takers reported feeling physically back to normal about five and a half months after birth. Emotionally, though, they said it took slightly longer: almost six months. (Hidden lesson: Just because a new mom looks pretty okay, don't assume that's how she feels.) So, once again, we're dealing with a challenging gap: Even mothers lucky enough to qualify for and afford twelve-week FMLA leave are stuck with three whole months, on average, of emotional boat-rocking. (And if your situation is truly debilitating to the point where you fear you can't work, please see page 272 in Chapter 12 for advice on how to take medical leave beyond maternity leave.)

And these are just the numbers related to time at work. In your previous life, pre-children, your hours away from work were likely restorative. TGIF, Sunday Funday, etc. But as new moms, 79 percent of the women I polled said that they spent one hour or less per week doing something for themselves during their first three months back at work. Many of them, I'd imagine, would opt to spend that hour napping, given that their babies weren't sleeping through the night until an average age of just over seven months. (In fact, if you would like to take a nap right now, instead of reading this chapter, please, please do!)

The technical term here, I believe, is "shit show."

But do not panic. If there is one thing we mothers are good at, it's anticipating shit and cleaning it up. Consider this chapter one giant organic cotton, scent-free, soothing-aloe emotional baby wipe.

The simplest way to feel good again: Ask this one question

As long as I'm letting it all hang out, I'll share this: Before I did my research, I thought that this chapter was going to have a lot of checklists. You know, things to help you understand what you're feeling, and the severity of those feelings, and whether or not you need a doctor's care.

I asked at least five experts—doctors, social workers, real pros: How do you know when you need professional help? Is there a list of symptoms? What's the time frame? All very reasonable questions, and things you may be wondering, too.

Here's the sad truth: It's not that simple.

Here's the reassuring truth: It's not that simple.

Don't worry. If you have a mood or anxiety disorder that necessitates professional care, I want you to know it, and I want you to get that care, and I've got more info on that coming up. I've been there, and I wish that I'd had that clarity. But I've learned that there's a lot that we can all do, together, as circles of friends and as a larger society, to help one another identify our emotional needs more conclusively and more quickly—and maybe even ward off problems before they become full-blown capital-*P* Problems.

Wendy N. Davis, PhD, the executive director of Postpartum Support International, was one of the several experts who paused, meaningfully, when I rattled off my picky black-and-white question, "How do you know when you really need a doctor?"

"The way we've learned to ask that question is part of what delays us from seeking the help that we need when we need it," admonished Dr. Davis, kindly. "What we do, as hard-working, high-achieving moms, as modern women, is that we wait until there is something really wrong before we ask for what we need. And that isn't healthy. The question for me is not 'How do I know when this is beyond normal and I need help?' The question is 'What do I need right now?' Asking this question is part of our creativity and intelligence as a parent. It's a strength, not a weakness."

Try it.

What do you need right now?

If I had asked that very question on day one. Or on day seven, or day fourteen, or at week twelve, I wonder—I really do—if I would have spiraled quite as severely as I did.

On day one: I needed my husband at the hospital with me overnight. He was, dutifully, at my urging, out to dinner with our six wonderful grandparents and a great aunt, celebrating . . . I minded but I didn't say so, and that night it was painful beyond belief just to sit up in bed, let alone to retrieve my crying son from his Isolette a few steps away. I wish I had asked Ben to stay. He would have.

On day seven: Sorry, Sweetie, this one's about you, too. I needed my husband to tell his employer to be reasonable, that he needed longer than a three-day paternity leave. I needed him home with me through the ticking hours, to make the calls to the five lactation consultants who weren't available until we found one that was. And then to ask her to come back again, the next day, and the next, not just once. I needed my insurance to cover that, too. And I needed someone to do that paperwork for me.

On day fourteen: I needed someone to help clean my apartment, or to carry my groceries home from the store so I didn't start bleeding again after I thought that I'd healed.

On day twenty-eight: I really needed someone to talk to, a friend with a newborn. My mom and my two mothers-in-law and my sister and my best girlfriends were amazing. But none of them had a new baby right then like me.

And on and on.

Back at work two months after that, I needed a part-time schedule for a couple of weeks. I needed an extra breast pump. I needed a ride home in a car, not on the sweaty subway. I needed an intern's assistance on a big project that was too much, too soon. I didn't ask for any of it. I'm telling you: *Ask.*

And it's not just me. Yes, I'll admit that I'm a perfectionist Virgo who likes to do everything herself. But we are living in a massive, woman-wide epidemic of outsized expectations and minuscule resources that contributes heavily to the emotional distress of returning to work with a newborn. "When you really look at the culture that we have created in the United States, we expect more and more of mothers, but we haven't given them any more support," says Dr. Davis. "The result of that is that you have mothers thinking that they should be able to work and have a baby, and somehow find that magic balance—even though no one is giving them the message at work, or at home, or on TV, that new parents need extra support. So the result is that everyone is likely to feel as though they are failing and falling behind."

Sarah Serafin, a work-at-home mom and medical transcriptionist in Chagrin Falls, Ohio, describes this as "America 'shoulding' on new parents. Whenever I get on a mentally self-destructive kick," she says, "I always think of an old favorite therapist saying to me, 'Quit shoulding all over yourself.'" I love that and am adopting it immediately.

Chirlane McCray, first lady of New York City, and an outspoken advocate for maternal mental health, told me and a handful of women invited to her home to discuss the issue, that she recalls being shoulded on in the ugliest way: "I don't know if you saw my face on the front page of the *New York Post,* with the words 'BAD MOM' over it?" she asked us. She had mentioned publicly that it had been difficult to be a new mom after age forty, and the *Post* had latched onto that one detail as something worth shaming. "It was just crazy—and my daughter's face when she saw that . . . ," she recalled, lowering her eyes. "It's not helpful to women who are struggling. Of course women love their children and want to do their best. But we're people. And this disease is real."

A little historical perspective helps here. "In ancient or primitive societies, families in villages shared the tasks of daily living—transportation, meals, cleaning, socializing. That's biologically how we are built," says Dr. Davis. "But in modern society, the more developed a country gets, the further away we get from that natural support network, although we still *act* as if we have that level of support." More families are structured nontraditionally. More parents move geographically far away from their families of origin. But our expectations of ourselves are unchanged.

This is where the vital question comes in: What do you need?

Dr. Davis struggled through postpartum depression and anxiety herself twenty-one years ago when she had her first child, and even though she was already a trained therapist (specializing in depression and anxiety!), she didn't recognize her own suffering. "I had no idea," she says. "It was like being a geophysicist and being *in* an earthquake and not knowing it's an earthquake." After she recovered, she immediately knew she'd found her life's work. Since then, she's passed on what she's learned to her patients and other therapists who come to her for training, and she always conveys this central message:

"I wish that I had had more understanding that becoming a working mother was a creative problem to solve, but the problem to solve is not 'How do I be a perfect mother?' The problem to solve is 'How do I maintain my emotional wellness?' Get creative about it, talk to your friends and confidants, go to a counselor, brainstorm! Working mothers would never hesitate to have a meeting to talk about a project, or to bring in a consultant. It's almost like working mothers put all this proactive creativity into their work life, and in our home life, we try to use a bad working model."

Here's your new model: "During this transition, make sure you are taking care of your physical, social, and emotional needs, so you can be the best mommy you can be," says Dr. Davis. "What do you need today? It might be a walk, or a phone call. It might be protein. All of the other chapters in this book only work if a mother feels she deserves to read them and if she's emotionally well enough to take action."

So, no checklists, sorry. Except for this one:

- ☐ THINK ABOUT WHAT YOU NEED.
- ☐ ASK FOR IT.

Okay, but *really,* when is it more than "just" the baby blues?

General consensus among the experts I talked to: *You're experiencing more than just the baby blues when it lasts more than two weeks and gets in the way of daily functioning.*

But—there are so many buts!

1ST BUT: The "it" varies tremendously among women. The symptoms of postpartum depression look different from those of postpartum anxiety, which look different from postpartum obsessive compulsive disorder. "There's a much more varied presentation than typical depression," says Christin Drake, MD, a psychiatrist and new mom in Brooklyn, who treats pregnant and postpartum women. "It's really kind of unreasonable to expect a person who is struggling *so* to figure it out on their own." Dr. Davis adds: "Some women might have crying and depression and a flat feeling toward their family and their baby. Other women might have intrusive thoughts, repetitive thoughts, anxiety, and it doesn't look at all like depression. It just doesn't feel right." Also common: irritability, difficulties sleeping even while the baby is sleeping, difficulty bonding. ("Who are these women who bond with their babies immediately?" one interviewee asked me, half-jokingly. "Did they go home from the hospital with a four-month supply of really great drugs that my OB didn't provide?")

2ND BUT: Those two weeks *don't* have to occur right after the birth. Postpartum issues can crop up months after birth, particularly during transitional times, like when you go back to work.

3RD BUT: You certainly shouldn't wait out the two weeks if the situation is urgent. "If someone is having suicidal thoughts, or thoughts about hurting the baby, or if your function is really impaired, the time line goes out the window," says Dr. Drake. "That's a medical emergency."

4TH BUT: You don't necessarily have to make an appointment with Dr. Freud. Look, I am a psychiatrist's wife. I love shrinks. (I sleep with a shrink!) But some people aren't comfortable with the whole idea. You do have other options. Dr. Drake says that a lot of patients come to her after their pediatrician picks up on something at the baby's checkup. "Many women don't see their OB until the six-week point, but pediatricians, who you'll see much earlier than that, are trained to help, too," she says, noting that this issue of timing is a uniquely American problem. "In other parts of the world people who are trained to look for mood difficulties are coming to the home to check on the mom in the earliest days." (In fact, in much of Latin America and Asia, a lying-in period of a month or more is common: Sex is forbidden, healthy foods are delivered, rest is mandated.) As I was editing this chapter, the U.S. Preventive Services Task Force made breaking news by issuing new recommendations from a national panel of experts: All pregnant women and new mothers should be screened for depression. The new recommendations and guidelines will help ob-gyns and pediatricians step in and ask the right questions. Raise the issue with anyone you're comfortable with: your OB, your primary care physician, a nurse, a therapist, a pastor, a rabbi. Or call an organization like Dr. Davis's (postpartum.net), where they know the language and are well equipped to answer any questions. "It can really be anyone who's knowledgeable and supportive," says Dr. Davis. "The most important thing is to start talking about 'Is this normal? Is this expected?'"

5TH BUT: You can be clearheaded and rational and still need care. One symptom of postpartum OCD, as I mentioned, is intrusive thoughts—something several women bravely revealed to me in their interviews. ("I pictured hurling the baby out the window. Or myself. Or both of us," one told me. From another: "I would cross the street and imagine the bus flattening the stroller.")

I'm terrified to write about this even now: I had them, these unimaginably gruesome flashbulb thoughts of all the ways my baby could die, including by my own errors. I absolutely knew that I would never, ever hurt this baby that I loved so much. So, I assumed, it was just my imagination on hormonal overdrive, nothing real. But the self-loathing I had over those thoughts *was* real. No one should have to live with that. That deserved treatment I wish I'd gotten. (And Dr. Davis told me something wonderfully comforting, too: "There has been research done that shows that the part of the brain that lights up when they do brain mapping during those flashable thoughts is the protective instinct." Not violent, protective.)

————

Still hesitant? Know that you aren't committing to treatment and a diagnosis just by asking those first few questions. And even if you do end up getting treatment, it can go very quickly (good to know if you're worried about the time and financial commitment). "This isn't long-term therapy," says Dr. Davis. "It's mostly problem-solving, support, learning stress-reduction techniques, learning to communicate with your partner, and learning to ask for what you need. Even moms with really severe symptoms may only need to be seen five times." Honestly, I'm not even pregnant, and now I want to go. (And again, if your care necessitates missing work, see page 272 for how to address that with your supervisor.)

One more thing: All of this talking? All of this asking, what do I need, and is this normal? Let's do it for *one another,* not just for ourselves. "We have to treat this as a public health problem, not just an individual one," says Dr. Drake, who feels like we're on the cusp of real progress. "We'll all now talk to our friends about 'Did I take off the baby weight?'—now we need to ask one another: 'Do I seem okay? Do I seem like myself?'" And we need to look out for other new mothers, especially those who may be more marginalized. "This is a thing that happens in one in seven women in the general population, but it's closer to one in four in women who have less support, who are single, who are younger," she says. "We all need to talk openly so people recognize when they're struggling. It's not okay to be crying every time you go to take a shower for six weeks. It's not normal, and I find it so odd from a psychological perspective that we both expect so much from mothers and then can convince ourselves that they would continue to struggle for so long."

Let's fix that. I've told you my story. Start sharing yours.

Ever heard of a self-care plan?
At work, you need one now.

"Self-soothe, little dude, self-soothe." Seven years later, Ben and I will still crack up when we remember saying that to newborn baby Will, begging him to find his thumb, stop crying, and settle peacefully. Babies aren't born knowing how to chill themselves out. As an adult, you probably do know what it takes to make you feel better fast (besides a glass of something white or something red). But you might have to think about it. I'd suggest doing that thinking before you're hit with a bad day, or a bad meeting, or a gridlocked commute, or a colleague who says the wrong thing at the wrong time. Go back to work knowing that you will have at least one emotional outburst, and have your ripcord right there waiting for you to pull. To set yourself up for the easiest float back down to earth, follow these three steps:

1) Give yourself permission to feel the feelings.
2) Take into account your environment.
3) Self-soothe.

"This is a moment when knowing yourself really comes in handy," says psychotherapist Sarah Best. "Even if you don't necessarily have a perinatal mood or anxiety disorder but you suspect that you're going to have some emotional moments in your return to work, be real with yourself about that. Emote. Acknowledge that." Don't spiral and feel bad for having the feelings, for goodness' sake. "I'm a big believer that negative emotions are okay," says psychiatrist Samantha Boardman, MD, founder of the website PositivePrescription.com. "I think there is room for crying, and anger and frustration, and boredom, and anxiety. It's just what you do with those feelings that matters." Prepare for the fact that you may have a short fuse, or get teary over something that might not have bothered you previously. Then when that exact thing happens, you'll think: *Right. I told myself this would happen. I must know myself well. So my plan will work, too.*

Step two: Once you've acknowledged your feelings, you need to decide to what degree you can reveal them in your workplace.

Back in Chapter 2, I made a heartfelt case for bringing your whole self to work—including your new-mom imperfections. I think it will ultimately help us all to just be more real with one another. To get a little teary in public. To admit that it's hard to focus when you're not sleeping at night. I wish I could click my heels and make everyone's workplace receptive to those kinds of emotional admissions overnight. More realistically, many work environments require baby steps. One office's weepy group hug is another's plaster of paris baby handprint on an executive's desk that sends shock waves—shock waves—around the floor. So look at your environment and decide ahead of time: What can I show here that helps people understand a new working mother's mind-set in the short term without damaging my credibility in the long run?

Best-case scenario, "There are some environments where it's not going to be a problem to close your door and have some time to yourself," says Best, who coaches new moms through evaluating their workplaces for just such a moment. "Other women may work in a shared workspace where it's not going to be a problem if you become visibly upset—in which case, give yourself permission. But"—big but, I will add—"others are going to be in a more corporate or more masculine environment where that's not going to be warmly received." That's when you need your parachute plan (step three).

Best had one client who knew that there was no actual safe space at work where she could take five minutes to herself. "So her plan was five M&M's and a phone call to her mom," she says. "She would step outside only long enough to go to the newsstand to get a pack of M&M's," something anyone at the office would have done, so it didn't seem like she was dodging work. "And then she would call her mom, who lived out of state, for a little check-in. Not some big emotional conversation, just a quick hello to someone she knew cared how she was feeling and that she was taking care of herself." That was enough to get her through the moment and on with her day, knowing that she'd confidently met her own needs.

Maybe all you need is three deep breaths, or five minutes in the stall in the bathroom, or the temporary distraction of reading a favorite blog, or of texting a friend. Experts I talked to suggested classic coping tools like counting backward from ten, or pretending to be a fly on the wall while describing the situation (in fly speak, I guess?) to someone else. One new mom told me she loved nothing more than doing a page of an adult coloring book. Another carried *The New Yorker* with her and saved the "Shouts & Murmurs" humor page for just such a crisis moment. The specific action itself doesn't matter. "Just knowing that you've been proactive in your self-care plan is what makes it work," says Best.

Dr. Boardman describes that feeling as fortifying. It's empowering, she says, to know how to take care of yourself. "You need those tricks with you at work. Pack them right along with your breast pump."

There is, sometimes, a numbness that comes with feeling emotionally overwhelmed. What if you can't even think of one thing that will help you self-soothe? (Or what if your one thing really is a big fat glass of Montepulciano? Probably not okay before the 10:00 a.m. staff meeting.) Dr. Boardman recommends using a fantastic tool of the Positive Psychology movement called the VIA Survey. Developed by renowned psychologists Martin Seligman and Christopher Peterson, the survey ranks your twenty-four "character strengths" to determine what motivates you personally and helps you feel capable. Dr. Boardman's suggestion is that you identify your top strength and then make a self-care plan that employs it.

Oh, sure, I'll be your guinea pig. I am currently not postpartum, but I would still have a hard time telling you what my self-care plan should be beyond a cup of hot chocolate in the winter or ice cream in the summer (neither of which would make me feel particularly great about myself an hour later). So I tried the VIA Survey online (viacharacter.org). In 120 questions and ten minutes (I timed myself), I found out that my top character strength—above gratitude, perspective, leadership, self-regulation, and more—is: love. Clearly, I'm not a very complicated soul. But it's true. I do "value close relations with others," particularly "those in which caring and sharing are reciprocated" probably more than anything else in the world. My best bet for a self-care plan, then, would be to call my dad, who never, ever hangs up the phone without telling me that he loves me. Alternatively, I could come up with a plan that allows me to feel better by expressing my love: writing a quick note to my husband or best friend, say. That would bring me back to my senses and help me feel better fast, it's true.

"It's fun to look at your strengths in this new way," says Dr. Boardman. "For instance if you find out that you have an incredible love of beauty, maybe you find some way to experience nature in the middle of your workday. When you do things using your strength, you fortify yourself against your toughest days."

P.S.: Here are your magic words for when you can't employ your parachute quickly enough and (horrors) you've had a public, emotional outburst: "Yes, I am struggling a bit with this transition, but I am also confident that things will improve." (Thank you, Dr. Drake!)

How to act sane when the sleep situation is out of control

As I type these words, I am willing my fingers to press the correct keys. My knuckles feel eighty years old and arthritic, and my mind is way up there in decades, too—and not in a "Boy, she sure is sharp for an octogenarian" kind of way. What happened? I didn't sleep last night. Our younger son had nightmares, three of them, and ended up in a sleeping bag on our floor, from which he whimpered and cried about monsters, and asked questions about why we celebrate both Christmas and Chanukah, for what felt like hours. We pleaded, we soothed, we promised presents, we threatened to take away presents. Eventually, I yelled, and then, upset with myself for losing it, I tossed and turned for another two hours while he finally slept. Yet here I am, pressing the keys on my trusty MacBook Air, working.

In our house, we have one good sleeper and one spotty sleeper. Both boys were sleep trained the down and dirty cry-it-out way at 3.5 months old, after I'd been back at work for a couple of weeks and realized the situation was unsustainable. If I had a third baby we'd use the same method again. But there is no way in the world I'd be qualified to give you advice about how to get your baby to sleep through the night. It's an incredibly personal process. My cousin cosleeps; my best friend fed her baby multiple times a night until she was almost a year old. Another family I know hired a $1,400, one-night sleep coach who arrived at their baby's nursery with a white noise machine and a roll of duct tape to darken the windows and then proceeded to lie prostrate under the crib texting the parents sleep updates. That six-week-old baby is now a champion twelve-hours-a-night sleeper. Like I said, to each his own. Unfortunately, Mama still has to function at work no matter what her chosen method. And the hundreds of mothers I surveyed said that their babies weren't allowing them a decent night's sleep until seven-plus months, on average.

So instead of giving you tips on how to get your baby to sleep, I hunted down expert, scientific advice about how to deal with sleep deprivation. You know who's really good at that? The military. They've started using sleep deprivation as a weapon of war, testing drugs and sleep patterns that allow soldiers to perform on less sleep with the lowest degree of cognitive impairment.

"Sleep deprivation is a form of torture because the effects are so profound," says Wendy Troxel, PhD, Senior Behavioral and Social Scientist at the RAND Corporation, and an adjunct professor of psychiatry and psychology at the University of Pittsburgh, where she studies behavioral sleep medicine. "Lack of sleep affects every aspect of you: your ability to think, your mood, your physical strength, your focus," says Dr. Troxel, who has researched sleep among military service members and their partners. Maternal postpartum sleep is also (as you know!) highly fragmented. Those frequent interruptions have been proven to have the same effect over time of going one entire night without sleep. "After four to five nights, when healthy human subjects are subjected to five or less hours of sleep per night," Dr. Troxel explains, "they will function on performance tasks at a level of impairment that equates with being legally drunk."

Basically, you're going to work drunk at 9 a.m.

Not hungover. Drunk.

Troxel has also studied sleep among couples and families, and she says the sleep challenges new parents face really are somewhat akin to those of soldiers at war. "You feel the weight of the world on your shoulders to protect this precious baby," she says. "In some ways, this is similar to the experience of service members: There is a reduced opportunity for sleep, but the need to be constantly vigilant is overwhelming. The sleep deprivation and high-stress environment feed into each other." Even once babies start sleeping through the night, Troxel's (as yet unpublished) research shows, the quality of mothers' sleep tends to be poor: About 44 percent of mothers with two-and-a-half-year-old children experience moderate to excessive daytime sleepiness. "There's that conditioned response to be ever vigilant," says Dr. Troxel. "It can be ongoing for a long time, and although this will be at the forefront of your mind because you are living it, others [your coworkers, for instance] will forget because, frankly, it's not their life. So you may have to do some gentle reminding, know your limitations, and work through it the best that you can."

I tell you all this not to scare you but to earn your trust of this expert. Wendy Troxel isn't sugarcoating anything, so you can know that the advice she offers here—to help you deal with lack of sleep, and improve the quality of the little sleep you're getting—is valid. And did I mention she's a mom, too? Her best coping strategies:

NAP EFFECTIVELY. Nap? I know: Ha! But seriously, even weekend-only snoozing can help. "In the military and in other shift-work environments where you can't avoid lack of sleep, napping is very effective at combating fatigue—if it's well scheduled," says Troxel. That means under sixty minutes, so you don't wake up from a sleep so deep that you just want to keep sleeping, and before 4:00 p.m. so the nap doesn't hinder your ability to sleep at night. The tricky twist to the weekend nap is actually convincing yourself to take one, especially if you have company. "Even in our most depleted times, we feel societal pressure to somehow entertain," says Dr. Troxel. "It's become socially unacceptable to say, 'Hi, thank you for coming over . . . I'm going for a nap now.'" But you must. My advice: Set up the expectation before the visit. That way your visitor might actually remind you of your intention, letting you off the hook.

GIVE YOURSELF FIFTEEN MINUTES OF WIND-DOWN TIME BEFORE BED. Your baby has a going-to-bed routine. You need one, too. "The instinct of new mothers, who are so exhausted, is to rush to bed as soon as the baby is in bed, but your brain just may not be ready yet," says Dr. Troxel. "If you spend your day, up to that minute, just giving giving giving, and only caring for others' needs, you may not have allowed yourself the appropriate amount of time to wind down for sleep. Take a bath, do some deep breathing, do some sensory relaxation exercises, something to help your brain shut down," and your sleep will be of higher quality.

DO NOT USE SCREENS DURING NIGHTTIME FEEDINGS. This one comes straight from a study by a collaborator of Troxel's, Hawley Montgomery-Downs, PhD, at West Virginia University. Montgomery-Downs and her coauthor titled their paper, "What Are Postpartum Women Doing While the Rest of the World Is Asleep?" The answer: using a smartphone (59 percent), a back-lit tablet (25 percent), TV (20 percent), or a computer (16 percent). Plenty of the mothers who were surveyed used a lamp or a nightlight with no problem, but those who watched TV or used a computer had longer nocturnal awakenings. And no one wants that.

HAVE SOME COFFEE—AND SOME PERSPECTIVE. "The single best strategy for coping with fatigue is caffeine," says my new favorite non-bullshitter Dr. Troxel. You heard it here first. "Well-scheduled caffeine, early in the day, in reasonable doses is fine—but I'd avoid any other stimulants, including energy drinks, because they have so many other ingredients." What if you're pumping or nursing? Dr. T. says that one cup of joe in the morning, after pumping or nursing, isn't likely to do anything other than make you a better woman. But, as with anything, she says, "having a balanced perspective is important, and if a woman is dying from exhaustion at work, the idea of stopping breastfeeding early will probably cross her mind, which of course isn't ideal, but neither is falling asleep in a board meeting or having poor decision-making skills while trying to piece together a million-dollar business deal. So whether it's caffeine, taking extra time before you return to work, stopping breastfeeding before you planned, or just toughing it out . . . all of these have a risk/benefit ratio to explore. Talk to your doctor about it, but also talk to your spouse and to yourself."

GAME THE 2:00 P.M. SLUMP. That post-lunchtime sleepiness is real. "There's a dip in the circadian signal for wakefulness around this time of day," says Dr. Troxel. "Get up, take a walk, get some sunlight on your face—even if it's just from the window or a lightbox." And try to schedule your day, if you can, so that any long meetings where you're just sitting and listening aren't in the early afternoon. Paradoxically, if you have to speak or be onstage, 2:00 p.m. can be a great time, she says: "Your adrenaline will be pumping while you present to and engage with others. You won't fall asleep on your feet. Hopefully."

STRATEGIZE NIGHTS WITH YOUR PARTNER. My friend Leigh nails the relationship implications of sleeplessness: "You know that adage about not going to sleep angry?" she asks. "When you have a baby who's up three times a night, you're going to sleep angry three times a night, every single night." It's not easy. Some partners split the night wake-ups evenly. In other couples, especially if the mother is breastfeeding exclusively, they may all fall on Mom.

If that's you, consider pumping and switching off now and then if you can. "It's the cumulative sleep deprivation that is so awful, and so costly to our ability to function," says Dr. Troxel. "So doing some amount of trade-off is very important. We've all dealt with one or two bad nights. This is not the end of the world. So if you can get a bit of a respite, that's huge."

That actual, practical division of labor is important to your sleep when you are back at work—but so is the sense of peace that comes from having logically, preemptively discussed your plan for nights with your partner (if you have one . . . again, single moms, you are my heroes). "No matter what decision you make, make it as a family," says Dr. Troxel. "Some couples decide to have separate beds or bedrooms while the baby is very small so that one parent getting up doesn't disturb the other. An on-duty room and off-duty room, earplugs included, can be a good decision to ensure the deepest sleep possible." What you really don't want is to fall into a resentment trap. If you're pissed as hell and you're lying there in bed stewing, you're not going to sleep, she warns. "Your cortisol and your adrenaline are pumping because you're angry and resentful. So for both partners, attempting to deal with these conflicts before bedtime is very important."

So how do you ask to be the one who gets sleep tonight when you both have to work in the morning? Remember, says Dr. Troxel, that sleep will help the more rested partner contribute to the family more actively during the day. "You may want to say, 'I need to sleep downstairs tonight so I can get more rest and treat you better.' Just having the discussion can make a huge difference."

What if your job is an emotionally demanding job?

Liz, a teacher in Philadelphia, had a terrifying case of postpartum anxiety with her first daughter—"white-knuckle level fear all the time about her," as she puts it—and it hadn't fully passed by the time she went back to work in September. "My first day back, I could not manage. I cried the entire day. Thankfully, class hadn't started yet. It was meant to be a teacher bonding day, with a team-building ropes course, and I just remember thinking, 'I don't want to do a trust fall with this guy's hand on my ass. I want to be with my baby. I'm worried she's not eating. It didn't help that I was in a fairly new job, and people didn't know me well enough yet to know that this wasn't the real me."

Shira Epstein is a rabbi. Her first son was born two weeks after she finished her training and was ordained, ready to start her long-anticipated career supporting a vast community of Jewish families with everything from marriage advice to grief counseling. Still, she tabled her job plans initially, out of worry. "I had worked in congregations as a student and I knew it was going to be over-whelmingly demanding to meet both my baby's and my congre-gants' needs," she says. "So I chose to go into organizational work for a year instead." But the organizational job wasn't a great fit logistically or emotionally. By her second baby, she was back at work as a rabbi, and happier.

A week after Cristyn Zett went back to work as a vice-squad detective (now lieutenant) on the Pittsburgh police force, three officers were killed there in an attack that made national headlines. "We were just plunged into chaos," she recalls. "I was actually probably a little more focused at work than I would have been otherwise. I had to be. But I kept worrying, What if something happens to me? What happens to my son then? I mean, I could walk out today and get hit by a bus, too, but you know you're just walking into a lion's den when you're in service."

I asked these three women: What helps? How do you find the strength to help other people, when you're in a fragile state your-self?

For Liz, maintaining a sense of control of the things that she could, in fact, control was key. Her teenage students' needs varied unpredictably day to day, but her classroom was her refuge, a space that she spent time organizing to suit her needs—including mak-ing room to pump (see Chapter 7 for that great story). Same went for her schedule. "I made my free period right before lunch so I would have an extra-long window to go see my baby at daycare if needed." Knowing she had that one daily escape hatch helped her stay steady for her students.

Cristyn credits her evolving relationship with her husband, Rick, for her ability to deal with her physically and emotionally draining job. He is on the police force as well, and they usually work opposite shifts. Their son, Gavin, has Down syndrome, and most of his doctor appointments were in the morning, when only Rick could take him. Very quickly, Cristyn had to empower her husband to be their conduit to the doctors, and in doing so, she saw how capable he was: "To be honest, he kind of wasn't a baby guy, but he really just didn't have a choice! At work, I'm surrounded by guys who don't know their kids' teachers—and I'm not knocking that, that's how their lives are set up. I know that Rick knows the doctors, the therapists, and now the teachers." And she doesn't say so, but my guess is that helps at those moments when she feels vulnerable. If something terrible were to happen to her on the job, Rick is capable and involved, and she knows it.

Shira, with her second baby, knew that she'd be needed by her temple's congregants at challenging hours—for everything from prayers as people died, to Tot Shabbat services on Friday evenings for other people's children (when her own were too young). She made her life simpler by living within walking distance of the synagogue—five blocks. And she got comfortable, fast, with the fact that the work environment she'd chosen, while demanding, was inherently family-friendly. "My nanny would bring the baby in because we were so close, and I would nurse in staff meetings," she says. That bonding time made her more able to draw the line and separate, too, when she needed to. "I never had my baby there when I was interacting with a congregant in need, or speaking to a parent about their child. Having my own child there would have undermined the help I was giving, like I wasn't really putting their needs at the top of my list."

Shira also told me that she realized that the emotional obligations of her job would become more challenging as her children got older and needed more complicated support themselves. Babies are draining, but they don't ask questions or get their feelings hurt the way five-year-olds do. So here's her other great takeaway for women in emotionally demanding careers: Pivot. Use your skills to move between jobs that have different emotional requirements as your needs at home change. These days, Shira is executive director of a major Jewish nonprofit, the 14th Street Y in New York City, where, she says, "I can be more emotionally available to my children now that they are school-age." She's maintained her career—grown it, even—but kept her heart and head open for when they're needed at home.

Emotional triage from women who've been there: a speed round of good tips

"There are so many women out there who are fine . . . but they're not *good*," says Dr. Boardman when I ask her about what I've begun to call the In-betweeners—new moms who aren't technically, diagnosably mentally ill, but who are back at work while they're still emotionally raw. "In society now, we put so much pressure on women to bounce back, physically, obviously, but also mentally to get it together and move forward," she says. "There's a bit of intolerance of negative emotion. Give yourself permission to feel that in-between feeling." And know that you'll get past it, too.

A handful of strategies have been proven by researchers to help when you just feel like quitting—turn back to Chapter 3 for those. But sometimes you simply want to hear what worked for your friends. A shocking percentage of new moms, 87 percent, say that they experience feelings of isolation. Well, no more. Think of the women quoted here—self-described recovered In-betweeners, and some experts and PPD/PPA sufferers, too—as your compatriots: They've been there, they've felt all the feelings, and they're full of good advice about making it through the emotions of the Fifth Trimester. Their quick hits of wisdom for you:

KNOW THAT WHAT YOU'RE FEELING ISN'T NECESSARILY WHAT EVERY-ONE IS SEEING. We have a tendency to spiral, says Nitzia Logothetis, MSc, MA, founder and executive chairwoman of the Seleni Institute for maternal mental health. "It could be over the simplest thing," she explains. "Let's say you miss an email from someone. You may beat yourself up for not having sent yourself a reminder to reply. Pretty soon you're thinking, Oh my goodness, they must think I'm not capable at all, that I don't have it together. You're thinking it over and over. But in reality it's *just one email*—the other hundred you've sent in a timely fashion have made a much bigger impression!"

PRETEND THIS IS YOUR THIRD BABY. "Having been through new motherhood three times now, my instinct is to say to myself, 'You've got this,'" Logothetis says. In reality, things are only more complicated with three children. But that confidence goes a long way. "Now, when I feel anxiety trying to balance and care for my third baby, I just remember this feeling is familiar. It's just part of caring for a baby. And it won't last forever."

PUT A DATE ON YOUR CALENDAR THREE MONTHS FROM NOW TO REEVALUATE. "If you feel like you're in the woods at work, I promise in the next three months you'll feel different," says writer and single mom by choice Wendy Shanker. "Three months is a season, ninety days. Maybe it's because our womanly bodies are so smart. Get through it and cope however you need to cope—and then know that you've gotten through it with an understanding of what's going to get you through the next season, too." Sarah Best, the therapist, sets the exact same time frame: "Inevitably, at week two or three, a patient will come into my office tearful, saying that they need to quit, or pull their kid out of daycare and hire a nanny they can't afford because commuting is too intense, and I always, always say, 'Let's give it three months.'"

FEEL FREE TO CANCEL AS OFTEN AS YOU WANT. There is no relief as wonderful as a lunch hour reclaimed, or a night when you can go to bed early and sober (instead of late and cocktail-partied-up). "I was always on time, always followed through, never canceled anything," says Superfly's Jennifer Justice, who's a single mom of twins. "Finally, I just gave myself a break. You have to just let it happen. It's not going to last forever, this stage." If a "fun" plan is stressing you out, cancel! Tell them Jay Z's lawyer told you to.

BUT ALSO: DO THE SEEMINGLY OVERWHELMING THING. When you have a baby, and something that used to be completely normal in your life becomes exponentially more challenging, it's really quite defeating—and depressing. Lydia, the Christie's auction house executive, fought that feeling by ripping off the Band-Aid and traveling home on her own to see her parents in Louisiana, with her toddler and her baby. It was a confidence-inducing rush, she says. "People were like, How are you going to fly with two tiny kids? And I was like, If I don't do it now, I'm going to get scared of it, and then I really won't ever do it. I remember as a child, my siblings would force me to do things like hurling myself off of a rock into this waterfall in Montana. It was like that. With anything you do in the working world, or with your kids, sometimes you have to just do it—because if you don't it seems so much more overwhelming than it actually is."

FIND YOUR SPIRIT CELEBRITY. Tia, the beauty editor who had one of those lovely Fifth Trimesters that came with a side of divorce, ended up with migraines so debilitating that she was hospitalized. New baby, new job, failing marriage, hospital. Midcrisis, in her hospital bed, she emailed a friend and colleague who said just the right thing. "I was sick, and my marriage was falling apart, and I was like, 'Who's going to date this unlovable, chubby person, who's in pain and has a baby?'" Tia recalls. "My friend Charlotte reminded me, Look, your favorite person on earth is Elizabeth Taylor, right? She was always in the hospital, she had chronic back pain, and she was married eight times! All these men were obsessed with her. She didn't give a fuck. She got up and accepted her Oscar with a huge tracheotomy scar and was like, 'This is who I am, and if you don't like it, you don't have to be in my life.' " It was a turning point for Tia: "At that moment, I realized, I'm not apologizing for who I am. It really helped."

IF YOU "WORK ON" ANYTHING RIGHT NOW, MAKE IT YOUR EXPECTATIONS. "Before I had my son Will, I was able to burn the work candle at both ends," says Koty Sharp, a marine biologist in Rhode Island. "And after I had Will, I had this idea in my head that I wouldn't have to rearrange things just because I had a child. That was crazy. I had to accept that my schedule would not be the same, or that sometimes my body wouldn't have as much energy. So the biggest thing for me during the first few months coming back to work was just trying to renegotiate with myself. I worked on changing my expectations. Not changing my professional contribution, but figuring out how to redesign my approach. And I think I actually got better at my job."

Be careful in this transition not to attempt the impossible, says Dr. Drake, who recommends scheduling some time back at work well in advance of any high-stakes presentation or meeting. Yes, even if that means coming back a few days early. "It's much easier to keep your perspective if you are not facing down a huge display of your readiness—or not-so-readiness," Dr. Drake explains.

THINK OF THIS TIME AS A (MUCH FASTER) ADOLESCENCE. Do you know a single person who liked her teenage years? I don't either. And yet, most of my friends are now happy and successful and look back on those awful, transitional years as formative! Same thing applies during the Fifth Trimester. "It felt just like being twelve again," says Tia of the loss of footing she felt going back to work as a new mother: the identity shift, the body changes, the heightened emotions, and the insecurity. You've actually done all this before, years ago. And that's a comfort. Says Tia: "I somehow found strength in the fact that I'd been through hell and come out stronger."

SPEAKING OF HORMONES: DON'T DENY YOURS. Robin Fredriksz is a Hollywood makeup artist (maybe you've heard of her clients, Cameron and Drew?) and single mom who was lucky enough to have her older sister be her surrogate when she couldn't carry the baby herself. "When you don't carry a child, you're not going through the same emotional upheaval," says Robin. "The doctor who delivered my son put it in a nutshell. At the birth, he said to me, 'I want to show you something.' It was literally a plastic bucket of afterbirth. 'Your sister just lost a ton of hormones, just like that. So be aware of that, be gentle with her,' he told me. Seeing that, I realized: How could you not be an emotional wreck?" Robin shares this story with her friends and tells them: Be aware; be gentle with yourself.

REFRAME STRESS AS EXHILARATION. Corey, the start-up culture expert, says she feels almost like she had two babies the year that her son was born: the actual baby, and her new job, which was at— what else?—a rapidly expanding start-up. "It was really intense, and having both of those experiences in tandem is the type of thing that could drive people crazy. Nothing could have prepared me for that." The one thing that helped was for her just to accept the pace. "I realized: Okay, things are crazy at work, and things are crazy at home, and that's just the new normal." And then her whole outlook shifted from panic to enjoyment. "To have experienced that kind of growth both in work and in life, I realized, was amazing."

MAKE A BIG HOO-HA OUT OF YOUR MOM MILESTONES. Baby rolled over to the left! Baby rolled over to the right! Well, guess what? Mommy just did something awesome, too: She realized she was getting better. Liz, the teacher in Philly with the rotten case of anxiety, was so distraught with fear for months that she could barely even let anyone else hold her baby. "Going back to work was almost an impossible thought," she says. But she did. And a couple of months later, after baby Bailey started solids, Liz recognized how far she'd come: "One day, food fell on the floor and I popped it back into Bailey's mouth and I thought: Well, look at that. We are all going to be okay." It's important to recognize those milestones to see just how much time helps you grow.

OPT OUT OF THE COMPARE-ATHON. Quiz: Can you name three celebrities who were pregnant at the same time you were? I sure can (lucky me, I got gorgeous Jessica Alba for both of my pregnancies!). Sadly, I remember how much they went out and how high their shoes were, and their chosen brands of stroller, and how rapidly they lost the baby weight. Not a good use of brain cells. "Do not go down that rabbit hole of Facebook and Twitter and all of the self-comparison with celebrities or the friend who had her baby ten days ago and is now back to a size two and is already posting from her business trip," warns Dr. Boardman. "If you want to inoculate yourself against inevitable stress, *really* try to avoid comparison. Of course it's okay to leaf through *US Weekly,* or scroll through Instagram if that's what relaxes you, but know that it's not real. No one's posting pictures of their pimples." It's a tough reflex to control, so if that requires taking a social media hiatus, do it.

JUST ROLE-MODEL THE HELL OUT OF ANY SITUATION. I loved this simple, moving insight from my interview with tech exec Stephanie, a director and sales team leader, who had breast cancer during her pregnancy and a mastectomy during her maternity leave with daughter Caroline: "One of the big ongoing jokes—but also a true guiding force for my husband and me—was saying to myself, 'What would Caroline's mom do?' and also, 'What would I want my daughter to do in this same situation?' "

DO NOT MAKE ANY MAJOR CAREER DECISION NOW. "In the absence of any mood or anxiety disorder, it is important to hold tight and not make any major decisions for the first couple of weeks back, knowing that these will be the toughest," says Dr. Drake. "My daughter went on a bottle strike during my first week back to work, and I was either running home to feed her or having her brought to my office for feedings during that week. It was horrible for us both." Of course, she had her doubts about working. "But it passed quickly as these things do," she says. "If I had made any real decisions about my professional life during those first couple of weeks, I really would have limited myself."

MAKE MEETING SCHEDULING YOUR BITCH. There are an awful lot of things at work that you can and should delegate. Meeting scheduling isn't one of them. Take that crap on, says Koty, the marine biologist, and make the schedule accommodate your needs to help keep you calm and in control. Koty and a bunch of her colleagues had a five-hour meeting session to schedule when her son was about five months old. She raised her hand for the heretofore thankless task of making the schedule, which included—ta da!—two breaks timed perfectly for pumping. "Believe me, it wasn't some great honor to coordinate the thing, but doing so put me in the position of power. When my older male colleagues asked why we needed 'bathroom' breaks at all, I explained and everyone was very supportive."

BLAME THE MACHINE. I am an over-apologizer, the kind of person who bumps into furniture and then stupidly says "I'm sorry" to it. My husband is the exact opposite; he does something I call blaming the machine. If he can't figure out which remote control to use, he accuses the TV of misbehaving. If he gets a spot of salad dressing on his favorite tie and the dry cleaner can't get it out, he doesn't blame himself for spilling (or even the dry cleaner for being incapable). He blames the salad dressing for being oily. Stupid salad dressing, ruining his tie. "Babe," I'll say, "quit blaming the machine." Well, you know what? He might be the sane one. Because being able to convince yourself that you're not to blame for a shitty situation can really help in this back-to-work moment, says Dr. Drake. "There is a real gap between the reality of motherhood and the public understanding of motherhood, and certainly the pretending in the workplace about what motherhood is really like. Being aware of that gap is really important." In your darkest, most unbalanced moments, she suggests, say to yourself: "This is crazy, but it's not me that's crazy, it's the situation." The situation is hard, and here in the United States, parental leave and reentry into the workplace are not set up in a humane way. It sucks, but acknowledging the suckage helps. Blame the machine.

DO NOT FADE GENTLY INTO YOUR COUCH. "It's so tempting to just isolate yourself and stay home, especially when you have a new baby," says Dr. Boardman. "But our collective mother was right: Sometimes you just have to put on lipstick and leave the house. And you end up feeling better for it." I love my couch. I love it so much that I had to replace it once I was done breastfeeding both of my boys, but Dr. Boardman specifically warns new moms about something called Guilty Couch Potato Syndrome, which is, apparently, an actual scientifically studied phenomenon: The guilt you feel from wasting time vegging out can actually outweigh the benefits of relaxation; it depletes your ego. Everyone needs downtime, of course, but if there's something that pushes your limits a bit, give it a try. Robin, the makeup artist and single mom, says it's the one piece of advice she gives all her new-parent friends. "You can't be all about your child," she tells them. "There needs to be work, child, socializing. Yes, it's easy to just stay home, but don't do it. Seek the balance. Keep all of the parts of yourself alive."

THINK OF YOUR WORK AS A CAREER, NOT JUST A JOB. This one's a biggie. A number of women I interviewed mentioned that they started feeling genuinely good about going back to work when they stopped feeling oppressed by their jobs, and started feeling *im*pressed by their career potential. I related. Three weeks after coming back to work after having Will, I was approached by a competitor with a really tempting job offer that I didn't take (see: No Major Career Decisions, above). I felt so valued, and I saw, instantly, that I wasn't tearing myself away from my baby every morning for "the man" but for myself—for my own advancement. Part of what helped me see that big picture: I had to force myself to make time for the meeting, and to find something to wear, and to do my due diligence on the person who was recruiting me. Dr. Drake says this kind of prioritized career-building time is essential, something she struggled with herself: "I didn't actually have much difficulty managing the work of my medical practice," she recalls, "but it was all of the other things that go along with my professional identity that I struggled to prioritize: my extra teaching schedule, my meetings with old colleagues, even the blowout that I wanted to fit in before an important meeting." As soon as she had that epiphany, she felt more settled into her new life. "It's the intangible stuff that helps us stay in and move up," she says. Never forget: You work for you.

CHAPTER SEVEN

※

Pumping doesn't have to suck

Wee-woo, wee-woo. Lookiloo, lookiloo. Maaa-mo, maaa-mo. Ruuuh-roh? Ruuuh-roh? Are those Fisher-Price rain forest mobile noises? Yo Gabba Gabba language? Nope, just the sound of millions of women pumping breastmilk at work. If you decide to become one of them, prepare to be the kind of person whose pump also talks to her in its own special language. Yes, the process is that crazy-making. But for the 83 percent of working moms I surveyed who headed back to work while still breastfeeding, it was also incredibly worth it.

Logistically, pumping was one of the things I worried about most before my first day back. What equipment would I need? How would I commute with it? How much milk would I get? And how on earth would I find the time—and the privacy—in the middle of the workday?

One additional question I didn't know enough to worry about before I was in the thick of it: How would I find the *focus*? Toggling between doing something so personal and doing actual work required Herculean levels of discipline in those first few weeks back. Every day, three times a day, I would have just gotten into my groove editing some on-deadline story, and then I'd have to stop, set up the cursed/blessed Medela Pump in Style, and pray that my milk let down. If it didn't, I'd think of my sweet baby's little face, try to imagine the smell of his baby-shampooed, musky, warm head, feel him snuggled against me, and then . . . finally, there'd be milk. Damn if it wasn't hard, at first, to find my way back into that perfect headline for my story. But the whole process of pumping is a bit like working out: Eventually, your body learns what to do, even adapting to suit your meeting schedule. And your mind adjusts to the pivoting, making you feel like a lactating-deadline-meeting superhero. (What symbol does Boobwoman have on her chest? Boobs, I suppose.)

Unlike so much of the newborn phase, pumping is something you can actually plan for in advance—and that includes asking your workplace to make accommodations for your return, if they're not on the ball already. Studies—lots of them—have shown that several things significantly positively impact the duration of exclusive breastfeeding/pumping for new working moms. These include: lactation rooms, flexible scheduling, supportive bosses, and a sensitive work environment. A supportive spouse or partner back at home helps, too.

The biology of whether pumping works perfectly for your body, your baby, and your job isn't entirely within your control, but you can set yourself up for as much success as possible by getting your baby into the groove of taking a bottle and by having the right gear—and realistic expectations. "Before, I was so judgmental toward moms who didn't breastfeed," says Her Campus cofounder Windsor Hanger Western. "And then I started breastfeeding, and it is *so hard*. Storing up the supply, the pumping, the feeding, the bottle training which somehow feels so mean . . . And it's one hundred percent on you, no matter how supportive your partner is." In my survey, women said that on a scale of 0 to 10, they ranked the pressure they felt to breastfeed at about a 6.6. That pressure—or desire, or whatever you want to call it—doesn't magically dissipate when you go back to work. In my experience, it got stronger. It's pretty easy to slip into an adversarial relationship with your pump before you even put it to use.

There's a whole school of thought out there that the breast pump is evil, that it chains women to their home obligations even while they're at work. "It was not the vacuum that was keeping me and my 21st-century sisters down, but another sucking sound," wrote Hanna Rosin in her 2009 *Atlantic* story "The Case Against Breast-Feeding." Her pump. I understood that perspective just enough to reject it. As much as I hated the planning, the washing, the storing, the schlepping, the all-day-long micromortification, the fact that my husband never even had to think about milk mid-meeting . . . I was grateful to be able to make it work. Grateful to be able to do something for my baby while I was busy at work doing something for the world.

We all have our reasons. My friend Francesca Donner, who works at *The New York Times* and was an editor at *The Wall Street Journal* when her first son, August, was born, pumped largely because Aug was allergic to cow's milk (and therefore the enzymes in most formula). "Was pumping a chain to my motherly duties? Not really," Francesca says. "I won't downplay it: It was undoubt-edly time-consuming. But it was my choice. And in the grand scheme not such a burden. People should do what's right for them. Pump. Don't pump. I was happy with my choice . . . and happier still to be in a place that made it easy for me to pursue my deci-sion." Laura, a top business-school professor and mother of three admits, "Pumping was hard, but it assuaged my guilt over being at the office, and the oxytocin release was so good for de-stressing. I still remember it and wish I had access to that hormone at work now!" Vivian Howard, chef and restaurant owner of Chef & the Farmer in Kinston, North Carolina, doesn't think of herself as very maternal, but says that she was, nevertheless, "hell-bent" on breast-feeding. "It made me feel better about working. And I remember it being something that I leaned on for a long time . . . well, six months," she says, laughing. "With twins that's a long time."

When that sobering *Atlantic* feature damning pumps came out,

I was seven months into pumping and very much in the zone. I was tempted to read the story during a pumping session, but I waited until my commute home. This was the magical solution for me: Three times a day, pumping time was focused, uninterruptable work time—a blessing in disguise, actually, for my job productivity. I'd figured out how to swing that thanks to a few nursing hacks and some decent self-discipline. I was also lucky to have a private office (albeit one without a lock) and understanding, unsqueamish colleagues, and luckier still that my body was up to the task. I made enough milk. If your body doesn't, or if you want to switch right on over to formula, I judge you not.

Here are some very good reasons *not* to pump for a newborn at work:

- You did not give birth to your baby and therefore do not make her milk.
- Breastfeeding just didn't work for you—physically, emotionally, whatever—and you're already formula feeding entirely.
- You hate pumping. Passionately.

In my opinion, those are all valid reasons to skip the whole thing. Here are some other reasons you might *think* you can't pump:

- Your workplace makes privacy impossible.
- Your work schedule is too unpredictable.
- Your boss and colleagues are lame.
- Your baby won't take a bottle.

These concerns are still valid but often surmountable. In my poll, 81 percent of women who tried to pump at work said that it affected their ability to feed their babies breastmilk negatively—41 percent found that they had to supplement with more formula (or switch to it entirely). But, but! The average working-pumping mom still made it to almost eleven months before quitting. That's amazing, given the challenges. There are possible work-arounds to all these issues if you want to try. This chapter is meant to help with that and to cheer you on through the marathon of being a working-pumping mom. And at the end you get something a *lot* more satisfying than a "26.2" sticker for the back of your car: You get to throw your pump the fuck away. (Or, okay, recycle it at medela.com.)

Get your gear

There's this temptation to think of baby gear as a total racket. Do you really need a wipe warmer? Or Pee-pee Teepees? In my experience, no and no. But with the pumping gear, I'm telling you: Get it all. Start with the basics before the baby is born, and then once you've established that pumping works for you, go nuts. Buy a triple set of tubing and flanges (horns) and extra valves (those things get nasty). It seems like a lot of money at the time, but learn from my mistakes: If your tubing cracks in the middle of your workday, you will absolutely spend $50 having a new set rush-messengered to your office from the baby store. Overfull boobs spend money faster than tourists at Duty Free. Here's what you need:

THE PUMP: In a perfect world (dream it with me), your workplace would have one for you: a "hospital-grade" pump (actually several) installed in a mothers' lactation room. Those are the gold standard, says Johns Hopkins Hospital specialty nurse and lactation consultant in pediatrics Julie Murphy, RN, BSN, IBCLC (I'll add WMOF to that list of acronyms, too, because this woman is also a Working Mother of Five—five!). "Personally, I believe that hospital-grade pumps hold up longer and allow many moms to pump in much less time," says Murphy. Hopefully, soon, more employers will invest in mothers in this way. But what if your employer just isn't there yet? You can rent hospital-grade pumps—two popular ones are the Ameda Platinum and the Medela Symphony—by the month (buying one will set you back about $2K). And regular old portable pumps may be fine. I was partial to the Medela Pump in Style (in spite of its name). I've heard from several experts that the Ameda Purely Yours works well, too.

And thanks to President Obama (actually, probably thanks to Michelle) and the Affordable Care Act, pumps are now covered by insurance. "I really encourage moms to take advantage of that benefit," says Amanda Cole, owner and founder of the NYC-based breastfeeding supply mecca Yummy Mummy and yummymummystore.com, which sells pumps but also has more than five hundred rental units currently in circulation nationally. "Most providers will ship those pumps prior to the delivery of the baby, so you might as well get one at the same time that you're getting your crib set up."

Since one pump is covered, I'm just going to be tacky and set money on fire and tell you to get two: one for home and one for work, so you don't have to deal with commuting with one or, God forbid, going back to the office on a Friday night to pick up the one you left there by accident when you euphorically bolted out of work for the weekend. I tried to make do with one pump and then did the math and realized that buying an extra worked out to less than $1 per commute. So worth it. As a moderately paranoid person, I also got an inexpensive hand pump to carry, just in case the motor petered out on me while I was, I don't know, on assignment in a helicopter flying over a glacier or something.

THE ACCESSORIES: Namely, tubing and flanges (the horn-shaped things). With the flanges, I know they look crazy and like torture devices and you don't want to think about it yet, but here's the story: Size is key. Do not be prideful. The "medium"-size flanges fit only a percentage of the population. Everyone I've ever met has needed to size up. You are interested not just in the size of the circular horn part but the diameter of the cylinder that sucks in the nipple; if it's too small, things will really hurt. "Moms change the size of their flanges generally based on three things," says Murphy. "One: What it looks like—it should be wide enough that the nipple never touches the sides of the tunnel. Two: What it feels like—some moms just feel like too much of the breast is being sucked in if it's too big, or that it rubs or pinches if it's too small. And three: How much milk you get. I recently had a mom who looked like she was in the right size but her supply was at a standstill. We sized up and she immediately got more milk."

THE TRANSPORTING STUFF: Get yourself a little cooler bag and icepacks. Most of the pumps come in their own unattractive cases. "I never used that fugly thing," says my friend Ashley, a fashion magazine editor. "With many models, you can detach the pump and carry it in your regular bag." Keep a few milk storage baggies in there too in case you ever run out of room in the bottles that you pump into.

THE "FASHION": Yes, in quotes. Something I didn't think about until my first morning back at work was that I needed clothes that made pumping easy. I had been so worried about what would fit and be stylish that I completely ignored the logistics of the fact that, three times a day, I would be taking it on and off.

Here's what doesn't work:

- dresses with zippers down the back
- beautiful underwire non-nursing bras (they will be yours again, one day . . .)
- silk (because: milk drips)
- anything so clingy that it shows your nursing pads, or gets marked up by deodorant when you pull it off and on
- anything low-cut enough to show the top of your high-cut nursing bra

Here's what does work:

- button-down shirts
- wrap dresses
- any stretchy shirt with a tank top underneath—excellent for covering your belly while pumping

- pretty camisoles with a jacket
- patterns (better for hiding milk leaks)
- nursing shirts—and if they look a little too obviously like nursing shirts (as I was always afraid they did), layer them under a chic little cardigan or blazer.

A quick word about bras: Some women can wear underwire nursing bras. There are plenty out there, and they teased and taunted me. I was one of those lucky people who got mastitis (a horrible feverish breast infection) just from looking at my boobs the wrong way, so I had to go underwire-free the whole time. And I never tried one of those hands-free nursing bras that the flanges of your pump attach to (the picture of the smiling woman on the box terrified me), but many women I interviewed said that that makes me a fool. "It's one of the things that moms at our store say they live and die for," says Cole. "I wrote every single baby gift thank-you note while pumping thanks to that thing."

Do some advance work (in your freezer)

Before I had my firstborn, my mother kindly suggested that I bake a lot of bran muffins and freeze them to eat after the birth when I might need a little help moving things along in the intestinal department. Not a bad idea, particularly if you're like me and think of muffins as essentially a vehicle for chocolate chips. By the time the muffins were all gone, about a month after the birth, the freezer space was suddenly available for something much more precious: milk. I had terrible engorgement issues in the first few weeks, so I had actually already started pumping a bit at a lactation consultant's suggestion. Though some LCs might tell you to wait a bit longer to sort out your body's supply-and-demand equilibrium, Murphy is all for pumping a bottle a day as soon as breastfeeding is "established." What does "established" mean? "That's when the baby's weight gain is appropriate—they're back up to their birth weight—and the mom feels like things are falling into place," she explains. That could be as soon as a week after birth.

I know women who kept one day's worth of milk in the freezer all the time. I've also talked to women who had whole separate freezers (like in the garage!) just for milk. You will, as you become part of the frozen milk club, also hear horror stories of power outages and milk gone bad, and weird enzyme issues that make stored milk taste metallic (that was me), and people who wept as they poured their "liquid gold" down the drain. It happens, so give yourself a break and know that it's a possibility and not actually the End Times, all Shakespearean in its level of tragedy. Formula is a wonderful invention our great-great-grandmothers would have loved.

The amount of milk to save up is entirely up to you. Yummy Mummy's Amanda Cole recommends having, ideally, two days' worth stored before going back to work. "That way, if your caregiver gives 50 percent more than she's supposed to"—an honest mistake if she's getting used to the baby's cues—"you're not in a hole from day one." If you have to travel for work, like the 25 percent of pumping moms I surveyed, you *can* really save up. Eileen Yam, a researcher with an international development NGO/nonprofit in Washington, D.C., had to leave eight-month-old baby Everett at home for eight days to travel to Burma. Transporting milk home was impossible, so she pumped and dumped the whole time. She also had a husband who respected her wishes and used her stored-up stock judiciously. "The milk was important, but having a partner who could deal mattered just as much for my peace of mind," Eileen says.

I found that I always wanted to have about two and a half days' worth of milk in my freezer. In my raised-by-a-Jewish-mother mind, that was the sweet spot of how long I could possibly need to be away from the baby for some unexpected hospitalization. (Any major disease or car crash that required longer than that was clearly a bigger deal than opening a can of formula.) I used good old Ziplocs, Sharpied on the date and ounces, and then froze them flat in half-bottle portions. Once they were frozen solid, I would stand them up, like cards to be flipped through, arranged with the oldest ones at the front.

As with all of this, whatever works for you, do it. But to give you an example, here's how I handled stocking up before going back to work (and Murphy says she did the exact same thing): While home during my last month of leave, I would nurse the baby first thing in the morning and then put him in his bouncy seat to be wildly entertained watching me pump a few additional ounces to store away. (BTW: The milk at the end of a session, the "hindmilk," is richest, so pumping after you've fed the baby lets you know that she's had her fill and that what you're saving is quality stuff.) Before bed, I'd pump another bottle and give it to my husband so he could give the baby a half-conscious late-night dream-feed. That plan did three things: One, it allowed me to stock up the freezer. Two, it got the baby used to the bottle. And three, it helped train my body to overproduce when I went back to work. The pump—as you'll hear approximately ten thousand times—is less efficient than the baby. ("It took me months to figure it out: You just have to pump more than you'd breastfeed," says Monica, mom of twin boys.) Once I was back at work, this plan also helped make that first pumping session of the day my biggest one—reassuring if any of the others got screwed up by a day gone to hell.

At work, find your space

Here's a fun game. You can take almost any old idiom and sub in "full boobs" and have an accurate statement: Hell hath no fury like a woman with full boobs. Full boobs are the mother of invention. Home is where the full boobs are. You get my point: When you have to pump, you have to pump. Here are some places women told me they pumped for work: in the parking lot of a Boston elementary school in the winter, in the backseat of a taxi in the West Bank, in a sweater factory closet in China, backstage at the Emmy Awards, in the Eisenhower Executive Office Building for White House staff, and my favorite: in the sperm collection room of a fertility clinic (that poor woman was doing her residency in endocrinology, and I just hope she had a lot of hand sanitizer and a high tolerance for irony). Almost anything is possible with the right support, says Murphy. "I've helped female construction workers and farmworkers pump on the job," she says proudly of her work in the more rural parts of the community the hospital serves. With chronically sick, hospitalized babies, and parents who can't risk losing their jobs to be with them, Murphy says, "pumping milk is one of the ways these moms can have a part in taking care of their babies. So we figure it out." How's that for inspiring?

I pumped in a boring old office and thanked my lucky stars daily. The door had no lock, but it was frosted glass, so as long as I put a cheerfully life-threatening Post-it note up, it was relatively private. By my second pregnancy, our company had opened a "mothers' room," conveniently located on my own floor of the building, but I still preferred my office, because to me, a pumping space was only a good pumping space if it allowed me to work. (And indeed a 2013 study published by the American College of Nurse-Midwives found that technical support at the office was significantly associated with the duration of exclusive breastfeeding.) Bottom line: I had options, none perfect, but options all the same. I had it pretty good.

Thanks to 2010's Affordable Care Act, things have much improved. Workplaces of a certain size with hourly employees are now required by federal law to provide a space (other than a bathroom) for expressing breastmilk—and if it's not used exclusively for that purpose, "it must be available when needed . . . shielded from view, and free from any intrusion from coworkers and the public."

In many states, the laws are more inclusive of professional, non-hourly workers (those of us who are otherwise exempt from the Fair Labor Standards Act's overtime pay requirements).

Still, in my survey of hundreds of moms, 36 percent of those who pumped at work used a makeshift or not-entirely-private space (think: a supply closet). And 22 percent of those used a bathroom. A bathroom. I find that infuriating. (Murphy does, too, but she also, characteristically, offers helpful advice: "Hang up one of those zippy multipocketed toiletry kits so none of your pumping parts ever has to touch a surface. Then use hand sanitizer and do not touch *anything* else, other than your body or your pump parts, until your bottles of milk are back in your breastmilk tote bag. And then be careful as you clean your supplies *over* the sink, not in the sink. Bring your own dry towel—don't put it down on a surface—and put everything away in a Ziploc bag that you change once a day.") Clearly, women are capable of making do. But they shouldn't have to.

Even when lactation rooms are available, some women feel their employers have simply checked off a box without much regard for how they'll be used. "Until recently, our lactation room was located right in the middle of the trading floor," says Lila, who works in human capital at a big finance firm. "It was basically 250 men, and if I wanted to pump, I would have to walk across the floor with my Medela bag." Margot (not her real name), who worked as a trader herself when her first child was born, says that her firm's lactation room had it all: hospital-grade pumps, lavish decor, even a top-floor view of the Manhattan skyline, but all that didn't do a thing about the culture. "I'm sure the room worked well for the female assistants and the women who worked in HR," says Margot. "But in order to use it, I would have to stand up in the middle of the trading floor and announce where I was going because there was no excuse not to be at your desk. And all of the guys would just cover their eyes and go, 'Uuuuugggghhh.' " Margot tells me this as we sit on a pile of coats and backpacks at our first graders' basketball practice at 3:30 on a Thursday afternoon. She no longer works, and while she's happy with that choice, she recognizes the catch-22 of having jumped off the ladder. "The problem is there's no female leadership. Until more of the bosses are women, there's no incentive to change. No reason for those guys not to react like that."

And these are office scenarios! Places with walls and heat and chairs and running water. Pittsburgh Police Lieutenant Cristyn Zett, whose male colleagues were very supportive—Wall Street tough guys could learn a lot from Pennsylvania cop tough guys—told me about how she had to wrap herself in blankets to pump in her station's unheated locker room. "I'd take off my shirt, my bulletproof vest, my gun belt, and pump in this ice cold room in December," she says. "I laugh about it now, but it wasn't fun then. Our stations are in bad shape."

Turns out, workplace setup is the key to pumping-mom satisfaction and productivity. In my poll I found that, per session, the typical pumping mom spends about twenty minutes on the actual pumping and an additional twelve minutes dealing with the logistics of setup, cleanup, and travel to and from the pumping space. Multiply by three times a day, and a woman typically spends ninety-six minutes of her workday pumping total—but thirty-six minutes of that could be made more efficient if the resources and circumstances were right. Here's the other thing: Those minutes spent pumping can also be spent working: on calls, writing, at a computer. But the logistical minutes? Those are just lost time.

So what's the ideal situation? It looks like this:

- a private office with a lock, or a nearby lactation room with all the conveniences (phone, computer, access to files and server, Wi-Fi) of a private office, and soundproofing (32 percent of women I surveyed said that their pumping was often audible)

- a designated space in a refrigerator that is right there by the pumping area—and not shared with your colleagues' leftover Moo Goo Gai Pan and two-year-old diet salad dressing
- clean space to store multiple sets of pump parts to cut down on the time spent washing and sterilizing three times a day
- water, lots of fresh water (snacks too!)

These are not unreasonable things to ask for, especially if you make the case loud and clear that pumping time can be working time. Nothing moves mountains faster than dollars saved. See Chapter 12 for advice having that conversation if you need it. I have a feeling that bosses who are unfamiliar with pumping—either they've never done it themselves or never had partners go through it—think that it involves some kind of yogic meditation. To be fair, the first few days can require a little inner-peace-finding to get to that first crucial milk letdown. But after that, you can write game-changing code, negotiate a late-night talk show host contract, or practice your first TED Talk—all while milk comes out of your body for twenty minutes. Heck, maybe you can even spend that time building a better breast pump—MIT held a breast-pump hackathon in 2014, and there are several in early development now. (One, Babyation, which uses only small disks on the nipples to allow for fully clothed pumping, far exceeded its $50,000 Kickstarter goal for funds in early 2016, and looks really promising.) But we're not there yet.

So ask for what you need. And if you don't get it, make your own solution—ideally one you can share with other coworkers who may need it one day, too.

I give you the story of Liz's "Narnia."

Liz, a high school English teacher in the suburbs of Philadelphia, had an adorable but stubborn first baby who wouldn't take a bottle. So when Liz's second baby had no such drama, she was thrilled to be able to pump for her at work. However, Liz's school didn't have a lactation room for its staff. "My only option really was a bathroom," she says. "So instead I turned a supply closet at the back of my classroom into the school's de facto pumping station." Yes, even while high schoolers were having class. The space inside the closet was surprisingly homey. Liz filled it with books and lighting and a place to do some grading, and, ever the English teacher, started calling the closet Narnia, like the world beyond the wardrobe door in the C. S. Lewis classic, *The Lion, the Witch, and the Wardrobe*. She put up a sign: NARNIA, DO NOT ENTER.

In the process, she educated a whole bunch of Philly high schoolers. "Early on, an eleventh-grade boy walked in on me, and I screamed, and he immediately closed the door," she recalls. "I don't think he saw anything, but as I sat there and finished pumping I realized anything he's going to think I was doing is so much worse than what I was actually doing. So I found him later and said, 'Just so you know, here's what's up . . .'" After that, Liz made a general announcement to her whole class about "how nursing working mothers feed their kids when their kids aren't there." Instead of giggles, she got respect.

Liz started talking about Narnia outside of the classroom, too, making lighthearted mentions of it in the faculty lounge so other teachers and staff would know that it was available to them. "I felt like I was proving a point," Liz recalls. "The administration talked about finding another room for pumping moms, and I was like, That's wonderful, that's great! And until you do, I want any nursing mom in this building to know that she can use my space." Two years after Liz finished pumping, Narnia remains. Other teachers and the school receptionist have used it, knowing that they could pop into a classroom full of high schoolers who no longer even bat an eyelash. Liz's hope is that she's helping bring up a generation of future bosses who will do everything they can to help new parents. And until then, she says, "this is just the kind of thing women do for each other."

The secrets of (sorta, kinda, good enough) scheduling

Pumping moms that I polled most commonly said that they pumped three times during the workday: once in the morning, once around lunchtime, and again in the late afternoon. That was my own experience as well. We've already talked about the time spent on pumping versus logistics, so instead I'll address the concern so many women say they have about fitting in pumping: You can make the schedule, but *how* do you stick with it? Quick answer: You don't always. You can't. But you learn to read your body well enough to get by.

Technically, federal law mandates adequate break time for pumping to mothers of infants under age one. However, this only applies if you're an hourly worker. (And again, many states and workplaces, thankfully, go way above and beyond the federal requirements for non-hourly workers as well.) In practice, though, here's what "It's time to pump!" looks like:

10:30 a.m.: Meeting with boss is supposed to start. You chug a bottle of water to keep your supply up so you can pump on schedule at 11:00 a.m. Always . . . so . . . thirsty.

10:45 a.m.: Should you pump now? A few minutes early? Because still no meeting. Nah.

10:57 a.m.: Shit. Totally should have pumped.

11:02 a.m.: Oh? A different meeting while you're waiting for that one to start? Sure thing.

11:05 a.m.: Pop-up meeting interrupted by call from sitter who thinks baby has an ear infection. Your boobs ache with the thought of baby in pain. Thank you, breast pads.

11:10 a.m.: New email: Original meeting will begin in ten minutes. Apologies for delay.

11:11 a.m.: Boss's Boss (BB!!) may also join.

11:12 a.m.: P.P.S.: Is anyone allergic? BB's Pugadoodle will attend. Claritin available.

11:20 a.m.: Meeting begins.

12:30 p.m.: Meeting ends. You immediately start pumping, exactly ninety minutes late, and ninety minutes before you're somehow due to pump again. Simultaneously scarf a sandwich.

I am here to tell you: It will be fine. A full 44 percent of women who pumped at work said that they had to miss a session or pump off schedule at least a few times a week. These are the same people who, on average, made it to eleven months before quitting. Do not skip the meeting with the company's CEO or your biggest-ever client. Your body was made to deal with these things. Think of it this way: It's not that different, really, than if you were home and your baby took an extra-long nap.

Go ahead and schedule your pumping sessions into your calendar, and then make your own personal rules for what to do when the day goes to hell. "It's stressful, staying true to that every-three-hours rule," recalls Yummy Mummy's Cole, who often felt like she prioritized a customer's needs over her own while launching her store. "My phone alarm would go off, and I'd be in the middle of helping a new desperate mom buy her pumping supplies, and I'd be needing to get to the back of the store to my own pump at the same time."

The irony of that story doesn't even begin to compare with this one's: Shira, the young rabbi, found herself desperate to pump while officiating at a winter funeral that had gone on far longer than expected, in twenty-degree weather. With nowhere to go and her breasts so full she felt close to vomiting, Shira holed up in a car in the snow, covering the windows with her coat. "My job was to bury someone when they needed to be buried, and that trumped my baby's need for food, but eventually my physical need to relieve the pressure had taken over," she says. "I remember calling my rabbi friend and saying, 'I just pumped in a cemetery.' Now I can laugh, but back then I cried."

Sarah Serafin had to return to her waitressing job almost immediately after the birth of her daughter; her husband had just lost his job. Stopping to pump—in the employee bathroom—could have meant unhappy customers and missed tips, so she was incredibly grateful to the other servers who covered her tables. Still, it wasn't easy. "I would pump just before the dinner rush and right after," she says. "But then a family would come in with a crying baby and all my milk would let down again. I finally started lining my nursing bra with diapers because nursing pads aren't made to do that kind of triage. You figure out ways to make it work."

As a woman with a decent but not prolific milk supply, I found that I could be as much as about an hour and a half late to pump and then delay the next pumping by about thirty minutes and still be fine. What was important to my supply was to not skip a session entirely. If it was absolutely impossible to find three pumping times during the workday, I would add one more on to the end of the day before bedtime. I've heard of moms who would wake themselves up in the night to get an extra bottle pumped—but I am simply not that selfless of a human being. (Another terrifying strategy if you miss a session at work: "I pumped while commuting some days," says business school professor Laura, which, she admits, "was kind of terrible.") As I got more and more comfortable with the whole thing, I learned which meetings I could speed along or duck out of during those last few minutes of chitchat. I also learned to tell the assistants in the office (confidentially) what was up. I wasn't secretive at all, but with lots of outside VIPs coming into our meetings it felt polite to be a bit discreet. Plus, the assistant would often have the most realistic sense of the boss's scheduling.

Murphy suggests being a little stricter, at least at first. What causes your supply to fall off, she explains, is letting your breasts get super full—and then not relieving them. "In general, if you know you're going to be busy, pump ahead of schedule," she says. "You can pump forty-five minutes or an hour after you last pumped. Or if you know that you only have a few minutes, not enough for a full session, pump just enough to get rid of that 'full' feeling and then come back and finish later."

If you're truly in a bind, with no place to pump, or no container in which to store your milk, even a five-minute break to hand express into the sink helps, says pediatrician and lactation consultant Katie Kelter, MD, one of the founders of the New York Milk Bank. A milk-bank advocate would permit you to throw liquid gold down the drain? Maybe just this once, if that's what it takes to get through the day. "Frequent breast stimulation and milk removal is what maintains production," says Dr. Kelter. "So I really recommend learning how to do hand expression for those times when you can't get a full pumping session in. Some women find the technique works even better than pumping—an ER doc I knew from residency never even used a pump twenty years ago. She would just hand express into sterile urine specimen containers." For the best how-tos, look up videos on YouTube from Jane Morton, MD, at Stanford.

Another tip: Become an efficient and quick pumper. "Let's be honest," says Murphy. "The support of your work environment goes up if you can get your pumping done fast." Who knows? Maybe a coworker is frustrated that you've had two babies, and she's still trying to get pregnant. Maybe you have a boss who's way past the baby years and knows she's not going to get the same "breaks" that you do. "The quicker you can get it done, the better for you and your coworkers," she says. So, okay, how? First, snack like a preschooler so your milk supply stays strong. Eat breakfast. Perhaps have a second breakfast. Do not get to 2:00 p.m. without lunch. And Murphy's best tip for speeding things up is a bit counterintuitive: "Take three to four minutes before you start pumping to relax," she says. "Have a piece of fruit and look at some pictures of your baby on your phone. Do a bit of hand massaging of your breasts before pumping to replicate the snuggling a baby would do and to release oxytocin. Then, while you pump, use your hands to massage a bit too so you can feel where the pockets of milk are and release them. Empty breasts make more milk!"

And now, the "what abouts"

WHAT ABOUT TRAVEL?

In a perfect world, every one of those 25 percent of new working moms who has to travel for work would be able to take her baby with her, along with a nanny, and fresh 500-thread-count hotel crib sheets. Or we'd all work for a company like Accenture, IBM, or EY, where they now pay to ship your milk home for you. (Insert sound of angels singing on high.) More realistically, if you have to travel, you'll want to make the trip as short as possible, and you'll need to pump—a lot. Add an extra session or two daily to make up for the fact that (say it with me) the pump isn't as efficient as the baby. If you want to save what you pump, rent a mini-freezer for your hotel room. That's what Windsor Hanger Western, cofounder of Her Campus, did when she traveled just weeks after her daughter was born. "Oh, and I bookmarked the TSA web page on my phone that said that it was okay to fly with milk," she says, "Just in case anyone gave me trouble—I was ready."

Another "What About": What about planes? Especially flights that last more than a couple of hours? "I did it twice," says Yummy Mummy's Cole. "I flew by myself to California when my daughter was two months old and I was terrified that she was never going to take my breast again. But I was committed." One mother, Rebecca, then a French teacher, told me that the flight attendants actually stood guard at the lav door to shoo away people while she pumped. But Cole found it easier to just pump in her seat (call the airline to see if outlets are available in your row). The engine noise mostly hides the sound of the pump. Bring extra batteries just in case and a cover if you like, ask to be seated by the window, and you're all good.

WHAT ABOUT BEING WALKED IN ON?

It happens. Thirty-three percent of women I polled who pumped at work reported having someone bust in on them. As with everything else: Act like what you're doing is perfectly natural (because it is) and everyone else will, too. "That, and master the one-arm-across-the-boobs pump hold, so you can be mostly covered up in an instant," says Ellen, who, as an unshy mom of a special needs baby was my own early pumping-working mentor, years before I had my first son.

I was once walked in on by a delivery service guy who knocked on my door, ignoring my PRIVACY PLEASE sign. I yelled, "Don't come in! Don't come in!" in my most panicked voice, and the poor guy took my muffled shrieks to be a sign of distress. He came in, took in the scene, made a conscious decision to swallow his pride—I think he really didn't know what the pump was—and just asked again if I was okay. He was worried about me! Lesson learned: Don't yell, and make sure your sign is crystal clear. From that point on, mine was DO NOT ENTER! With a smiley face. After our interview for this book, Eileen, in D.C., sent me a photo of her sign: a cartoon picture of a smiling cow with a warning in both English and Spanish. Smart lady.

WHAT ABOUT COORDINATING WITH YOUR CAREGIVER?

You're in the game. You're producing enough milk and making it to meetings. But: What's going on with the baby? How do you make sure that your nanny or daycare is giving her the right amount of milk?

"During the first couple of weeks, ask your caregiver to write down the timing of the bottles and the number of ounces," instructs Cole. She should feed on demand, but if it's 6:00 p.m. and you're seven minutes away from home, most caregivers can hold a baby off—*if* they know that that's what you want. Think about it: If you're the nanny, do you want Mom walking in to a screaming, hungry baby? Nope, not unless she's explicitly told you that it's okay. "Constant communication builds trust and alleviates stress," says Cole. And don't forget to rely on the biggest tool of all to tell you if your baby is being over- or underfed: the scale! Many babies will drink more milk from a bottle than they would from the breast simply because the mechanics are easier. "Keep an eye on his weight and height changes after you go back to work, and ask your pediatrician if you're unsure," says Murphy. "If those numbers are on track, he's getting plenty."

My advice? After those first couple of weeks, chill as much as you can and don't hypermanage the baby's feedings from afar (your baby is not a Nest thermostat!).

WHAT ABOUT WHEN YOU'RE DONE?

Ready to wean? Mazel tov! This is the one thing that pumping makes easier. Simply shave a few minutes off of one of your pumping sessions every day until you feel like you can skip it. Your supply will adjust. I was pumping three times a day, so I dropped the middle session first, then the late afternoon one. The last to go was the always-abundant midmorning session. I was still nursing the baby at home once in the morning and once at night, so I dropped one and then the other the same way until, poof, the milk was gone. I was making things up as I went along, but the lactation consultants I've talked to since said that my ad hoc plan is just what they recommend.

That takes care of the boob part of the equation. What about the baby? With both of my boys I weaned at ten months, so I didn't quite have doctor's permission to switch over to cow's milk yet. So, formula. And you know what? It really wasn't as stinky/messy/gas-provoking/annoying as everyone said it was back when I was struggling to be an exclusive breastfeeder. My second son switched right over to Nestlé Good Start like it was from the tit of the Greek goddess Hera herself. My first son, not so much. So, we gave him mixed bottles: three-quarters milk at first, with one-quarter formula, increasing the proportion of formula every few days until he learned to deal. He remains a picky eater to this day, God love him. Pass the organic macaroni and cheese.

CHAPTER EIGHT

❧

The easiest way to win at reentry

Manage Up, Manage Down, Manage Sideways

In college, I lived in a disgusting but extremely happy little row house on South Forty-Second Street in West Philadelphia with six other girls and an uncountable number of significant others. There were the actual boyfriends and girlfriends, the one-night stands, and then what we dubbed "the Nebs." Short for the Nebulous People. Those were the in-betweeners who spent the night but weren't quite committing yet and kept us all wondering about their intentions over the next morning's toast with Nutella.

As the term caught on at 326 South Forty-Second, "neb" quickly moved beyond the realm of romance. Our checking accounts were neb, especially at the end of the month; PMS-ing (which we all did simultaneously, catastrophically) was neb. The red tape one roommate had to cut through to be able to accomplish a double major in engineering and fine arts—two departments that may not even have known each other existed—was neb. "Neb" was shorthand for anything hard to read, hard to get through, and generally pretty annoying.

You might have a sense of where I'm going with this.

Years later, as we roommates one by one started having our

babies and returning to our jobs—as an editor, a small-business owner, a visiting-care nurse, an investment banker—we found the first three months back at work . . . you guessed it . . . totally neb.

And the nebbest part of the whole adjustment for lots of women? Coworkers. They'll rip your heart out in one giant guessing game.

First, your peers. Are they genuinely relieved to have you back? Or did they resent taking on some of your work and/or make a play for your job (or your fancy stand-up desk) in your absence?

Then your boss. Is she doing cartwheels because she missed you so much and you're back-back-back in business? Or did she perhaps realize that she could conceivably get by without you (and your salary)? Cha-ching. Pass the P&L.

And the support staff . . . How do they really feel when you now race out the door at 5:25 p.m.? Are you showing them a future to aspire toward, or to fear? And what's with the fact that you never wear compliment-able shoes anymore (and can they even respect a woman who now changes into commuting shoes)? I kid. But only kinda.

Well, take a deep breath, because I know the temptation is there to say, "Screw you all, I have a job to do and some breast-milk to pump, and I don't really care what you think of me, and I'm going home to my real life at the end of the day." Rumor has it when you hit age thirty (or forty) or simply have read enough Nora Ephron, you're supposed to move into some blissful life state where you stop caring about what other people think. If you've gotten there already, cheers, but sorry, for this brief reentry period at work, you really do need to notice what other people think of you.

"Impossible," you're protesting. "I'm supposed to do my job and take care of a tiny human, and not completely ignore my marriage, *and* I have to care just what the heck the boss's assistant thinks of my shoes?" Okay, no, you absolutely get a pass on the shoes, unless you work at a fashion magazine like I did. But you do need to acknowledge that the way people see you at work changes the minute you walk back in that door after maternity leave. It's stupid and it shouldn't. But it's reality and it does. And you need to manage that, thoughtfully, from the top of the staff on down.

Done right (that is, with self-assurance *and* self-awareness), managing up, down, and sideways also offers you an opportunity to change your workplace culture for the better. You aren't just trying to keep your head above water as you tread in the swimming pool; you're redefining its surface with every ripple. And you should. It's our generational duty.

As I write this, the vast majority of women in their early baby years are either Gen Xers (born between 1965 and 1984) or Millennials (born between 1981 and 1997)—and yes, there's some overlap there called Generation Y, but it's basically ignorable. You know which side of the early Reagan years you fall on.

Pretty soon, thanks to biology, most of the new working mothers in America will be distinctly Millennial, and my hope is that the public disdain for that term will do a complete 180. Millennials have a "deserver" mentality? They lack respect for hierarchy and like to "disrupt"? Well, clutch my pearls, what if that leads to some actual social progress?

"When you talk about culture, I think Millennials have the potential to change everything," says Lindsey Pollak, a Millennial workplace expert who consults with the insurance company The Hartford. "They are the largest generation in the workforce, and everything is up for grabs, including the way we think of integrating parental leave into our careers. They're changing benefits that employers offer. They're changing *parenthood*." By 2025, Pollak predicts, Millennials will be 75 percent of the workplace. "And it's urgent for companies to realize that they want work/life balance." Pollak is being polite, but what she's saying is that corporate America will have a talent rebellion on its hands if it doesn't stop shaking its head and tsk-tsking.

So, permission granted to relate to your boss, colleagues, and underlings differently than you did before you had that baby. Yes, they see you differently now, but here's how to use that to your advantage and shift the earth (or the Flor brand carpet tiles, as it were) under your feet.

Let's start at the top: Manage up

A couple of surprising things emerged when I asked the women I surveyed about their bosses. (1) I was expecting complaints, but most women said their bosses acted pretty nicely—the vast majority asked about their baby and how they were doing; 70 percent of my survey takers even recalled their supervisor giving them a baby gift. So that's good (the most challenging thank-you note, though, right?). But then here's the other revelation: (2) Almost half of new moms, 45 percent, said that they found their boss harder to please than their newborn baby. It was trickier for them to satisfy a grown, competent adult they knew well than it was to soothe a perpetually hungry infant with an underdeveloped digestive system, who is constantly chilly because he loses heat through his massive head that he can't yet hold up by himself. Hum. Interesting.

So, here's what I deduced: We have a problem with bosses, but *the problem with bosses is not bad bosses.* Not usually, anyway.

The problem is circumstantial. And that's great news. Because while you can't change someone's personality, you can change your circumstances. Your relationship and your work are different now that you're a parent. Managing up requires thinking clearly about how your work/life circumstances affect your boss and dealing with that in a way that's advantageous to both of you.

Meet Jennifer Dorian, the boss you want: "Here's my opinion on the fourth and fifth months of your baby's life," says the General Manager of Turner Classic Movies and mother of two school-aged girls, in Atlanta. "You have to give yourself a break on every level. If you can show up at work in clean clothes and be alert and awake and can contribute, that's good enough for me as an employer. I'm just glad you're back and you're contributing. We missed you; we need you desperately back. But I don't expect you to schmooze or take on new leadership or growth-and-development assignments for those first three months back. I just need you to cover your part of the factory."

Possibly your superiors are all this outstandingly empathetic and reasonable. With hard work and endurance, hopefully you will be this kind of leader yourself one day, if you aren't already.

Seventy-one percent of the women I surveyed said that their boss, like Jennifer, had children, too. And every single person I interviewed who cited a specifically encouraging boss noted that that boss was a parent. It's a bit like going to a female gynecologist, I suppose: You're comforted just knowing that she's felt the same pain. Truly, bosses who have children anticipate needs you couldn't even predict for yourself. "I have several pregnant employees right now," says Alice Shillingsburg, mother of three, who is the director of an intervention program for kids with autism in the South. "I realize that they're a little bit uncomfortable all the time, because I've been there. I know that they need to leave meetings to go to the bathroom, often. I really try to pay attention to their needs." Once they're back from leave, Alice specifically asks her employees to come to her if they have any issues with scheduling pumping. "I'm happy to move a meeting by fifteen minutes, because I find it just as important as you do," she says. "But I never would have done that before I had my own kids—it just wouldn't have occurred to me."

If your boss is anything like Jennifer or Alice, be grateful for your supervisor's empathy and thoughtfulness, tell him or her so, and promise to pay it forward. **That's the first step of managing up as a new parent: appreciating how good you've got it.**

Next point: Women told me that even bosses without children were pretty darn supportive, and here's where things get interesting: When I cross tabulated some answers to try to figure out what impact a boss's parenthood would have on their employees' happiness, I came up with—notably—*not much*. There was only a tiny correlation between how often women had to miss pumping sessions and whether or not their boss had kids (those with kid-less bosses had 5 percent higher rates of getting off schedule). Similarly, there was virtually *no* correlation between how much the women stressed out about getting to work on time and whether or not their bosses were parents. I asked women about how critical their bosses were, expecting a big chasm of percentage points between those with kids and those without. Not at all. Women whose bosses didn't have kids were only 10 percent more likely to describe them as "harder to please than a newborn."

Huh. Perhaps there really isn't much of a bias that childless bosses have against parents as employees. In reality, maybe it works the other way around: It's the employees who make false assumptions about their childless bosses. This is an important thing to understand if you're trying to manage up well.

Back to the gynecologist analogy for a minute. It's only partially true. Years ago, when my husband was in medical school trying to decide which specialty to pursue, he thought briefly about becoming an ob-gyn. It's one of the few truly happy fields of medicine, bringing life into the world, he explained to his slightly dubious fiancée (me), and it's complicated and fascinating to be treating two lives simultaneously. "But as a man, how could you ever know what it feels like to get a Pap smear?" I asked him. "Or how much pain someone could tolerate during birth?" On the contrary, he explained. Because he's a man, *because* he'd never go through it himself, he'd err on the side of more sympathy, not less. Similarly, nonparents are not worse bosses of new parents, regardless of what you may have expected. **And there we have the second step of managing up as a new parent: Be aware of your own biases against your boss, so you stop feeling so victimized.**

(Big parenthetical aside: "Difficult" bosses, as described by the women I interviewed, were rare, but they came in all shapes and sizes: Sure, there were big, old, white dudes who'd seemingly never faced any kind of discrimination—one mom told me about how one such buffoon referred to the pumping room as "the Dairy," as in, "go ahead and start the meeting without Amanda. She's in the Dairy." But there were also other youngish C-level moms who were tougher and less flexible than anyone. It doesn't take a residency in psychiatry [the specialty my husband eventually decided on] to realize that these women may have taken some of their own frustrations and regrets out on other newbie moms. This kind of assholic behavior may look like sexism or age discrimination, but those are really just the ugly costumes it's dressed up in. Unclothed, it's just a bad personality. You and your kid have nothing to do with it.)

Third step of managing up: Recognize and deal with generational differences. Millennials have the potential to change everything, as The Hartford's Pollak noted above, but in the process, they also have the potential to scare or annoy the crap out of their bosses. Let's manage that! When Pollak goes into companies to do Q&A sessions about Millennials, she says she gets a lot of questions from senior managers about what that younger generation wants. "They often think of Millennials as kids, but I explain that Millennials are *parents* now, and business leaders themselves, and they're going to want these kinds of benefits," says Pollak. That's eye-opening. It's easier for a Baby Boomer (those born in the years 1946 to 1964) or a Gen Xer to understand a request for work/life balance when there's a baby involved. (Have you ever had that problem when you walk into your parents' house and immediately feel like a preteen again? It's a little bit like that, and I promise you, having a baby helps tremendously. As soon as they become grandparents, your parents treat you more like an adult . . . probably because you act more like one, too.)

But intra-office peace between the generations is a work in progress:

- 70 percent of Gen Xers feel that too much attention is given to Millennials, and 55 percent of Gen Xers consequently feel that they are being ignored in the workplace.

- 86 percent of Gen Xers think that "the entitlement generation" is an apt nickname for Millennials.
- 74 percent of Boomers and Gen Xers believe that Millennials do not accept feedback well.

Do not be depressed if you're a Millennial or a young Gen Xer; this is useful information, as each of the three upsetting stats above inspires a clear antidote:

- When you ask for something that requires personal attention, don't make your case only about your particular needs. Address the greater good for company efficiency and culture. (Asking for flextime to care for your baby is no different than another, older employee asking for flextime to care for a spouse or an elderly parent.)
- When you ask for something—an accommodation for your new work/life balance, different duties, different compensation—do not come across as entitled. Be polite and do your research. Yes, of course you deserve to be treated fairly—that's the whole point of this book. I believe you actually are entitled to a work situation that lets you have a life. But before initiating a conversation with your boss, put in the time and do your research to make your case.
- And lastly, accept feedback well. Sorry if this sounds didactic, but as a chronic interrupter, this is what I remind myself: Listen. Don't interrupt. Don't act defensive. And do ask your superiors for advice. It's flattering and usually pretty useful.

You can make small culture corrections with your boss that go a long way. Many Boomers simply aren't aware that they project an old-school bias. At a minimum, it's your duty not to perpetuate sexism, and if possible, you might even be able to squelch it. Corey McAveeney, a culture analytics expert at the consultancy Culture Amp, has learned that some companies that have a hard time with inclusion find that it stems from things as basic as the language managers use. "One woman told me about how the guys in a friend's workplace all praised one another with sports metaphors," says McAveeney. "But maybe Susan in Marketing doesn't want to be a 'baller.'" Talking the problem through made it clear that the senior men didn't have ill intentions (they weren't the bully bosses I described a few pages back). "They were like, Oh, we just thought everyone would want to have that status," McAveeney recalls. "So many industries have been male dominated for so long, but the gradual shift in our economy as more women are the primary earners and have higher degrees gives us an opportunity to course correct. We just have to be willing to say something."

We also have to be willing to show real support for managers who get it right, especially in industries that are mid-evolution right now. Anna (I've changed her name), a nurse, has two superiors: One is old-school in his (lack of) regard for gender equality and vocabulary and the like; the other is forward-minded and feminist, and encourages a professionalization of what was once a blue-collar field. You can guess which one Anna praises to her colleagues and the staff beneath her.

Fourth step: Recognize the pressures of bosshood. Yes, their paychecks are bigger, but with those dollars comes a boatload of responsibility. Understanding that stress helps as you navigate your new relationship. Because, like it or not, you add to your boss's stress at this moment. It's okay. She's paid to deal; it's the natural order of things. But compassion is helpful in both directions.

"I've got forty-something lives at work counting on me to make decisions for their job happiness and satisfaction," says Alice, the autism program director, whom I talked to a couple of weeks after she came back to work following the birth of her third child. She offers her employees as much flexibility as possible but can't always be as generous with herself. "It's tricky. I *have* to be at the 8:00 a.m. directors' meeting. It's not an option for me not to be there," she says.

Alice is one of those bosses who shares openly about her own kids. But it's not hard to see how the pressure could make other leaders uncomfortable baring that side of themselves. Of the women I surveyed whose bosses had children, 19 percent say those superiors rarely or never talked about them, and 26 percent didn't acknowledge their kids' existence with photos or artwork at the office. As an executive editor, I marched back into work after my second son, hauling my breast pump and a stack of six framed photos of my kids. It was important to me to "have" them there, and I liked that their little faces reminded every deskside visitor that I had a life beyond the office. But not everyone feels that way. If you don't see your boss's kids on her desk, it doesn't mean she doesn't love their sweet dimples or the time-traveling underwater rocket ship drawing they made her this morning. More likely, she's under the kind of pressure that requires compartmentalization—or that her own boss doesn't approve.

You're going to do better than that when it's your turn to lead. But it helps for now to understand.

And step five: Now you're ready to reset your boundaries. My dad recently told me a story from his childhood that I'd never heard before. He was twelve years old. It was 1962, and John Glenn had just orbited the Earth three times, magnificently, historically. Schoolchildren all over the United States stopped their lessons as their teachers clicked on the radio to listen, live, to Glenn's reentry into the atmosphere, back down to Earth. "It was supposed to take two minutes of silence, maybe three," my dad recalled. The nuns at his parochial dayschool in Cincinnati exchanged meaningful looks, no doubt, as the seconds and then the minutes ticked on, and the commentators talked of a possible heat shield malfunction, awkwardly filling the airwaves. "Then it was silent," my dad said, his green eyes wide, looking a bit, I imagine, like the boy he was back then. "Just silent. For four minutes and then five, and six." And finally, in Dad's recollection, at minute seven, Glenn's voice slices the silence, crackling, "Boy, that was a real fireball!" and cheers erupted all over the country. Little kids jumped out of their desks, pumped with the thrill of victory; teachers dabbed their eyes discreetly, overcome with relief.

Glenn went dark.

With all due respect to that heroic man and his patriotic mission, you're going to, too.

For a minimum of a couple of hours, every workday, hopefully more, you will be unreachable. And your boss is going to be okay with it.

You've probably heard countless female executives, in beautiful jackets with no spit-up on them, say things like, "You can have it all, just not all at once." I actually *do* think you can have it all going on in your life at the same time, to a degree: the baby, the marriage, the big job, the friends, even the community contributions and the phone calls with your mother. But good God, woman, you can't actually do all those things in the same minute, or even in the same hour. So, like it or not, you have to reset some boundaries with your boss: Now that you're a parent, are you going to be on email over the weekends? How often? Are you going to work on vacation? (You are going to take vacation, right?) And, most significantly, are you going to have any periods during the day (probably in the evening) when you pull a John Glenn and simply go dark? Bath/feeding/bedtime, I'm looking at you.

Simone (not her real name), who works in private equity, says that prior to having her first baby, and even to an extent before having her second, she was online always, available always. That's what her team was used to, and when she came back to work after her second child, she realized she was going to need to announce a change, starting at the top. "I'm still the person who is on my BlackBerry the minute I wake up, at six in the morning," she says. "I just hate to disappoint people. But a few weeks ago, I literally said to my boss, 'From seven to nine at night, I am offline.'"

The temptation is to be sneaky and avoid the conversation. You deserve this time to devote to things other than your job, and you'll BRB on email as soon as it's over, right? Well . . .

Choose instead to be a grown-up about it, like Simone, and be transparent with your boss. All any supervisor ever wants to know is that you have a plan that allows you to get your work done well. Now it's your job to sell him or her on the specifics.

Over in Chapter 12, experienced negotiators will give you the exact words and strategies to use for all kinds of circumstances, but right now, it's important to think big picture about your approach.

Pollak's suggestions for acing this moment are textbook managing up: "You always want to know your manager's style," she says. "Does that person respond well to statistics? To an emotional request? To your showing your loyalty to the company? Think about what that person values in his or her own career and in his or her employees, and let that knowledge be helpful." I'd recommend a big combo platter of all of the above. Go in with your research done (remember, your boss probably has a boss too and might need to manage up to *that* person): What precedent has been set by other employees either at your firm, or elsewhere in your industry? What actual written policies already exist? And how will you manage to get your work done and be available to the rest of the team if you're out of pocket for this time? Make a plan.

"I wrote everything out, down to what I hoped my pumping schedule would be," says Sarah, the curriculum manager at the huge museum. "And the two bosses above me didn't question me at all. I think that's because I established myself early on as being on top of things. There was no question that I wanted to make sure that motherhood and work worked for them and for me."

Next, speak from the heart about how much you value your position and the work you do. Remind your boss—who might actually be worried that you'll just up and quit—that you see yourself staying and continuing to grow and learn and contribute.

And finally, says Pollak, remember the bigger picture. No matter how much your boss does (or doesn't) like you personally, you are one piece of a larger machine. "Think about what is best for the company," Pollak advises. "What is best for the long-term success of the organization and ask yourself: How will my personal situation fit into the larger picture?"

Again, I'm breezing through this to make the general point about how managing up—getting what you want by thinking of your boss's needs—can make all the difference. But Chapter 12 is your playbook for conversations about flextime, compensation changes, a shift of duties, and more.

You've got the big idea. A handful of lesser-known, but key, things to keep in mind:

It's your job to propose the plan. Just like in your pre-kid life, if you're bringing your boss a problem, you should also bring a solution, possibly *solutions,* plural. Let's say, like Simone, you want to be completely John Glenn–dark from seven to nine in the evening. That's reasonable. So, what if there's an emergency? What if—I'll use an example from my magazine job—a story is due on press but a factual error emerges, and someone has to decide if it's worth thousands of dollars to (literally!) stop the presses; if they can't reach you, the error prints. (Ah, print journalism, so modern.) Easy. Solution number one is that you designate someone who's qualified as your proxy when you're unreachable. Solution two: You give a couple of key people your home phone number. Not your cell—you're not looking at that puppy for two hours, remember?—but your home phone, which will only ring from work in a true emergency.

This plan is for now, not forever. A quick warning not to act like this "accommodation" is the biggest and ballsiest thing you're ever going to ask for. Maybe, eventually, you'll want some additional dark time (a vacation that's completely off limits, say). Or you'll want to drop your three-year-old off at preschool in the morning and arrive at work a half hour later. Your needs and wants will change as your baby does. And approaching your current proposal as a trial, just for now, gives you an opportunity to renegotiate later down the road, and lets your boss exhale a little deeper, too.

Remember: Your boss's daily rhythms are different from yours. As a former boss, I winced when Jennifer, the cable TV exec, told me that the leaders who "break my heart for working parents" are the ones who view 5:00 p.m. to 8:00 p.m. as a crucial part of their own workday. "It's not that they're against the idea of flexibility," she explained. "It's that they are stuck in meetings all day long." That chunk of time at the end of their day becomes their catch-up time, and often their face time with their employees. "It makes me so angry when I see that," says Jennifer. "I have known a lot of people who—not my own bosses, thank God—expect you to be available to them because that is when they're doing their work and that's when they need you."

I certainly didn't require my staff to stick around waiting for an in-person meeting with me. But I did do that last sprint at the end of my workday, bombarding countless people by email with their next to-dos. Even if I didn't expect those things to be done that evening—the next day would have been fine—my staffers may have felt pressured to deliver right then and there. So, what do you do if you have a chronic evening-orders-giving boss? "Try to get them to see it through your eyes," says Jennifer. "If they're not parents themselves, they may just be clueless about those magical evening hours at home." Barring that, suggest a standing daily or weekly meeting during the day, and at night make yourself available on a limited basis. Jennifer's counsel for a truly challenging case: "I would say, Hey, boss, I want you to know that two nights a week, I can stay late and be there for you, and the other nights of the week, I can be reachable but will be writing you back around 9:00 p.m."

Finally, sixth step: Don't shy away from autonomy now. Along with motherhood comes a wonderful status shift: You are now seen as someone capable of great, great things (like producing and keeping alive a human baby child). Consciously or not, your boss knows that the thing you just did at home for the past several weeks or months was hard. Ergo, you are skilled. Run with that!

In my experience, there's a little window of opportunity when you first come back when the leadership is waiting to see what your first move will be. Will you jump right back into the old rhythms and hierarchy? Or will you wither a bit with uncertainty and look for more guidance than you did previously? Or: Will you become ever so slightly less patient with "the way things are done" and take more initiative and ownership than you did before? Go for option C.

If "more initiative and ownership" sounds daunting, think of it this way: It's more efficient. It will also make you happier. A study out of the Wake Forest School of Medicine looked at what job factors give people a better work/life facilitation, and autonomy was right up there. Another, similar study out of Germany took a broader look at what motivates women in transitional moments in their careers, specifically when they come back from maternity leave. It showed similar results, with a twist: Women who were motivated by goals—the ones who wanted to achieve measurable success at work (i.e., *you!*)—soared when given autonomy, with higher rates of work adjustment and learning.

What's all that mean? Having more agency at work gives you a feeling of more control over your entire life. And bosses are pretty psyched about it, too.

Now for your peers
(we'll call this managing sideways)

A long, long time ago, in the early 1980s, in a world that was very different from ours now (and also kind of not), *The American Journal of Psychiatry* published an account of a group of psychiatry residents gone completely haywire over issues surrounding working parenthood. It's well known now that almost half of medical school graduates are women, but back in the dark days of the early eighties, it was somewhat carousel tipping that women had begun flocking to the specialty of psychiatry. And over at the Payne Whitney Clinic at New York Hospital-Cornell Medical Center, one of the most prestigious training programs in the country, all hell had broken loose because of that simple biological fact.

Of the twelve second-year residents, six were women, and three of those six had become pregnant around the same time. All was congratulatory and quiet when the first pregnancy was announced. The mother-to-be worked out a plan with her supervisor: She'd take one month of maternity leave (three weeks of which would come from her vacation time), and once back, she would make up the overnight call shifts she'd missed while away. Only in reality—surprise, medical professionals!—once back, she didn't feel physically or emotionally capable of leaving her month-old baby for twenty-four-hour overnight shifts. Her colleagues, realizing that their other two pregnant associates might feel the same way when their babies arrived as well, freaked out. And the administration responded to the crisis the very same way my mother handled me and my little brother when we fought over a toy: They told them to work it out among themselves.

Ha. Right.

In a move that foreshadowed several reality survival TV shows of the early twenty-first century, the men formed an alliance and held a secret all-male meeting. The remaining two pregnant women, the men decided, would make up the overnight call that the first pregnant woman refused to do. Yep, the super-pregnant residents would take on extra shifts. Word of the plan leaked, the women flipped out, and it was, the *Journal* reported, "a battle between the sexes that reflected issues long ignored or suppressed." Being psychiatrists, the twelve residents worked it all out in— what else?—a group therapy session. There were "feelings of rage, envy, and competition"; the men believed that the women were favored generally, not just in this moment (and likely, the women *were* very talented, standouts in a male-dominated field). "The men saw themselves as the drones of the program," the article's author, Elizabeth Auchincloss, MD, wrote, "doing all the work while the women enjoyed the fruits of motherhood and professional success." One man worried that his own wife would have to take time off from her job to care for their child while he covered the pregnant woman's shift (see? this dilemma had all kinds of sides to it). *Eventually,* they all came to an agreement and split up the call shifts fairly.

So, what's this story from thirty-plus years ago doing in this book? It's here to show you that while circumstances have changed, the emotions colleagues experience when one of their own goes on leave haven't, at least not entirely. I called the paper's author, Dr. Auchincloss, who, back in 1982, was the chief resident of the group. These days, she's Vice Chairman of Education and also—full disclosure—a senior colleague of my husband's. "I have noticed a huge change since back then," Dr. Auchincloss says. "I'd like to think that's because, as an administrator, I like to run a family-friendly program."

Dr. A. notes that a residency class from a handful of years ago had more pregnancies than any had had before. This time around, the administration handled the reallocation of the extra shifts swiftly and authoritatively, and the residents used the experience as fodder for a skit in their annual holiday show. "If I recall, it was about the guys getting pregnant; it was very funny. But it was good-natured," she says. A big change. Still, she wonders now, as we're talking, about the happiness of the nonparents in the class: "It was such a very strong parent group, and the people who were not in it must have felt like outsiders," she muses.

The feelings of the haves and the have–nots may never go away, says Dr. A., putting on her psychotherapist's hat. "There are conflicts between parents and nonparents forever. As natural groups, they probably do have prejudices against each other," she says.

Notice which natural groups occur among your peers in your workplace. Some possibilities:

The parents versus the nonparents.
The new parents versus the seasoned ones.
Men versus women.

"Lately, people say to me that the biggest pushback they get is from other childless women who feel kind of upset I guess that their lives are taking a different turn," says Dr. A. That they don't have the partner and the child. I heard that, too, in many interviews. Female colleagues were often the hardest on other female colleagues.

These kinds of divisions are clearest to see among your peer group at work because everything else is fairly even. You're at the same level, and likely paid similarly, too.

If you understand the allegiances and assumptions that each of these groups has about the other, you'll help yourself tremendously. In my survey, 30 percent of mothers admitted that before having children of their own, they resented other colleagues who were working parents. "Absolutely the biggest change I experienced at work after having my daughter was how much more empathetic I am now to people whose kids are sick and have to leave the office," says Katie Fiamingo, a senior brand manager in charge of innovation at Nestlé Purina PetCare in Saint Louis. "Before, I distinctly remember having thoughts of, Oh, geez, again? Can't she get a sitter or have her husband be home?" Remember how you once felt and manage to that. Katie is now hyperconscious of not dumping work on her colleagues when her own child is sick.

TWO STRATEGIES THAT HELP WITH RESENTFUL COLLEAGUES

1) **PRACTICE GIVE AND TAKE.** It's a lot easier to ask a favor of someone (and believe me, you will be asking) when they know you'll cover for them, too. Or, better, that you already *have* covered for them.

I've mentioned my former work wife, Wendy, back in Chapter 2, bless her wonderfulness. Wendy and I played a constant game of hacky-sack, keeping the beanbag in the air. We made a pact, very simply, to be honest with each other. We covered each other's vacations, never scheduling them at the same time and always with the agreement that we would handle whatever crises arose but also call if there was something that the vacationer would have a faster or easier answer to. Same for babysitter emergencies and school appointments. We took turns playing good cop and bad cop—both with the junior staffers, and with our boss. Sometimes our boss would tell one of us something but forget to tell the other. Wendy and I had a solution: We compared notes almost every time one of us had a one-on-one with her. It was a relationship years in the making, but it worked. So: Get a work wife. Woo her with flowers on her desk, or cocktails after work, or Marvin Gaye playlists, or whatever it takes. Listen and be interested in her life outside the office. You'll make your own little couple bubble of trust.

But what if you don't have a good candidate? What if the dating pool of work wives at your office is small or lousy? Or if it feels too late? Just adopt some of the same practices with . . . lots of people. "It's what I tell my own daughters," says Dr. Auchincloss. "Get a lot of credibility in the bank with people you can trust. You're going to need help. Then you have to help people back. Make sure you're not the needy person all the time. Be the helpful person too so when you need help you can get it."

2) DON'T ACT ALL MOM-PERIOR. You know what I'm talking about. Look, between you and me, we both think you're doing the most important work in the world by raising that baby. Your mother can join our little triangle of agreement on that, too. But outside of her and me, zippity lippity, as my boys say.

Every single one of your childless peers has something in his or her personal life that she values as much as you do your baby. "I've heard a lot of griping about workloads, and those who do have children and those who don't," says Corey McAveeney, the workplace culture expert at Culture Amp. "But we all have family members, many of us have aging parents, we all have friends and try to have lives outside of work." She teaches start-ups who seek her advice that it's important for everybody to have the same benefits. "If someone has to leave early to go to the doctor, or take their child to the doctor, or their parent to the doctor [*and yes, I'll add pet to the vet, too*], it's all the same." Corey's preaching to management, but we all need to listen. "Our economy will only improve when everyone can contribute and feel supported and be able to be as productive as possible. Inclusion is the theme right now." Amen!

YOUR ULTIMATE MANAGING SIDEWAYS TOOL: TRANSPARENCY. It's the twenty-first century's hottest, sexiest, and most overused HR buzzword, yes, but let's not hold that against the *concept* of transparency, which is a good one: Be honest, be yourself, don't try to hide your intentions. If there's one thing no new working mother has the brain space for, it's long, knotty strings of lies and half-truths and who's-aware-of-whats about the new circumstances you've managed to negotiate with your supervisor. All of that is way too complicated, and you're already dealing with something complicated enough: your colleagues' jealousy. I heard it again and again:

- "I haven't been asked to be secretive, exactly, but my new four-day week is a touchy subject when it comes up."
- "It always caught me off guard in 360 reviews that the hardest relationship you have is actually with your peers. I think it's because our peers are jealous when we have new flexibility."
- "My colleague who was pregnant before I was kept strolling in at 10:00 and leaving at 4:30. Maybe she was working through lunch? I don't know, but I was definitely resentful."

Ultimately, it doesn't even really matter what the "groups" are at your workplace and who's on which side of the "versus." Jealousy is the underlying drumbeat of all resentment. Your job is to act like you're doing nothing wrong (because you aren't).

Where things really get complicated—insert the panic-inducing cymbals into that drumbeat—is when you've been given special dispensation because you're actually more valuable and more talented than your peers. Quit blushing. It's nothing to be embarrassed about. My hope is that this book will be for everyone, but realistically, if you're reading it, it's in part because you really care about your work. You're a planner, and you're conscientious, and that probably makes you pretty damn good at your job.

So here's the dilemma: How do you keep things from being weird (or, shall I say, neb) with your colleagues?

Be ruthlessly, almost cluelessly (but actually stealthily) transparent. Here's how:

BE POLITICALLY TRANSPARENT. "When people ask about your new hours or whatever, tell them exactly how you got them," advises Jennifer, the cable TV dream boss in Atlanta. If they express jealousy, you can convey the idea that, hey, they're free to ask for that kind of thing, too. Karen, the marketer in Connecticut, says her boss was actually nice enough to make that suggestion to her himself. "He said, Look, you don't even need to engage people in conversation about it; send them to me," she recalls.

BE EMOTIONALLY TRANSPARENT about the challenges of new parenthood. It cuts right through the smugness when your colleague realizes you're doing the same job she is on only half the sleep. "If your workplace gives you that cultural permission to vent once in a while, it helps," says McAveeney. "It gives employees something to laugh about together." And if you're laughing together, you're on the same team. Never mind that the other members of the team got margaritas and a full eight hours last night. (See? Who's jealous now?)

This emotional transparency is especially helpful if you are in the tight spot of being told to keep your accommodation a complete secret from your peers—something that often happens when the higher-ups are worried about setting a precedent they can't afford on a larger scale. Remember: You may not be able to openly advertise your new hours; but no one's stopping you from talking about your feelings, your love of your baby, or the push-pull of a very full life.

BE VISIBLY TRANSPARENT. Whaaa? My mother would say that's an oxymoron as bad as "jumbo shrimp." But really, make sure you're visible. Don't sneak around. Other people need to know when you're available and just what exactly it is that you're doing all day. Sarah, at the museum, says she learned the importance of this kind of transparency by watching a former colleague get it wrong. The colleague's challenging pregnancy had necessitated some work accommodations, but she hadn't made it clear to Sarah and other colleagues what her arrangement was. "I felt so in the dark all the time," Sarah recalls. "She'd email me requests at 7:00 a.m. but then never be available after 4:00 p.m. but also never just said, 'Hey, these are my new hours.'" So when it was Sarah's turn, she communicated these kinds of logistical things explicitly. She understands the desire for privacy that many women feel but says, "I think the more secretive you are, the more people are going to call into question your motives and wonder what you're really doing."

And finally, the fun part: managing down

There's only one thing that wakes me up faster than a screaming baby: a text from our nanny saying she's sick and can't come in. I bolt upright: 6:05 a.m. I text our backup babysitter who's a bartender-slash-actress, praying she doesn't have an audition. Delivered. But no "Read." She's probably still asleep from last night's last call. Anxiously, I scroll through the day ahead in my mind, thinking of all the Meetings I Cannot Miss and all the Patients My Husband Cannot Ignore and watch the clock click toward 7:00 a.m., when I know my office's backup daycare center (such an amazing benefit) will start accepting calls from panicked parents like me. I pray there's a spot for a four-month-old baby in the infant room and a three-year-old in the preschool area.

"This is Joe at Bright Horizons. How can I help with your childcare needs?" Joe. Wonderful wacky Joe. Please please please let there be room today. And there is.

Forty-five minutes later, we're on the subway, baby Teddy in the Ergobaby carrier and Will holding my hand. I adjust the heavy diaper bag, the breast pump, and my work tote, exhausted with only fourteen hours, five meetings, and twenty pages of copy to go 'til bedtime. At work, I fall into the elevator buttons, automatically pressing sixteen for *Glamour*'s floor instead of three for the daycare. Fine, I'll throw all these bags in my office and then take the boys back down.

Not so fast. When you work in an office that's 85 percent female, the grand (de)tour avec new bébé and a precocious, bespectacled toddler is significant. "Oh my God! So cute! When did Will get glasses?" "He's the kid from Jerry Maguire. No joke, like that actual kid." "Hey, LSB, here's the copy I owed you—just in time for the production meeting. Oh, hiring the interns young, I see." "So your babies are going to be downstairs in daycare? Won't you be thinking about them *all day*?"

Finally, we wend our way out of the crowd and hit the art department on our way to the elevator. My favorite trio of brilliant-childless-people-younger-than-me is standing at the lightbox in the middle, looking at images for a birth control story, when they stop my little menagerie of walking birth control.

> WANYI: "People: I'm claiming this one. This Brody is mine. Danielle, you can have Teddy. But Harry Potter here is all mine."
> DANIELLE: "It's a deal, girl. Hi, little baby future husband."
> BRENDEN: "Hi, baby. Oh shit! I mean shoot. I made the baby cry. All I did was look at him!"
> DANIELLE: "You always make the babies cry."
> BRENDEN: "Sigh. That's because they see the evil underneath the handsome. Babies are smart like that."

It was all fun, all cute, ten seemingly wasted minutes that brightened my whole challenging day. And yet: not wasted at all. Four years later, as I write this, neither Wanyi, nor Danielle, nor Brenden has children yet. But I've had conversations with all three of them, real talks, about career and parenthood. They've asked, because I put it all out there on days like the one above. "One of the most fulfilling parts of staying in the workforce is being able to pass on what you've learned to other moms," Facebook leader Liisa Hunter told me in our interview. "For me that even includes the ways in which I was very naive with my first pregnancy and baby." Me, too.

There's a saying Ben taught me when he was in medical school, learning basic doctorly things like how to do sutures: See one, do one, teach one.

Managing down, as a new parent, covers both the "do one" and the "teach one" parts that benefit those who are in the "see one" stage. In my opinion, we're obligated to show junior colleagues what so-called balance looks like, sick nannies and all. We're also obligated, as managers, to be thoughtful and attentive and not so distracted by life outside of the office that we look like a walking disaster. It's called role-*model*ing, and you really do want to be on model behavior around your subordinates, no matter how tempting it is to let your guard down completely. All of those coos and remarks above from the *Glamour* girls (and guy)? I'm telling you, ten minutes, tops. But it was important to me that everyone see me as Mom and then as Boss, on time to our next meeting, minutes later.

The number one workplace issue that Millennial women say they want to tackle as leaders one day is work/life balance. Your biggest duty right now—the way you can help them the most—is to succeed in your job. You don't have to blow it out of the water and get promoted tomorrow, but if your junior colleagues see that you're managing *up* well and that you're managing *sideways* well, you're already role-modeling for them.

The rest of managing *down* comes down to strategic transparency (that word again!) and sensitivity. As an homage to the wonderful, spirited *Glamour* office, I'll do it up as a list of dos and don'ts.

DO BE OPEN ABOUT THE PHYSICAL REALITIES OF WORKING MOTHERHOOD. You're pumping? Fine. Say you're pumping. Better yet, say you're pumping and working (because you are working while you pump, right? See Chapter 7 immediately if not!). But don't pussy-

foot around the biology of being away from your newborn by saying something like, "Oh, I just need privacy for a few minutes."
Most people will be astute enough to figure out what's what, and
all you've taught them is that pumping breastmilk is something to
be embarrassed about. It's not!

Christie's, the auction house where Lydia Fenet works as an
SVP, has a gorgeous lactation room, but she preferred to pump in
her office so she could keep working. She says: "I remember saying
to my team—they were all women—from day one, 'Guys, here's
the deal. I'm already going to be leaving earlier and getting in
later given the fact that I have to nurse. So you can either lose me
for another hour and a half a day as I go up to the pumping room
three times, or you can realize that we're all women here, and at
some point in your life if you do want children and you continue
to work, this is the reality of it. I'm pumping in my office.'"

More than that, Lydia actually pumped *in front of* her staff, in
meetings and on conference calls. This is highly optional extra-
credit territory and obviously would not fly in 95 percent of workplaces. But Lydia knew it could work in hers. "I told them, 'This
is going to be the most horrible five minutes of your life when you
have to see this for the first time, then I swear to God after that
you probably won't notice.'" And they didn't. At least she says they
didn't.

Now, I'm not particularly modest myself. I had my breasts out
nursing all over New York City, and I still couldn't have done
what Lydia did. But the woman deserves some ink in this book
for that kind of next-level frankness. And now anyone else in her
workplace has an open invitation to use her office, too, for pumping post–maternity leave, or for putting their feet up on the couch
when they're tired or pregnant. "It's just a nice feeling to know that
when you're going through it, there are people above you who are
really okay with it all," Lydia says.

I attended a small roundtable with Chelsea Clinton at Clinton
campaign headquarters the day that Hillary clinched the Dem-
ocratic nomination. Chelsea was less than two weeks away from

the birth of her second child, and while we spent the majority of the hour talking about poverty, family leave, childcare, and other family-related issues important to her mom's campaign, Chelsea wrapped up the talk with this: "Admittedly, I'm running to the bathroom. I don't think the biology of being pregnant is something we should be weirded out by." This is a woman who is very, *very* careful with her words. And she went there.

Simply talking about the physical challenges goes a long way. As a three-time mom, Alice, the autism program director, likes to help pregnant employees anticipate the uncomfortable-to-talk-about stuff: "Usually when someone tells me that they're pregnant, I say I know there's a bunch of things that you probably haven't thought of yet that will come up once you're back. Please feel free to ask me about them." Some take her up on it, some don't, but they all seem to appreciate the invitation. "I want to help other women not create their own obstacles. I open the door for them to think, 'Okay, she thinks this is legitimate; I don't have to feel weird about it,'" Alice says.

Helping other women not feel weird about natural stuff: That's a do!

DON'T SHY AWAY FROM MONEY CONVERSATIONS. As a new parent, you know your value more than ever. You're needed—really needed, too needed!—at work and at home. Encourage those who work for you to see their value, too, and to have long-term perspective about their earning power. Right now, your paycheck is paying for more needs and fewer wants than it used to. And while it might not be advisable to tell your salary to people who work for you, you can certainly share with them valuable information about what it costs to be a parent.

"I oversee a lot of Millennials, and I think, frankly, they value their free time more than anyone," says Lydia. "So many have said to me, 'Oh, I don't need a pay raise, just give me more vacation days.'" No, no, no, says Lydia, who instructs them *never* to say don't pay me for my work. "Don't even get me started! I'm like you have got to get paid for your work, that is rule number one as a woman." And every little raise will help with future working-parent success.

DO TAKE YOUR EMPLOYEES' OUTSIDE-OF-WORK LIVES SERIOUSLY. Halloween. I can't even tell you how many mothers I interviewed brought up the importance of being able to leave the office early on Halloween, and how much that says about workplace culture. Well, I have to be honest, before I had kids I routinely worked late on Halloween covering for the moms, and I tried to understand. But Halloween? Really? This wasn't a sick child, or an accident on the playground. Then, eventually, one October 31, I dressed my four-month-old baby up as a lobster and only then did I get it.

As a manager, try to give everyone underneath you the benefit of the doubt on some Halloween-like "important" life thing that seems perhaps only borderline important to you. Everyone's got one. A volunteer shift at four o'clock every other Thursday. A cat with IBS and lots of vet visits (shout-out to my little sister). "It's not just parents. Everyone wants flexibility," says Millennial expert Pollak. "Everyone wants to bring their whole selves to work." And that means wildly different things to different people.

"Just because it's not children doesn't mean it's not important," says Alice, who had an employee recently who was training for a marathon. "She had to train for several hour stretches at a time, so she and I talked about one or two days a week leaving a little bit early so she wouldn't have to run by herself in the dark. To me that's a work/life balance thing."

DON'T ASSUME THEY'RE MOTIVATED BY THE SAME THINGS YOU ARE NOW. Coming back to work, here are the top three things that motivated me: The free coffee in the office kitchen, the flexibility to get my work done and go home on time, and my husband's unwavering belief in my ability to supposedly do it all. On the other hand, my assistant at that time—while likely also motivated by the free coffee—was driven by things like overtime pay and a plum assignment to interview a TV star, even if that celebrity was only available at 8 a.m. on a Saturday.

This bit of advice from Jennifer, the cable TV exec, was eye-opening to me: "Be aware. Be attuned to what the needs are of your staff. Because they're likely different than yours," she says. So don't get tunnel vision. "People reporting to you might care more about visibility, or advancement, or recognition. Different people get turned on by different things." Manage to their motivators and recognize their successes, however they define them.

DON'T PULL MOM RANK ON OTHER PARENTS. You may have people working under you who are parents. You're senior to them, so your time at work might, technically, be more valuable to the company. But their job at home as a parent is exactly as high ranking as yours is to you. We are all C-level at home. Manage accordingly and give your employees the same flexibility of schedule and respect for their conscientiousness that you'd hope for from your boss. "Becoming a stepmother made me look at so many more aspects of my job through the lens of a parent," says Jesse Lutz, a freelance producer in L.A. "Now, when I delegate I think, maybe Ginger should be assigned task A, on the early shift, so she can be freed up to do school pick-up." And Jesse has rethought the quality and mission of the work she's got her team doing as well. "When I think about what we are creating, and buying, and supporting as a business, I think: Is this good not just for the child I'm helping to raise, but for children everywhere? Is this content helpful and inspiring to other mothers and fathers out there trying to do their best, too?"

DO RESIST THE URGE TO HYPERMANAGE (YOU'RE A MOM BUT NOT *THEIR* MOM). Remember the studies about embracing autonomy several pages back? Give some to these guys, too. It's not cheating to manage your team members with a little less scrutiny than you used to. It can be truly beneficial for you (frees you up to see the bigger picture) and for them (lets them own their successes). Micromanaging is almost a reflex given how much you have rolling around in your brain right now to keep track of. But don't. Just don't. And see what happens.

"Before I left on maternity leave I needed everyone to be here exactly on time every single day and I was so impressed by face time," says Lydia. Not anymore. Lydia knew that *she* wasn't getting any less work done with her own new, looser schedule, and she was happier, too, so she offered her staff that same flexibility. She crossed her fingers and watched it work. "I said to them, 'Look, you are fully formed individuals. You're in your late twenties and I am not your mom. I am someone else's mom, not yours. My job is to make sure that you are learning and growing.'" And they have. Her team works hard and happily and smart. And when they're on deadline, they crank it.

Ultimately, Lydia realizes, she's grooming the next generation of leaders, and their successes are hers, too. "As a boss, as a woman, as a mom, I want to show them that it is possible to have a life."

CHAPTER NINE

❊

That whole 50/50 partnership thing

(Aka: The Chapter That Keeps You Married)

The baby is the easy part of having a baby," my friend Janie (not her real name) told me over lunchtime ramen one day when I managed to sneak her away from work. It was too humid out for spicy food, but then again, maybe it was the conversation that was making me sweat. "What's been rough is my marriage," Janie continued, as I nodded, thankful to have my noodles to slurp. "He helps out, and I'm so appreciative of that, but there is only so much trying to explain that 'this is truly harder on me than it is on you' that I can do before I start sounding like an ungrateful dickhead."

Not a dickhead. Fifty-fifty. In theory, that's what you want, right? A marriage of two people who, likely, are both working, and both raising the baby, and both keeping your home from looking like an episode of *Hoarders*. In my experience—and in Janie's—it takes a while to get there after having your first kid, and the return to work provides a perfect storm of challenges.

Probably you've been home on leave while your partner has returned to work much sooner; away all day, he may be unaware of the minutiae of baby care that you've just begun to master.

Now it's your turn to head back to the office, where you may feel shockingly out of your element for the first time since your intern days.

Then throw in the physical stuff: If you're nursing, your body is the one making the food, around the clock—and yes, most babies of mothers I polled were still waking up in the night, until about seven months old on average. Pumping at work brings its own pressures—again, handled by default, by you, lucky mom.

And money. Going back to work reminds you of why you work in the first place—because they pay you—and new parents start to worry about finances at this point, too. The first few weeks of your baby's life were all about survival mode, and in truth, she didn't need much—diapers, maybe some formula, swaddle blankets if you didn't swipe enough of them from the maternity ward. But a few months in, the larger financial commitment crystallizes. You start crunching the numbers on daycare versus nanny versus having one parent stay home. (Pop quiz: Add eighteen years of your current salary, adjusted for raises and cost of living increases and 401(k) contributions—don't forget the compound interest. Now subtract eighteen years of childcare costs, also adjusted for inflation. Then factor in your potential earnings during the college years if you stay at work all the way through, versus quitting temporarily for five years of baby time . . . or maybe ten years if you have three children. This is a math problem with seemingly infinite answers.)

It all adds up to Superstorm Sophie la girafe (named for the $25 teething toy) of relationships. In my survey, 71 percent of partnered respondents said that they fought more with their partners in their first three months back at work than they had before. But there's hope, and good news: 60 percent of partnered respondents also said that this time period brought them closer as a couple, even if they fought more along the way.

Really? A huge number of women were saying that, after going back to work, they fought more with their partners than ever but *also* became closer than ever. I wondered: What did the happily married subgroup do right? And what did the unhappy—even divorced—minority do wrong, if anything? Some of the "brought us closer" variables were predictable. Date night helps, of course, but you didn't need this book to tell you that. There are several other more subtle factors that cropped up, and you'll find them in the advice throughout this chapter. But the bottom line, which I heard again and again as I talked to women who'd made it through the storm, is this: You have to prioritize each other. Not the baby, not your job. Each other.

HAHAHAHAHAHAHA.

I know, I know. Go ahead, laugh some more.

HAHAHAHAHAHAHAHAHAHAHAHAHAAHAHAHAHA-HAHA all the way across this damn page and back.

But really, I mean it. Just maybe not in the ways you're imagining. This chapter is not about clearing your calendar for a weekly night of gazing across a candlelit table at each other. (There will be time for that . . . eventually.) It's about giving each other the benefit of the doubt in the smaller moments, about getting past resentment, about realizing that your individual career and parenting goals have to matter to each other for you to succeed as a family.

A big, huge, superstitious knock-on-wood caveat here: In my career in women's magazines, I edited hundreds of relationship advice articles and watched, wincing, as many of the self-dubbed "relationship experts" we interviewed would end up . . . consciously uncoupled. I'm no expert. My relationship isn't everyone's definition of perfect. (In fact, I'm already dreading the fallout when my husband reads this chapter.) Still, I'll throw a little salt over my shoulder and wish for the best and share what I've learned to be true about those first few months of parenting/working/living together.

But let's pause a sec for this important message . . .

It wakes you up in the night. It ruins a lovely dinner out. Often, it is shitty.

Nope, not The Baby. The Resentment.

Women mentioned it to me again and again: "If I'm honest, I resent him." "I'm not usually such a resentful person." "I just find myself constantly keeping score and resenting the unfairness." In almost every interview, coupled women brought up their feelings of resentment. It seems to be the one emotion that poisons everything else. I remember some mom of a classmate of mine back in high school sent in chocolate chip cookies once. But instead of the sugar, she'd accidentally used salt. The cookies were inedible. None of the butter or chocolate, or even the love baked in were palatable because the salt had poisoned everything. It's the same way with resentment. If you feel it and don't deal with it—especially with the compounding pressure of going back to work—it overpowers every bite of what should/could be your sweet time together as a new family.

Resentment is almost inevitable, because in the beginning of parenthood there are simply more things it's easier for the mom to do for the baby (i.e., lactate), and also because *dads just aren't willing to help with the rest.* Psych. Not. That last part's a deep-seated cultural lie, and it's just not true. Or it doesn't have to be. Let me explain.

I did an additional second survey, this one smaller, of one-hundred-plus dads/partners, and asked them a bunch of questions about *their* experience of your Fifth Trimester. (Sneaky, I know, but illuminating.) The results showed that 39 percent of them didn't maximize the time offered by their employers because it didn't feel tenable—at work, or at home. The majority of dads/partners, 61 percent, actually wish they had taken more leave. Sadly, the most enlightened husbands tend to feel this frustration most acutely, says Josh Levs, author of *All In: How Our Work-First Culture Fails Dads, Families, and Businesses—And How We Can Fix*

It Together. "It's really tough for guys even before the baby is born," says Levs, who famously sued his former employer, CNN, for discrimination against birth dads. "Because even though we recognize that we're going to need to make some changes, we have a whole lot of structures that don't want to work with us. There's a problem with our core culture. It's backward not to recognize that the dad's life is about to revolutionize as well." So please do your part to fight that cultural assumption in your own little family. You'll help yourself, your partner, and society at large—yes, really, just by letting him (or asking him to) change some diapers.

The reality is, man-ineptitude blaming gets women only so far. More often, it's our own discomfort with letting other people pitch in that screws us in the end. If you don't want to feel like the only adult in your home going through this challenging transition, don't be! *Let* your partner share in the agony and the ecstasy and the to-dos—at the very least because if he does, you will get more sleep. And right now, sleep is the most enjoyable thing of all. And it makes everything else the next day—including work— more enjoyable, too.

As my husband would certainly tell you, I actually have no right to preach on this soapbox. I am a walking master class of resentment. I count things. I keep score. I simmer and remember and require actual apologies (not just "I'm sorry that you feel that way!") when I think I've been wronged. But I'm getting better, and I wish I could go back and have a stern talking-to with my new-working-mom self. I turned a big corner on resentment when (a) I had the above epiphany about how letting him do stuff gets me more sleep, and (b) I had two glasses of wine one night and admitted to myself that I was deriving some secret sense of satisfaction from resenting how much harder life was for me than it was for my husband. Pathetic, right? Apparently pretty common, though. "When you're frustrated, it kind of feels like scratching a mosquito bite; there's something sort of indulgent about just being mad or disappointed in someone," says psychotherapist Sarah Best. "It's easier in the moment to just complain, 'You don't help,' rather than actually communicating and saying, 'I find it frustrating when you . . .'" And then fill in the blank. I realized I was using resentment as a crutch, rolling my eyes, rather than dealing with the problem. And let me tell you, it got a lot less satisfying. Fast.

So, skip all the drama and learn from my mistakes. Some of the advice in this chapter will sync up with your particular love and work equation; some of it won't. But either way, I hope you take away a few strategies to make things feel more fair, more balanced, and far less resentful.

When in doubt, think, "save a bottle for dad"

This one comes straight from my mom, "Doctor" Grandma Susan, and the takeaway is crucial even if the specifics don't apply to your own circumstances. She made sure with all four of us Smith kids (three breastfed, one adopted and thus formula-fed) that our dad gave us at least one bottle a day from the very beginning. As I tend to do when my mom makes suggestions, I ignored her at first and then eventually adapted her idea to suit my own terms: To avoid so-called nipple confusion, I waited until the two-week growth spurt had come and gone (it was real and it was ravenous). By then I had enough extra milk to pump a bit and saved up one bottle's worth a day for my husband to feed the baby. Because I am not so entirely stubborn as to ignore my mother's good advice completely (try as I might), I made that saved-up pumped milk the baby's 11 p.m. "dream-feed" bottle. That meant so many wonderful things:

1) Ben got to hold and soothe our baby and then get him ready to go back to sleep. It was no football toss in Central Park, but that's about as good as father/son bonding gets at that age.
2) Ben also then got to put Will down in his crib for the big "This is bedtime now, son" sleep each night. That made

Will maybe ever so slightly less dependent on mommy cuddles to drift off. I was adamant that my kids not have to nurse to go to sleep. Snuggling my baby into dream-land sounded like heaven actually—that sweet little pop as you pry them off of your nipple, the dribble of milk unswallowed—but it wouldn't have left me functional for work in the morning.

3) Speaking of: I got sleep. Like actual 9:30 p.m. to 1:30 a.m. sleep even in the very earliest days. Four hours counts! And four hours really counts when you're back at work.

4) I hesitate to say that this fourth thing was the most impor-tant wonderful thing, because it's just not in my nature to rank *anything* above sleep, but: It was really good in the long run for me to let go of this one little duty. That bot-tle was only one of seven daily feedings Will was getting when I returned to work, but it felt huge. Ben was able to do this small heroic thing for me. And I was grateful.

Maybe you're bottle feeding already. Maybe your husband is already wearing one of those cool/crazy milk tube things taped to his waxed-for-this-purpose chest. Maybe this isn't your family's perfect option for letting your partner help out in a significant way. But do *choose another significant way then,* please. When there are onesies to be folded, or puked-on crib sheets to be changed, or a puked-on baby to be bathed, or an ugly shower gift to be returned, or a painful ear that needs checking at the pediatrician (and you both have client meetings), think to yourself: "Save him a bottle" and let your partner (*ask* your partner to) do it. The momentary discomfort of asking for help is well worth it for the monumental relationship shift.

Also: Single moms, I salute you for the millionth time at this moment.

Also, also: My friend Allison, the travel partnerships exec, says that I must warn you that whatever duty you do hand off to your partner should be one you're prepared to lose entirely. Jon, her husband, did bath time from the first evening they brought their twin sons home from the NICU. To this day, at age three, they insist on Daddy Bath. Mommy Bath—whenever it has to happen—is a drama and a struggle. And it's wet and a mess. "It makes me sad, honestly, that they don't want me doing it," says Allison. "But I have seen too many wives complain that their husbands do nothing. I didn't want us to be like that." The trade-off is worth it.

Trust him with this baby
(easier said than done, but here's how)

One of the other wonderful benefits of the "save him a bottle" strategy is that it forces you to actually trust your partner, particularly if you're meant to be sleeping and unconscious while he's caring for the baby. I remember the very first evening Ben and I tried the hand off; I showed him how to warm up the bottle and then dawdled around, spending more time brushing my teeth and washing my face than I had in weeks. Finally, I laid my head down on the pillow and . . . just couldn't sleep. Couldn't close my eyes. Was just so scared something would go wrong. And you know what? Something did. I crept back out to the living room to take a peek, and horror of postpartum-craziness horrors, my husband was mouth-open asleep on the couch, while baby Will lay awake on the floor, on his little play mat, staring at a jingling jangling monkey rattle. I was livid. Maybe you're livid on my behalf right now. (Thank you.) But I have to tell you: I was wrong to freak out. Yes, Ben had dozed off while on duty. But Will was nowhere near mobile yet or even able to roll over. This we knew. And Ben had put him in a safe place. Playing happily, in a clean diaper, ready to cry and wake Ben up when he got hungry. Will was fine. And after a calmer discussion the next day, so was I. ("You know, at the hospital, I take care of sixty-four patients overnight," Ben pointed out. "And they're all very sick.") Ben's internal rules of baby care were different than mine, but I had to trust that he loved our son enough to keep him safe. The next evening, I sucked it up and forced myself to sleep.

"A lot of our issues with trust have to do with guilt," says Carolyn Pirak, LCSW, and founding director of the Bringing Baby Home Program at The Gottman Institute, which studies marriage and relationship longevity. The guiltier you feel about not taking care of the baby yourself (in my case, choosing sleep over a feeding), the more you undersell your partner's ability to do the task that you're bowing out of. You think you're the only one who can do it well. And then you treat him accordingly. "The first step for a lot of couples is to help them recognize that they are equal in their parenting," says Pirak. "And that is a really deep-seated thing."

So let's look at that sense of equality. In my survey, I asked new mothers when they fell in love with their new babies; 47 percent said it happened for them at minute one, right after birth. Furthermore, 51 percent said that their partners fell in love with the baby at that very first moment as well. Which means: As mothers we think that our partners love the baby even sooner than we do. That's really sweet. (For the record, the dads/partners I surveyed recalled their own feelings coming on even more swiftly: 62 percent say they were in love from that first instant.)

But things change a bit when you ask new moms about *caring* for the newborn. Of the women I polled, 65 percent reported that they felt confident taking care of the baby by the seven-week mark. When I asked mothers about when their partners became confident caring for the baby, 49 percent said it took the dads at *least* seven weeks. Stay with me here, because it's worth it: In my poll of dads and partners, only 24 percent of those fathers said it took them that long, seven weeks or more, to get confident. Possibly, our definitions of "confident" are different?

Now, here's what's hard to figure out: Do these dads actually take longer to get confident caring for their children? Or do we just think that they aren't confident until later? Or—my guess, based on dozens of interviews with new working moms—do we *assume* they aren't capable and thus prevent them from getting the practice they need to appear confident in their baby skills from the beginning?

This is very bad. Women of the world, we can't ask our partners to meet us 50/50 if we don't let them participate and learn.

In my experience, going back to work does sort of force your hand one way or the other. You either let go a bit and just trust him, or you change your work structure entirely. I had an internal rule that I set for myself that I would always, without question, be at every pediatrician appointment personally. That was all well and good until baby Will needed to go twice in one week when I was just back at work. Work fail. So I asked Ben to leave work and go. He was still in his residency and still working those frequent overnight shifts, some consecutively for a week at a time. So he was honestly happy to have the time with our baby during daylight hours. And it's something I've trusted him to take turns doing with me ever since. On the flip side, Alaina, a financial news writer in Doylestown, Pennsylvania, found her hand forced in the other direction. Alaina went back to work after having her twins and then very quickly decided to quit her full-time job, in part because of what she calls the "post-maternity-leave hangover" she experienced at home: "When you go back to work and you've already set up those patterns at home during your leave of who does what . . . you definitely end up with the most work." Alaina is happy with her decision to work part-time freelance from home but only regrets that she reached it at a moment of stress.

Here's my two-part advice for you if trust doesn't come easily and you're looking down the barrel of going back to work:

1) **Learn some small bit of baby care together** so you can appreciate being a newbie right alongside your partner. It's helpful for you to see him master something in person— and for him to see you flounder a bit as a nonexpert. Plus, doing new things together is highly bonding, research has shown. Years later, Ben and I still laugh when we think about the crazy lady who came to our apartment for a

baby CPR class. (She took one look at my necklace—
big, chunky, white beads I'd worn to work that day—and
asked if we both knew exactly how many beads were on it
just in case it ever broke and one went missing . . . down
the throat of our child. Alarmist much?) Don't take for
granted the opportunity you have to be in the same place
at the same time, learning together.

2) **Give your partner the trust you would have if you
didn't have the *luxury* of doubting him,** the trust you
would in an emergency. Because work—at first—feels like
a mini-emergency, but lots and lots of women out there
deal with real ones. When I talked to women who *had*
to trust their partners to take over, they had one thing
in common: Not one of them said that their husbands
screwed up.

Simone, who works in private equity in New York, found out
only days after having her second child that her mother was diagnosed with stage-four ovarian cancer. Caring for her mother and
saying goodbye consumed Simone's maternity leave. Heartbroken
to leave her newborn at home, she was nevertheless resolute about
what needed to happen. "I focused all of my energy on my mom,"
Simone recalls. "I would take the train out to her four days a week,
pumping under my coat. I was gone 7:00 a.m. until 9:00 p.m., and
my husband dealt with the kids entirely. There was no choice." She
trusted him completely with the baby and their older daughter. "I
know you can't write this book and say 'get a new husband,'" she
told me when recalling how incredibly capable her husband was
during that time. "But he was so good, so good with the baby, as a
dad, and even making sure we still had Friday nights out the two
of us. I couldn't have gotten through it without him."

Like Simone, Ellen, a blogger and editor, didn't have a minute
to waste doubting her husband's abilities. When her first child,
Max, was just born, he had a stroke and doctors realized he'd sus-
tained brain damage. Ellen's and Dave's expectations of their child

and of each other changed almost immediately. "I'm usually the practical one in our relationship. But after Max was born, I was a grieving wreck while Dave was pretty stoic," Ellen recalls, thinking back on how Dave would step in and take over the baby care when she lost it. "Once, as I sat in our bed crying and holding Max, I blurted, 'This is my worst nightmare.' Dave said, 'Honey, look at him, he's beautiful. He's not a nightmare.'" Ellen now runs an incredible, award-winning blog for special-needs parents called Love That Max. "My community has shown me that special needs moms have a tendency to be ubermoms. But don't be the martyr," she advises. "Share your work and your worries." Allow your partner the privilege and burden of being helpful.

These stories aren't meant to make the run-of-the-mill challenges of working motherhood seem trivial. They're not! But remind yourself in those moments of doubt just exactly why you chose this partner in the first place—and how very much you can depend on him when emergencies happen. And then give him that trust in the everyday, now.

Then, *really* clearly ask him for the help and support you need

Lexi Petronis, a content producer in Albuquerque, New Mexico, went through more than I can even imagine with her first baby, Rowan. Ro was a surprise, from the moment she appeared as a faint pink line on just-engaged Lexi's peed-on stick, to the early June morning when the surgeon lifted her out of her mom's belly five weeks early—amazingly, on the one-year anniversary of Lexi's mother's death. It had been a year of remarkable life upheaval and change, and now Lexi, who'd never even had the chance to wrap things up at work, was driving to the hospital every two hours through the night to nurse her preemie in the NICU. Her husband, Dave, an orchestra conductor, made every 2:00 a.m. trip with her. She loved that she didn't even have to ask—he just came.

But once Ro was home, tiny and beautiful, things started to feel less balanced. Lexi essentially didn't take a maternity leave. She went into the office almost immediately and brought a lot of work home, editing in every little crevice of day that she wasn't nursing. "I remember very explicitly I would need to proofread at night," she recalls. "And I'd have Rowan on her Boppy pillow, in my lap at the computer. And I'd still be working when she woke up at 2:00 a.m. to nurse." Dave, who was rehearsing big concertos until ten o'clock every night, helped by bringing home dinner when he could, but it wasn't enough. Lexi was fried, resentful, and frustrated. "When he was around he was emotionally supportive, but often I was like, 'You're gone . . . all we do is tag team, and I'm the one who's buying diapers, and working all the time, and up all night, and we're living in my house that I bought, and I need you to step up . . .'" She needed to say it all, and he needed to hear it, but "step up" wasn't clear enough.

That long list of Lexi's isn't just some imagined feeling of being overwhelmed. When I interviewed Bringing Baby Home's Pirak, she mentioned a study that the institute's founder, John Gottman, had done about the relationship tasks that come up after a baby is born. "There were approximately three hundred additional tasks *per day*," says Pirak. "If you were at work and your boss came in and said, Hey, we just acquired a new company, and you're going to have three hundred additional tasks per day, the first thing that you would do is say, 'I need help—and a raise!'"

Things finally improved when Lexi got specific and pulled out a pencil: "I actually sat down with Dave and made a diagram of everything and everybody that I 'report' to in my life. Like, here are all of the things I do in a day and here are all of the people— the baby, my boss, my dad—who need me. I was a little box in the middle." And that made the difference. Now when she asks him to take on a specific task or to handle childcare in between work commitments, he understands her needs—and his value.

Maybe, like Lexi, you need your partner to have a broad-sweeping understanding of the stress you're under. Maybe you just need him to do something specific like put gas in your car on Sundays. Either way, the same takeaway applies. Know what you want, and ask him for it; don't expect him to read your mind. (As one veteran mother of three told me: "Don't assume he knows anything. When you talk about relationships, assumption is the mother of all fuck-ups.")

Because, take it from me, and the one-hundred-plus men I surveyed: They want to help—but they're not sure how you most need them. The majority of dads/partners felt that you needed them primarily for emotional (versus logistical) support. Ask yourself this: If you allowed him to be more helpful with the logistics, wouldn't that help your emotional well-being, too? "Outside of breastfeeding, your husband can do literally everything," says Josh Levs. "And the overwhelming majority of guys want to—so keep in mind that he's struggling with this sense of equality as well." So share your emotional struggles—*and* the tasks that would help you both feel better. Here's a crowd-sourced suggestion: The dads/partners reported stepping up particularly with non–baby tasks: 62 percent report taking primary responsibility for the housework during your Fifth Trimester, and 69 percent say they handled dinner duty most nights.

"I always encourage a frustrated mom to tune into what *kind* of support she wants from her partner and to communicate it really clearly," says Sarah Best. "Because 'I need you to help more' is definitely a heartfelt plea, but it's not particularly instructive. For one mom, it might be, 'I need you to unload the dishwasher so I can get a little more sleep.' For another, it might be, 'I need you to sit and listen to me vent when I get home from work about what a terrible mom I feel like because I'm not with my baby during the day . . . and then I need you to tell me that I'm crazy to feel like a bad mom and I'm great.'" I love the scene that comedian Jill Kargman wrote for herself in the first season of her Bravo show *Odd Mom Out*. Jill's character (also, suspiciously, named Jill) is picking a fight with her husband late one night, and finally he just asks: "What do you *want* from me?" Jill's response: "I just wish that every once in a while people annoyed you as much as they annoyed me!" I think Sarah Best would approve!

Learn how never to fight over household crap again

Okay, now that you've decided to trust him and to let him help, here's how to make the division of labor fair: Do what you're good at and let him do what he's good at.

(We'll pause for a moment here while you have the thought that you're good at two million things and he is good at only one: remembering to buy AA batteries. You had the thought. It was mean. And untrue. Now we'll move on.)

I challenge you to find one single couple in all of America who takes turns making their bed. He does M/W/F, she does T/Th, and on weekends they sleep in and then each grab one side of the scrumptiously fluffy white duvet and make the bed together. If that couple exists, I haven't met them. Why? Because there is definitely one person in each marriage who is better at making beds, who cares more about hospital corners and making sure the decorative shams are used as decorative shams and not as sleeping pillows with your face on them. (Ahem.) But if he makes the bed and you redo it, you'll get annoyed and righteous, and he'll get his feelings hurt and wonder why he even bothered. Sound familiar?

Same goes with your new working parental life. There will be new things in your routine (buying diapers, washing the car-seat cover, paying the nanny) that need someone in charge of them. Here's an easy rule of thumb: Whoever is better at something (or enjoys it more, or does it well enough) should do the task. If that leaves you with a wildly unbalanced list, start changing your definition of "well enough." No one ever died from un-ironed pillow shams.

"My husband works in finance so he does our budget, and—his mother trained him well—he's now the laundry guy," says Sarah, who's a museum curriculum manager. "Before the baby I would do the laundry maybe forty percent of the time. Now, I'm guessing it's five percent. I gave it up entirely after going back to work. We realized that doing these things, caring for our home, is like caring for each other. It makes us better." (Sarah, by the way, handles all things tech in their family, down to the background on her husband's phone. "He'll be like, How did you *do* that?!")

What about taking turns, that preschool skill you assume you'll want to model for your toddler one day? Save it for the things you can genuinely both do equally well (or equally poorly). Hayley and Ryan, both lawyers in Cleveland with similar schedules, made a pact early on that if their baby needed to be picked up from daycare because he was sick, they'd alternate. "I'm about to go back to work after our third baby now—we have three under three—and so far it's always worked," says Hayley.

Crucial side note: let him do it *his* way (and you do your stuff yours)

"This part is a little trickier for a lot of us," says psychotherapist Sarah Best. "Working moms tend to be high-functioning go-getters who have been able to set goals and work toward them throughout their lives. We really like to control things." Oh, yes. We do. "And when we enlist even the most loving, supportive, capable partners, they're not going to do everything the way we want it done." Oh, no. They're not.

But here's the big adjustment you have to make, says Best: "You have to find a way to tolerate that your husband might hold the baby in a position that you wouldn't hold the baby in. Is Baby okay and safe? Then we have to tolerate it." The next example Best gives me is about being okay with crumbs left on the kitchen counter when he wipes it down. This kind of kills me. What about bugs? What about sticky counter areas?? Deal with it. Or do the task yourself and find something else for him to do. "For the sake of your family, you have to find a way to accept help that is not going to be exactly the way you want it to be all the time," says Best.

Kim, a neuroscientist and pediatrician in New York City, offers this advice for when you let your partner take over some of the childcare: Don't assume the baby is the same with him as she is with you! "When I first went back to work, Eric stepped in for three weeks," Kim says. "I would feel my milk let down at the office and call him and say, okay, time for her to eat." Eric dutifully and awesomely kept notes on a dry-erase board of their daughter's day: diapers, feedings, moods. "I remember one day I got home and saw that he'd written down '3:20 p.m. screaming bloody murder' and I was like no, no, that can't be right . . . something went wrong. Maybe he didn't warm up the milk right." Nope. Turns out, their baby's schedule really was just a little different when she was with her dad: She napped longer, ate later, and woke up famished. And Kim quickly learned that that had to be okay—and that micromanaging from afar wasn't worth the resulting fight.

Sarah, the museum curriculum expert, recalls the moment she realized her husband had great instincts. "When my son was a newborn, I was very emotional and Googled a million things, every little worry," she says. "But my husband's instincts were so good it was frightening." Convinced their cranky son had reflux, Sarah was making herself crazy researching causes and treatments. "Then my husband was like, There must be a reason . . . we just have to find the reason, and it's probably pretty simple. I wonder if he's just taking in too much milk. And he was right! We pulled back a little on the time of his feeds and it made all the difference." From that moment on, Sarah insisted that her husband's one day at home with the baby every week be called Daddy Day. "He had been calling it Daddy Daycare—big difference—and I was like, No, no, no, you're not the babysitter. You're the caregiver now."

And while you're cutting your partner some slack give *yourself* a break, too, if you can't suddenly do all the wonderful, thoughtful things you used to do in your marriage. Dry cleaning is so boring, but I have the perfect story here. I have two dear, dear friends I never would have met had we not stumbled sleeplessly into a new moms' support group and agreed to defect together when the other moms drove us crazy. We made our own support group, with wine, once a month-ish seven years ago and have mostly kept it up. Here's a conversation from one recent night out:

ALLISON *(professor, mother of three including a baby, and wife of a nice, reasonable man named Andrew):* Guys, I'm so sorry I'm late, I worked until three and then had to get one kid from school and then the other from daycare and then turn around and go back to the dry cleaner and then sit in all of this traffic because the dry cleaner is on the other side of town.

ME: No problem!

TARA: Don't worry at all! So glad you could come in to the city for tonight.

(Twenty minutes later, post-chitchat, mid-guacamole)

TARA: I don't get it about the dry cleaner.

ME: Yeah, there isn't another one closer?

ALLISON: Oh, a million, but this is the one that Andrew likes.

TARA: *(shock and silence)*

ME: Whaaaaaaat?

ALLISON: Well, he has a thing about how much starch and . . .

TARA: He can't just pick up his own shirts, then?

ALLISON: Well, their hours are weird and it doesn't work with his work schedule . . .

ME: But it works with yours?

TARA: Would he even notice if you switched?

ALLISON: Well . . . I don't know. Hey, did you guys want more wine?

TARA AND ME *(simultaneously)*: Allison, we do not mean to bully you here but you have to switch dry cleaners!!

We totally did bully her. Poor Allison. But we'd seen one another through surgeries, and surprise third babies, and job layoffs. The dry cleaner was fair game. Allison is a perfectionist, and she's pretty damn good at everything, but she had to give herself a break on this one. Surely her husband would, too.

Try this: If you feel like you're compromising, either your own standards or his, redefine that word in your mind. A compromise no longer means that one person loses and the other wins. Now the whole family wins because the balance and peace are worth it. The baby wins. Go baby, woooo!

Make your work lives real to each other

This is one lovely hidden benefit of going back to work: You two will have more in common again. With paternity-leave benefits improving by the minute in the PR–happy worlds of finance and tech, more fathers are sharing parental leave with their spouses, and it's making big, splashy headlines. But most of the women I interviewed reported a more old-fashioned leave setup: The dads/ partners took a couple of weeks, max. The moms took six or eight or twelve-ish. For many weeks, then, your days are strikingly different than your spouse's.

When one of you is home on leave with the baby and the other is at work, the end-of-the-day catch-up doesn't always come very naturally. (What did you do today, Honey? Oh, you know, I fed the baby, changed the baby, held the baby, soothed the baby! And how about you? Ummm. Well, the usual. Did my work. End scene.) Getting back into the groove of sharing the highs and lows of your workday, now that you have one again, can take some practice. In my experience, I was exhausted by the time I got home, and, at first, some of the office blah-blah that used to seem newsworthy over dinner now seemed . . . kind of silly. But I beg: Do not be one of those mothers who only wants to talk to her partner about the baby. You are more interesting than that, especially now that you're back at work!

As with everything, it's a balance, Karen, a marketing exec in

Connecticut, realized. Before having kids, she'd been at a job that consumed her—she was barely sleeping, sometimes even crashing at a hotel right next to her office, and when she was home work was all she could talk about. "My husband offered me such good perspective whenever I got too carried away with it all," says Karen, laughing. "He'd be like, 'Karen, you're just launching a new hot beverage system. It's coffee. This should not be your whole life.'"

Karen switched jobs, had a kid, returned to work, and made a decision to prioritize motherhood at home by not talking about work at all. But this opposite extreme wasn't healthy, either. Pretty quickly, Karen found herself bickering with her husband, and realized they were losing the key element of what made their relationship work in the past: friendship. The solution? She had to do a better job of sharing what went on in her day. "There's a happy medium, I realized. So much of your life is at work. You have to find those funny work stories to share with your husband—a lot of times, that's where the things come up that you bond over, that help you be friends with each other," she says. "Being able to share the silly, gossipy stuff about colleagues really helped."

Work is a language two working parents have in common. And talking about it lets you express feelings that go far beyond the walls of your office. "I really believe that the quality of our life is determined by the quality of our human relationships," says Best, when I run this idea by her. "Talking about the cast of characters at work every day is a way to get at what your emotional experience is; it's sharing the deepest part of what you're doing, not just 'I wrote twelve pages or I saw fifteen patients today.'" For instance, she continues: "To say, 'I don't like the girls in my office' is one thing. But to say, 'Gosh, I work with all of these twenty-two-year-olds who are going out until four in the morning, and they have no idea what it's like to look at the clock on the wall and realize that I have to go pump in a minute, or to have to choose between peeing and eating lunch because these are the only ten minutes I have.' What you're really getting at when you share a story like that is how you feel about this whole transitional period in your life." This is a particularly good example because if you're pumping at work, the logistics of that are tremendous. Partner support has been shown to extend the duration of breastfeeding and pumping among working moms. But to support it, he's got to understand it.

This kind of "Daily Stress-Reducing Conversation," as Pirak calls it, can help him emotionally, too, especially if he's not thrilled about your going back to work—a real possibility. A whole slew of (now incredibly dated) studies from the 1980s and 1990s found that marital satisfaction was higher for men whose wives didn't work after the birth of a child. La la la la, fingers in my ears, not listening! Except, actually, take them out for a minute, because the more modern version of that statistic is this from my own survey of dads and partners: If income were no issue at all, 58 percent of dads/partners wouldn't want you to work at all during the first year of your baby's life. And 50 percent guess that you feel the same way. In fact, the number one reason he thinks you went (or are going) back to work was because of your current or future income. (Your passion for what you do was a fairly distant second.)

So. What to do with this cheerful bit of insight? Talk. Talk about your work in terms that you share to instantly help even the playing field. "Regardless of how different your jobs are, you both have to navigate these social worlds," says Best. "We all have the same set of cards, really. We all have being frustrated by people, being jealous of people, being intimidated by people." Talk about those relationships, and about why you work and the conflicts you may feel about that. Make your work lives real to each other, and you'll find common ground.

Take a confidence pill

Whatever that pill may be for you. Maybe you need more of a dissolving tablet. Or a lozenge? Give yourself a pep talk, or ask a friend to tell you everything she loves about you, or just scroll through your own Instagram history for a glimpse of the greatest version of the life you're living. Do what it takes to feel confident in this wildly crooked moment because . . . well, because it helps your relationship. Research says so.

How you feel about yourself affects how you get through marital disagreements, especially now, and especially if you're in what researchers call a "high negative escalation marriage" (ahem, that means you fight a lot). If you have low self-esteem (or if your partner does), it'll really bite you in the butt during the postnatal period.

"Sometimes, I think women really retreat into exclusively focusing on the children, as opposed to their marriage, because they're not feeling physically their best," says Dr. Samantha Boardman, a psychiatrist and founder of the blog Positive Prescription. "That takes a toll on the relationship which becomes a place of neglect. And then the spouse is feeling like, 'Oh my gosh, this is what my life is just going to be from now on.'" But it's not.

Going back to work, in my experience, is a huge, wonderful opportunity to reclaim some confidence. On leave, you were new at being a mother; and, yes, now you're new at being a working mom, too. But the actual work you *know* how to do. I spent much of my first day back on the brink of tears, except for the moment that a beloved colleague (perhaps knowing just what I needed) burst into my office proclaiming, "Thank God, you're here. I need a headline and you're the one person I want to ask. I've been wanting to ask you for headline help every day for three months." This is when the sitcom sound-effects person makes the magic-wand noise. It helped—so much—to feel confident in my abilities at that moment. And I carried a piece of that home with me that night.

If you don't have your own confidence to draw on immediately, draw on someone else's. As I mentioned at the beginning of this chapter, I looked closely through my own survey data for any unexpected things that the "got closer even though we fought more" couples had working in their favor. One that popped up:

More of those women reported having a Working Mom Mentor (WMM). The Gottman Institute's Pirak says that makes sense: "Across the board, postnatally, I have seen that if the mom has someone they can talk to whom they've observed get through this time, it increases their confidence, their feeling of 'this too shall pass.'" Because it will. It will not be hard and new forever.

Jennifer, the cable TV executive in Atlanta, recalls a day when her own boss (a man, actually) gently sent her home when she had an embarrassing hormonal crying jag at the office. It helped tremendously; she took a deep breath and relaxed with her husband and came back the next day recovered and ready to pay that sensitivity forward one day as a boss herself. She now feels, she says, "a moral obligation" to provide that kind of mentorship to her own new-mom staffers and friends, recommending that they schedule pumping into their day, and advising them that "if you can just survive and hang on for those three months, you're going to be okay." At work and at home.

An important P.S. here, if what's keeping you from feeling confident is also what's keeping you from fitting into your prebaby black pants (i.e., unhappy body-related crap): 76 percent of dads/partners said that in the Fifth Trimester you are either mostly or very sexy. So there. If you're having a personal-appearance confidence crisis, it's mostly in your head.

And the biggie (you knew it was coming): Make time for each other

Here's what you've got to do: First get your hair done, then hire a babysitter (preferably with a British accent and a jolly bag of tricks), then bribe the reservationist at the best new little five-star in town, and then have a six-course dinner with your partner and never talk once about the baby. Repeat weekly. Preferably twice weekly.

No, no, no, no, no.

No!

That is *not* what you have to do. Although if you know who to call to get into that restaurant, now that my kids are a little older, please do let me know.

The best and most reassuring thing I found out from my survey data was this: Anything over one hour—one measly hour!—of alone time with your partner per week makes a difference. To be clear, the 12 percent of couples who somehow found more than five hours a week to spend together, alone, without the baby, felt closer and fought less than the rest of us mere mortals. But there was very, very little difference in relationship satisfaction between the couples who spent one, two, three, four, or five hours together. Anything over one hour was enough. And that hour does not require a babysitter. It can be time spent on the couch with Apple TV. For this finite, transitional period in your life, I'm here to tell you, it really, truly does count.

So at first: Adjust your expectations of how much and what kind of alone time you really need at this moment. Don't aim so high that you just give up entirely. A frightening 42 percent of the women I polled reported spending one hour or less per week on couple time. It's easy to imagine that they thought of a list of very valid reasons why date night was an impossibility (the nursing, the exhaustion, the money, the hangover-phobia), and immediately put on elastic-waist pants and a face mask. But the 47 percent who managed to prioritize each other just a bit more were markedly happier.

"Most nights we sit next to each other on our laptops working, it's true," says Kim, the pediatrician and neuroscientist, laughing. "But we try to save Saturday nights. Sometimes we will go out for an early dinner, but at a bare minimum we just spend time together at home and don't work. We go to bed earlier." Going to bed earlier while staying home and not working counts as date night? You bet. In my book (and this is my book!), it does.

"Your marriage is the easiest relationship in the house to ignore," says Karen. "If you run out of time for anyone, it's him. But that's really not okay." Karen's fix: "Watching *Shark Tank.*

Seriously. That's our date night. You don't have to take a Caribbean vacation. Half the time we fall asleep in the middle of the show. But even just acknowledging that need to have that little bit of time together made us both return to that mutual respect we'd been missing when life got so busy after I went back to work."

The mutual respect Karen mentions is important, because the dreaded hex of resentment goes both ways. When I polled all those dads and partners, one sad fact became achingly clear: He takes it personally when you don't pay attention to him. I asked the dads how thoughtful you were prebaby versus post-, and, well, it's not good. With other people (family, friends, strangers), in his estimation, you manage to be "mostly" thoughtful. But with him? Sixty-eight percent of husbands and partners say that you're only "somewhat" or "not at all" attentive to his needs during the Fifth Trimester (way up from a baseline of 24 percent who made the same assessment prebaby). Reading between the lines, he sees that you're able to be patient and kind with pretty much everyone else, but that you let your frustration creep in when it comes to him.

This is where making time for each other really saves the day. "It's not that I felt neglected, I just missed my wife," says Renée, whose wife, Nathalie, took the longer maternity leave following the birth of their daughter. "I missed having conversations that weren't about poop and breastmilk. I wanted time alone with her to reconnect, and to share with her that going back to work was hard for me, too, but couldn't say that; it felt so emotionally small in comparison to what she was going through."

Eventually, you *will* get to the holy grail of Dinner Out Just the Two of You. You'll know you're ready when that starts to sound good to one of you and half-good to the other, and then you just do it. Date nights help you see a future beyond this crazy period of barely treading water. They give you a glimpse of the marriage you'll have when your kids are old enough to sleep through the night, or go to summer camp, or have their own first boyfriends or girlfriends, or leave the nest entirely. You deserve a taste of that now, and your partner does, too. "It was hard at first, but we spend only the first fifteen minutes of our Saturday nights out together talking about the kids. And then we move on," says Ellen, the blogger whose son has special needs. "We end up talking about the big stuff. Our hopes and the future, and what our next big vacation is going to be." Those nights keep you moving forward, and—cheesy but true—they remind you of why you started dating in the first place.

If you skip to the end of this chapter and read only one thing, read this

Ellen nails it, according to every expert I talked to. To keep your relationship happy, you need to be able to acknowledge that this transition is temporary—and to see that distant, sparkling glimmer of why you first became a couple and why you want to continue to be one.

All of it—trust, asking for help, sharing your work experiences, making time for each other—that's all reliant on optimism. "If you approach things like, 'This is probably going to be okay, and our relationship is probably going to be okay, and I'm probably going to be a good mom,' the automatic relationship scores are going to be so much higher," says Pirak. In her workshops, she says, couples laugh knowingly when she reminds them of their underlying friendship. "I'll say, 'You were not randomly selected. You all chose each other!'"

You chose each other because you had a lot in common as individuals, and that carries over into what you have in common as parents. In my research, the study I found that blew my mind the most showed just how much moms and dads mirror each other emotionally: In Sweden, where fathers are legally allowed to share paid parental leave with mothers, researchers wanted to take a look at the "experiences of the first year as a father." Their big conclusion? Men reported three major experiences: (1) "to be over-whelmed," (2) "to master the new situation," and (3) I couldn't make this up if I tried: "to get a new completeness in life." Pretty sweet, huh? Let that bolster your own optimism. I hope it gives you hope.

CHAPTER TEN

❧

What if you're your own boss?

Ultimate Freedom, Ultimate Pressure

Andrea Olshan—a dynamic, beautiful, Harvard-educated mother of three—runs her family's real estate empire, Olshan Properties, in New York City. Started by her father back in 1954 with the purchase of one residential building on the Upper West Side, the business now spans eleven states across the country, with more than a thousand employees. Andrea, who had grown the company as its Chief Operating Officer during her first daughter's infancy, took over from her dad as CEO while pregnant with twins. Both *The Wall Street Journal* and *The New York Times* quickly profiled her success. As for her Fifth Trimesters? With her eldest, she gave herself one week of maternity leave before returning to work. With her twins, born just seventeen months later, she took a month. She would have gone back sooner, but one baby was in the NICU for two weeks.

Four hundred miles and three states west, Sarah Serafin runs her own little work-at-home empire while taking care of her two children as a single mom in Chagrin Falls, Ohio. These days, with her kids in grade school, Sarah works primarily as a freelance medical transcriptionist (she transcribed—at all hours of the night—many of the interviews I conducted for this book, including Andrea's). But over the years since her daughter and son were born and her marriage unraveled, Sarah has been many other things, too: a restaurant server, a restaurant hostess, an employee at a tae kwon do studio, and an in-home daycare provider. Along the way, she's also worked tirelessly (and not for pay), researching therapies for her daughter's Asperger's syndrome. Sarah, like Andrea, took just one week off after the birth of her daughter. Her husband had lost his job, and she was able to pick up late-night waitressing shifts.

On the surface, these women's lives are dramatically different, most obviously financially. Andrea, who travels quite a bit for work, has employed, at various points, multiple nannies and housekeepers, an eye-popping luxury that was not lost on Sarah when I sent her the audio file of our interview. ("It was interesting to listen to someone who had almost the complete opposite experience of my own," she wrote to me before attaching the transcript. To be honest, I almost sent the interview to a different transcriptionist to avoid having Sarah feel that sting. But I knew she needed and wanted the work.)

Still, talking to Andrea and Sarah, and reading through my interviews with several other women who identify as self-employed—writers, actresses, small business owners, nonprofit founders, website entrepreneurs—I was struck again and again not by their differences, but by their similarities and by one overarching theme:

Working for yourself as a new mother may sound like living the dream, but the responsibilities and pressure of that autonomy are sky-high—especially when you've got a baby.

We all like to complain about working for "the man," but "the man" provides structure—and often maternity leave—that can be challenging to define for yourself. Success as a lone ranger requires strength, discipline, conviction, and constant reassessment. So while the specifics each woman described were different, Sarah and Andrea had a lot in common when it came to determination and adaptability. The sentiments they described were at times nearly indistinguishable.

Here's a little quiz: See if you can guess which woman said which of these things about running her own show:

1) "Every time opportunity knocked on the door, I was smart enough to invite it in."
2) "You do not have backup. There is not more than one of you."
3) "My day is scheduled in fifteen-minute increments. You have to be flexible, but you also have to be regimented."
4) "Part of success is just accepting that some things have to give."

Answer key:

1) *"Every time opportunity knocked on the door, I was smart enough to invite it in."* That's Sarah, talking about how she started her at-home daycare when she couldn't find any centers in her former town that could accommodate her daughter's special needs. Sarah launched her business to generate income, socialize her daughter, and be home with her. Andrea was similarly optimistic and opportunistic, when she first took over as COO (before becoming CEO). "I remember I had an eight a.m. conference call and I was waiting and waiting and the COO didn't show up," Andrea says. It turns out, tragically, he'd actually died over the weekend. "In a family company, everyone just looked around and said, Okay, now you're going to do that job. By that afternoon, his emails were being forwarded to me. It's that moment when you go from being one of many to leading, and you never know when it's going to hap-

pen. But you have to jump on it when it does." Her next jump was to CEO. Unlike in law, medicine, academia, or garden-variety middle management, there is no set path when you work for yourself. There's also no coasting.

2) *"You do not have backup. There is not more than one of you."* That's Andrea, referring to how impossible it is to truly check out. "When you are an independent contractor or own your own business, there really isn't anyone else who can do what you can do," Andrea told me. "I have never ever put an 'away' message on my phone, not while getting married, not while having my kids. You don't ever turn off." Sarah's version of this always-on-call feeling is more about living on the financial edge. When work is available, she takes it (even, I'll admit, on national holidays when she gladly took work off my hands), because she never knows what's around the corner.

3) *"My day is scheduled in fifteen-minute increments. You have to be flexible, but you also have to be regimented."* That description of the discipline required to manage your own business and income comes from Sarah. I almost dropped the phone when she recounted her daily schedule: childcare tasks peppered with fifteen-minute transcribing intervals when she would draw a line around her desk and tell her daycare toddlers that they were only to approach in case of emergency (I could learn a lot from her on not helicoptering). "And you've got to do it all with a calm, cool exterior," Sarah said. "Because you know if you give off a stressed vibe, the kids pick up on it."

4) *"Part of success is just accepting that some things have to give."* That's Andrea, talking about how she's learned to manage her expectations of herself so she doesn't feel so consistently stretched in every arena—a really common side effect of being your own boss. As the master of her own destiny (and business, and home, and family), she decides

what's sacred and what's not. She knows, many nights, work will prevent her from getting home for her kids' dinnertime and has made peace with that in part because she'll get up early in the morning to prep their food. "So, at 6:30 a.m., you're cooking dinner for them. It's a little piece of Mommy that's there. It shows that I care," she told me. Sarah, who says she suffers from superwoman syndrome (more on that in a bit), learned to relax her expectations and ask for help, too. "That whole 'I can do this myself, I've got it covered, not gonna ask for help when I'm exhausted' thing? Yeah, don't do that! I ended up with adrenal fatigue because I burned myself out."

Sarah and Andrea are part of a significant trend. Between 1997 and 2015, the number of women-owned businesses grew by 74 percent, according to a report commissioned by American Express OPEN. Just a year earlier, the 2014 report found that 1,288 new woman-owned firms were launched *per day*. And while both privately held and male-owned companies have experienced a drop in employment rates in recent years, U.S. employment has grown overall, thanks to—you guessed it—publicly traded and *female*-owned companies. Clearly, there's a case to be made that women-owned businesses are good for the economy. But are they good for women, particularly new working mothers? A 2013 *Inc.* magazine story entitled "The Psychological Price of Entrepreneurship" argued that small-business owners are more susceptible to anxiety and depression—and won its author, Jessica Bruder, a prize from the New York City chapter of the Society of Professional Journalists (many of whom are freelancers themselves). That certainly raises flags for new mothers, already in the throes of a major life transition. And, indeed, the pressures are real. But so are the freedoms, especially for women who are unhappy with a more traditional corporate setup.

Want to be your own boss? You can: Shimmy to the top of the

totem pole and run/own a company like Andrea, above. Or cobble together a series of part-time gigs that let you work from home and avoid the cost of childcare, like Sarah has done.

Or, third option: Hang your own shingle. Ever had the fantasy?

Love it or hate it, the term "mompreneur" is now in the Oxford English Dictionary (along with "wine o'clock" and "hangry"—coincidence, or just low standards? I'm unsure). The mothers I talked to who had started their own businesses prior to having children—the ones who were entrepreneurs before some genius put "m-o-m" in front of the word—seemed to have weathered the transition well. Others used motherhood as an opportunity to ditch office life or follow a passion—with mixed results but seemingly no regrets.

I heard from women like Vivian Howard, chef and co-owner, with her husband, of the acclaimed restaurant Chef & the Farmer. Clearly, Vivian is ambitious, one of the best chefs in the country, but when I ask her about working motherhood, she laughs. "Are you sure you want to ask me about that? The mother part of it is not what I'm great at. But I know that about myself."

Lexi Petronis, in Albuquerque, has dipped in and out of the freelance life between full-time jobs, because it lets her maintain that working side of herself. "I love being home, love being a mother," she told me. "But it's rewarding to be somebody who's not just Mom, buying the milk and picking up the Legos. I need that. And if I'm inspired, I'm more *inspiring* to the kids, too."

Wendy Shanker, an author and event scriptwriter in Miami, quit her desk job years in advance of having a family (which she ended up doing on her own with donor sperm). "I gotta tell you, I don't miss meetings!" she said, still gleeful. "Working for yourself is a lot like living on your own for the first time. The first few days you eat a lot of pizza. Then you order salad. The next day you organize all your clothes by color. And then you jump in." She's grateful that she found that rhythm and set her own standards and rules for herself well in advance of having her baby.

Amy Solomon had no such prep time. Just a passion (baking) and a problem: As a TV producer for *The Rachael Ray Show,* she went back to work after a blissfully disconnected maternity leave and found the hours untenable. "Many days, I would get to the office before seven in the morning and leave after seven at night. Plus I had my commute," says Amy. "My boss was wonderful, and I loved my job, but in TV you just can't walk out the door and go home to your baby." She stayed for three months to transition; then Amy walked out the door permanently. Three months after that, Amy recruited her mom and sister and started a quickly successful cookie-making business, Just One Bite.

What if you're not even sure what your backup passion plan is? Emmy Laybourne bridged two careers until she figured it out. As a character actress in Los Angeles with a newborn, Emmy went to sleep the night before her first postbaby audition and dreamed that her agent—dressed up as a dominatrix—was standing on her neck in high heels. How's that for a sign? Emmy promptly quit acting and enrolled in a screenwriting program, which gave her the skills for the freelance career she's got now: young-adult novelist. "There's such a deep level of transformation when you have a kid, of this creative process of giving birth, creating another human being," says Emmy. "I know it's very hippie-dippy sounding, but I feel like it takes you to a very important place about being alive, and having a mission. Maybe it's about having somebody with so much potential in your care. You go, 'You know, I've got potential.'"

Working feels more worth it when it's something that's truly yours, these women told me. Before she was pregnant with her daughter Marlowe, Eva Amurri Martino, an actress turned big-time mom-lifestyle blogger (Happily Eva After), says that the whole "worth it" idea confused her. "I thought it just meant that work had to be something I felt creative and passionate about," she says. "What I realize now is that it means that what you're getting out of working has to be more than what you're giving up to get it." (Read that twice. It's worth it.) Acting was creative, she was passionate about it—but the projects weren't hers. "My experiences working with great people and having a nice working environment were few and far between by the time I had my daughter. I had been seeing the not-so-pretty side of the industry for a while, and I just kept thinking: Is this *it*?" she says. "I would find childcare. And then I would pump, and then sit in traffic, and I realized, here I am putting in all of this time and energy for somebody else's brand. I'm busting my ass, leaving my child, and I'm doing it for some guy who I don't even really know. I don't know his wife's name, or if he has kids. I thought, you know, I'd rather be working my ass off for my own company. And the more I looked into it, the more I realized there are so many women who have started their own companies, working for themselves, and you start to realize why." Here's the why: "Because if you're someone who has a great work ethic and you're going to be working hard, you want to be getting everything out of it that you possibly, possibly can."

So, yes, it's hard. And yes, it takes discipline and drive and all the rest of those enviable qualities to pave your own path. But it can be massively, gloriously fulfilling, too.

As I've said, this book is for *any* new mother who wants to keep working, however she defines that word. If you have your own business or are thinking of leaving your job to start one, I commend your moxie. I'm trying to do the same thing right now myself, sitting here at my sterile little workspace in the library writing these words in this book, on my own after years of working for massive media corporations. I really, really miss the automatic deposit in my checking account every other Thursday night at midnight. But I am happier and more energized by my work than ever before. I never thought I would say that again after having my babies. But there it is.

How to be a good, fair, and tough boss
(of yourself, new mom)

Here's a colossal perk of working for yourself with a newborn: You get to set your own goals and your own benefits. What holidays will you take off? What's your budget? What are your deliverables? How long will you have to achieve them? Will you adjust them as your baby's needs change? It's exhilarating to be in charge of that stuff yourself—but challenging, too.

"The best part of owning my own business while being a mother is the feeling that I can control my own destiny," says chef Vivian. "I don't have to ask anyone's permission except my own in order to spend the morning with my kids. But sometimes I feel it is more difficult to get my own permission than it would be to ask a boss." Give yourself some ground rules so you can be the boss you always wanted:

SET ACHIEVABLE INCOME GOALS—AND AIM TO BEAT THEM. That's scriptwriter Wendy's number one rule. She meets regularly with a financial adviser and planned for the expenses of motherhood far in advance of her pregnancy. "Before having Sunny, I sat down and tried to budget out what it would cost: diapers in the beginning, baby music classes a year down the road," she recalls. And thank God she prepared. Sunny was born at twenty-nine weeks and spent three months in the hospital. "I gave birth to a $499,000 baby. The majority was covered, but that still opened up a couple hundred grand of therapies and drugs that weren't insured," Wendy says. Because she was already in the habit of managing her money, she made it through and has done better than she'd hoped: "To this day, I never thought I was going to pay for private preschool, but I have," she says. Sunny is only four years old, but as a single mom, Wendy is looking decades ahead: "Now I worry about the cushion that I'm going to leave her once she's an adult."

KEEP YOUR OVERHEAD LOW. Wendy moved away from expensive New York City to Miami, where she would be closer to her parents. She paid much less for childcare than she had budgeted but increased her spending for things like travel (for face time with NYC- and L.A.-based clients) and communication (really good Skype-worthy Internet).

BUDGET IN ACTUAL BENEFITS. Your most intangible benefit is flexibility, but you need some of the boring tangible ones, too: health insurance for you and your child. Holidays. Comp time. Career counseling. Lindsey Pollak, a Millennial workplace expert who consults with the insurance company The Hartford (one of the largest group disability providers in the United States), advises, "If you are not a full-time employee, look at joining a professional association or other group that could provide benefits to you."

FIND YOUR BASELINE MEASURES OF PRODUCTIVITY AND DELIVER-ABLES. I'm big into deliverables in any kind of job. If you were lobbying your corporate boss for flextime, you would spell out, in writing, the work you'd achieve in those new hours. It would set your boss's mind at ease, right? Well, the best way to quiet your own self-doubt is exactly that method: Give yourself goals. It took Amy, the cookie company owner, a few months to get used to operating in work "bursts" instead of a long stretch at a desk in the city. "It's two hours here, two hours there, an hour off, then three hours on," she says. With a baby, she couldn't ever just sit down and get her whole day's work done at once, but at the end of the week, she *had* actually achieved her goals. "I had to wrap my head around that."

Wendy, whose work relies on creativity, thinks longer term and more abstractly about what she needs to achieve. "I know there are authors who say, 'Write a page a day and at the end of the year you will have a book.' Well, some days I have zero pages, and some days I have nineteen." She has learned to account for the time spent simply thinking. "That processing is work," she says, and it's also on her list of goals.

START THROWING AROUND THE TERM "ROI." That's "return on investment," and Emmy, the actress-turned-novelist, relies on it to help decide what work to take on. "I think there must be a matrix: Money earned, time spent, and future opportunity for work gigs.

It's like a three-bubble drawing, and for good ROI, you need to hit the sweet spot of all three of them. The work has to be worth it."

CHECK YOUR EGO. "Your ego has to change when you become a parent," says Wendy. "Suddenly the work you take on is a little more about what's good for your family, and a little less about bragging rights." Eventually, you may find the hybrid, but for now, don't be ashamed to fill your work plate with a big scoop of rice and a little less of the spicy dishes. With a young child, Wendy didn't have the bandwidth to write a book of her own in that first year, the way she had previously, so she signed on with a ghostwriting agency to help other authors find their voices. "I'm fulfilling some of my ego and creative needs, getting paid for it, expanding my skill set"—and supporting her little family. All things worth feeling pretty damn proud of.

So . . . Can you take a maternity leave when you work for yourself?

Short answer: Up to you. Longer answer: It shouldn't have to be. In my opinion, with the right pay structure, a federally mandated paid parental leave should be available even to women who work for themselves.

Realistically, though, this is something that even the most family-focused and sophisticated countries are still struggling to define. In the U.K., for instance, women who don't get statutory maternity pay are typically eligible, as independent contractors, for something called maternity allowance, but as of 2016, that amounts to only 139.58 pounds (or about $200) per week, a figure that would easily qualify a U.S. family for food stamps. Even in Sweden, a country seemingly flowing with breastmilk and honey, economists have found that self-employed mothers take forty-six fewer days of paid parental leave than their wage-earner counterparts. (This may seem like a self-correction—mothers saying, Hey, government, you're offering more than we actually need—but that same research suggests that women in Sweden actually avoid self-employment in part because of this challenge.) The state of California gets it close-ish to right, offering self-employed parents the ability to buy their own disability insurance at a rate of just under 5 percent of their income (or up to a max of almost $5,000 annually for those making over six figures). It exists, but it sure isn't cheap.

The challenge of taking self-employed maternity leave is about more than the immediate lost income, though. One freelance money manager shocked me when she told me that not only did she not take a maternity leave, she didn't even tell her clients that she was pregnant! She worked remotely, and was worried that they would write her off in the future if they knew she had a baby cooking. Christin Drake, a psychiatrist in a solo private practice who treats many new mothers, cautions her patients (and friends) not to be so terrified of the loss of future business. She took twelve weeks off, unpaid, with her first daughter and is now pregnant with a second baby and plans to do the same. Another physician will cover her practice for her, and she'll be available herself for emergencies, she tells me. "Not having an income for three months is simply not possible for everyone," Christin says, "but we planned carefully for years to make it happen. I don't feel like I could have gone back to work sooner. I tell people all the time, taking a three-month leave will not ruin the business, not if you plan for it."

Here's what maternity leave looked like for several of the self-employed women who talked to me:

> **Vivian Howard, chef and restaurant owner, Kinston, North Carolina: six weeks.** Vivian went back to work three weeks after her twins came home from their three-week NICU stay. "I regret this now, but I treated going back to work as an escape from home, where I often felt inadequate," she says. "Because of the C-section, I was not

able to lift things in the kitchen. But there was a lot of work I could still do. And it was a comfort being there."

Wendy Shanker, freelance writer, Miami, Florida: zero days. "I never had a maternity leave because I gave birth in the middle of my pregnancy. The morning Sunny was born, at twenty-nine weeks, I remember making a few phone calls to the VIPs in my life, and the third or fourth one was the producer of a TV treatment I was putting together. I told her I was going to need to put it on hold for a few days. But within a week or so I was back up and working."

Jessie Randall, creative director and founder of the fashion brand Loeffler Randall, Brooklyn, New York: about one month. That was after the birth of her twins, one of whom was in the NICU for most of that time. "It was very, very difficult for me," she says. "When you own your own small business you can't stop working for three months." The second time around, with her younger son, she went back to work "almost immediately for a couple of days a week," bringing him with her to the office for the first six months. "It was a great experience for me," she says, "because I could continue to breastfeed him during the day."

Amy Solomon, owner of Just One Bite cookies, Millburn, New Jersey: zero days. "With my second child, I took a big order in the afternoon, and then my son was born at five-forty-five the next morning. The day after that, from the hospital, I was worried about getting that order out," she says.

Windsor Hanger Western, cofounder of Her Campus, a new-media brand for college women, Atlanta, Georgia: two weeks. "Only you know best how much time you can take away from your business," she says. "I remember people being like, 'Oh, you can take unlimited leave,' and I'm like, 'No, I can take *no* maternity leave because it's my

company and my employees depend on me. And I care, a
lot. Before I had my daughter, my company was my baby.
Now I have two babies."

Renée Farster-Degenhardt, then-co-owner of a thera-
peutic spa, Boston, Massachusetts (she's since sold the
business and now works for a tech company): **four full**
weeks off, plus four part-time weeks off, spread out
over several months. "You're never disconnecting completely," she says. "I talked them through a complicated
hot-tub repair over the phone. And socially, it's a little
fuzzy, too. During my time away, my colleagues would
want to come see the baby, because we were friendly, but it
felt weird because I didn't really want to think about work
at that time."

"Look, if you're running a business, you do what you have to
do," Andrea Olshan, a real estate CEO, says. "And I think that you
shouldn't feel bad, shouldn't feel that you have to be home for three
months or six months if you can't." All these women preached: Go
easy on yourself if you do need (or want) to go back to work very
quickly. If you can't start back with a part-time schedule, at least
give yourself the benefit of part-time expectations.

For women in creative fields, that means being patient with
your inspiration. Lack of sleep (and dreaming, actually) is suspected
to affect creativity. And more than that, your brain is busy managing the early days of Keep Baby Alive in a way that may not allow
space for imagination. "Be patient, and know that there are all
these different chapters to come," says Wendy. "There's going to be
a phase that's more you-centric than child-centric eventually. You
may not write the next great American novel while breastfeeding.
But five years from now you might."

In a more analytical field? As Jennifer, the cable TV exec would
say, become a ninja about your time—precise and deliberate. And
realize that the creativity advice *does* apply to you, too. Having your
own business requires imagining the work that's going to bring

your next payday. You need to think and spin to pitch yourself, so if that doesn't come easily with a newborn on your lap, know that it will get easier. You haven't changed. Your circumstances have. And as your baby grows, they will continue to develop and reach some kind of magical equilibrium.

In the meantime, if you have employees, be aware of the example you're setting for other parents (or future parents). "I didn't want my maternity leave to be a Marissa Mayer situation," says Windsor, referring to the Yahoo CEO's famously short maternity leaves. "Obviously, I have the luxury of choosing what I'm going to do because I'm the business owner, but I made an announcement that this is a policy I'm setting only for myself. By no means does this mean that women here will only get two weeks of leave. In fact, right now we're trying to define our maternity *and* paternity policies because one of our guys has a wife who's pregnant. That's important."

The cozy, sticky truth about working from home

I am very lucky to have the freelancer's holy grail of New York City real estate, a little office in our apartment, with a door. You know how often I use it? Not very. Most days, instead, I hop from Starbucks, to the library, to the museum cafeteria, to the other library, in search of Wi-Fi and peace. After years of being out of the house eleven to fifteen hours a day at a corporate job, I just hate telling my kids that I'm home . . . but not available to get a sippy cup of water, or pinch a bloody nose and count to thirty, or put Lego Batman's head back on. The reason I'm able to work outside of the home, of course, is that I have in-home childcare.

Still, being home with your baby while working is a nice option, especially if you're breastfeeding. "I'm doing it right now, but probably won't forever," says Hannah Blumenthal, who has her own interior design firm and a nanny. "It's a bit isolating, and I never feel like I have time to focus—I'm always doing fourteen things at once, but I like being able to check on my son. And I never have to go the whole day without snuggles." The distraction struggle is real, however, and Hannah uses up lots of her work minutes deciding whether or not to work. When her son vomited recently, her nanny texted her from the other room asking if she wanted to see it. Um, not really? "Of course I'm going to go downstairs and make sure everything's okay," says Hannah. "But it might be easier if I didn't have that option."

Windsor Hanger Western talked to me when she was home working with her weeks-old daughter and no childcare. She feels the same tug that Hannah does. "My daughter is tiny, but I feel like I should be interacting with her more. But between conference calls the most I can do is keep her diaper changed and feed her. It's hard to feel like I'm doing everything as well as I want to." Eventually, Windsor knows that she and her husband will need to find childcare if she wants to work at the pace she likes—fast.

But for anyone who *needs* to work at home, with their children around, and without childcare, it is possible, at least part-time. First you'll use naptime, of course. Then when the naps start to dwindle, Sarah Serafin, who worked at home doing medical transcriptions while also running her small in-home daycare, offers these tips:

SCHEDULE *EVERYTHING*. "You have to schedule work into your day, just like you would schedule meetings or phone calls if you were at an office. You may be covered in juice and cracker crumbs, but you are still doing a job that brings you income. It becomes really important to understand where the 'sweet spots' in the day are—when everyone is fed, rested, and able to hang and play happily for short bursts without adult intervention. Those are your work times. Write them into your calendar right alongside nap time and lunchtime. And then hold yourself to it. Don't go throw in that load of laundry if you are scheduled to be working. Put laundry on the schedule in its own place. Work time is work time, unless, of course, something catastrophic is occurring."

WORK WHERE YOU CAN SEE YOUR KIDS. "My computer was in the basement where the playroom was, so I could work while they were playing, and observe them to gauge how much time I would have during each scheduled work session."

ENFORCE SERIOUS BOUNDARIES. "Kids need to understand that you are not a play toy. There are playtimes, and there are times when Mom is just not available unless it's blood or fire or something she deems worthy of the interruption. I took masking tape and taped off a square around my computer that allowed about a three-foot radius around my chair, and the kids understood that if they needed something, they could 'come and put their toes on the line and ask.' A lot of times, they were told to wait or to try to solve it on their own. If it was an emergency, of course I would stop working immediately, but most of the time, it was 'I can't get dolly's clothes on' or 'Ben is picking his nose,' and I would assure them that they could figure out a solution, or wait x number of minutes until I was available. They soon understood, and it helped them become more independent. I only had to give time-outs a couple times and everyone got the message. There was no wiggle room for bargaining. That kind of back-and-forth will eat *all* your productive time if you allow it. You have to be firm, true to your word, and kind."

Beware of superwoman syndrome

Compartmentalization is *hard,* these women told me. When you're sitting in an office with ugly carpeting and a boss breathing down your neck, it's infinitely easier to focus on a job deadline. Without that imposed structure, work bleeds into life, and life hemorrhages into work. Pretty soon, if you're not careful, you'll be saying yes to three new clients, throwing a baby shower for a friend, volunteering at the preschool down the street in case you want to enroll there one day, and Googling things like "How to make an Octonauts pod first birthday cake."

Hey, what's that between your shoulders there? Are you sprouting a . . . cape?! Hello, Superwoman Syndrome.

This is important: Do not let working for yourself rob you of the very freedom you sought when you decided to become your own boss. Here's what helps:

SET DAILY WORK-TIME LIMITS—WITH NO EXCUSES. "I can't talk to clients between 6:00 p.m. and 9:00 p.m. It's parenting duty, but they don't need to know that," says Wendy. "As women, we tend to overcompensate and overexplain. Pretend you're a dude and strap on your strap-on [author's note: how much do we love this woman?]. He would not say, 'I'm heating up a bottle and will be available in ten minutes.' Simply say when you're available and when you're not."

ADOPT A ROLLING ADMISSIONS MODEL FOR YOUR TO-DO LIST. More than a few women I talked to mentioned their problem with 11:00 p.m. It's when they should be going to bed, but it's also primo quiet work time. "I get through about a third of the things on my list every day and when eleven rolls around, I feel this urge to finish before going to bed," says Hannah, the interior designer. You will never be finished. That's part of the challenge of being self-employed. The work will still be there in the morning. So go to bed because, as Hannah says she tells herself, "it's much better for everyone: you and your baby and your husband if you're getting the appropriate amount of rest."

RETHINK YOUR WORK ENVIRONMENT. Make it work specifically to suit your needs. Vivian, the restaurant owner and chef, built a nursery in the back of her restaurant since she was almost never able to be home in the evenings. Why not, right? "Once I went back to work, and I came out of the depression fog, I started thinking, 'Well, I still really want to work, but I also feel like I want to be close to my kids.'" she says. "I laugh now, because it seems so ridiculous, a nursery in a restaurant. But that's the benefit of being my own boss: I had the space, and I didn't need anyone's permission. All I needed were two Pack-'n-Plays and a rug."

SCHEDULE MOMMY-AND-ME TIME. If you've got an hour blocked off for a music class or a stroll to look in the windows of the pet shop (squee!), you will be much less likely to cave on those boundaries that Sarah talked about enforcing a couple of pages back. You need alone time. And you also need simple downtime with your child. Jesse Lutz, a freelance producer in L.A., has an erratic work and travel schedule. When she and her husband got married and she became a stepmother to a wonderful six-year-old, she experienced a very unique kind of Fifth Trimester—she couldn't take maternity leave, but she still needed special time with her new daughter. "I was six years behind," she says. "And working the way I do, I'd get home for a little bedtime, maybe a meal." Jesse found it wasn't enough and started carving out time for the two of them to just be together. And here's where her experience starts to sound similar to a new birth mother's: "This transition is about getting to know your child as much as it is about getting to know yourself," Jesse says. "There was so much relationship to be nurtured." Take the nurturing time. You can't nurture and work simultaneously.

FORGET THE OLD OFFICE HOURS. "I almost feel beholden to my employees to prove how hard I'm working since I'm working remotely," says Windsor, the Her Campus cofounder, admitting it's a problem. "I'll feel like I need to be at my desk, available on my Gchat until 6:00 p.m. because they are, too. But in reality I've been up and working since 7:30 a.m. and they don't start until 10:00." You will inevitably fill up some of your personal hours— mornings, nights, weekends—with work. It's just the nature of being the boss. Grant yourself permission to use some traditional work hours for premeditated personal things, too.

MAKE PEACE WITH YOUR VACATION SITUATION. Ideally, you'd give yourself the A-plus benefits you'd want in a more traditional work setup—five weeks' vacation, anyone? And, please, if you can take a true, unplugged vacation without fear of losing future work, do! In reality, though? "Vacation? Hmm, no," muses Wendy. "I'll add a day onto a business trip to see friends, maybe, but any time off I handle really efficiently." Amy, the cookie business owner, can count on her mom and sister to pinch-hit if she takes a break. But even still, "time off is not really time off," Amy says. "Those lines are so blurred. It's a real challenge." To avoid feeling ripped off, remind yourself of all the good reasons you've chosen this path—and of the dozens of mini-"vacations" (lunch with a friend, snuggles with baby) that you are able to take regularly.

FIND SOME FORMS (PLURAL) OF BACKUP. When you run your own business, it's true: No one can replace you. There is no clone machine in Vivian's restaurant kitchen, but after ten years in business, and five as a mother, she is the rare and wise self-employed soul who *has* figured out how to take a vacation: "My husband and I are able to finally step away without all the wheels coming off the bus," she reports. "Instead of finding someone who I feel like can do my whole job—no one would have that same sense of ownership—I find several people who can each do small pieces of my job. Isolate people's strengths and let them do what they are good at and understand how that does in fact remove some pressure from you."

LET YOURSELF SEE THE PAYOFF OF LETTING GO. "For so long, I wouldn't allow myself to do anything away from the restaurant, but when I did, it was worth it. Personally, I have learned that there are things I want more out of life than just to have everything be completely my way," says Vivian. And—eureka moment—taking time to live life improves her work. "I get tired of Southern food," she says. "Whenever I travel, whether I'm eating simple street food or something from a fancy restaurant, it's inspirational and invigorating."

Is all this planning, all this responsibility and pressure, worth it? Universally, the women I talked to for this chapter said yes.

Yes to "this sense of accomplishment," says Wendy. And yes to this lack of fear. "Once you deliver your own baby, nothing is going to scare you on the work front."

Yes to "doing what I want to do," says Emmy. "As a parent, you are in service to another human being. You're in the service industry. There's a point where you feel like you're done taking care of other people at work, too, where you say, I want to do something for *me*."

Yes to finding a solution for now that'll serve an eventual future. Sarah Serafin asked her mother once if motherhood ever gets easier. "She told me, 'No, Sweetie, it just gets different,'" says Sarah. "Same way with life. But the more you make choices that nurture your inner self, your family, and the core values that you believe in, the more you will start to feel like you are living your own life, instead of waking up one day and thinking, 'Whose life *is* this? It sure doesn't feel like something I would have picked for myself . . .'" For that, and the freedom and flexibility her work offers her, Sarah is grateful. When her kids are older, she imagines, she may use her untouched photography and art degree, or the medical knowledge she's picked up through her transcribing. Or develop the skills she's gained working at tae kwon do. "When it's time, the opportunity will again present itself," she says. "And until then, I'm not going to stress about 'What am I going to do with my life,' because I'm already doing it. There is no destination, just a journey."

CHAPTER ELEVEN

✦

Master your new time "off"

Studies tell me that I am lucky to have been raised, in a true partnership, by a fantastic father. My dad's involvement in my childhood likely has helped make me more ambitious in my career, and more able to succeed in my own romantic relationship. But I don't need a bunch of PhDs to tell me that. I know how lucky I am because I rely on one crucial lesson my father taught me to get through most days as a working mother. Let me explain:

My dad is a giver, a guy who is currently spending his retirement rebuilding a local playground. Dad is the kind of man who crafts emails five hundred words long when you're down on your luck. "I love you, chin up" would be enough. Instead the guy writes a pep talk that would turn around the last at-bat at the bottom of the ninth of the most underdogged World Series of all time. My sister and I save his emails like they're pieces of jewelry. He supports, he encourages, he gives, gives, gives.

On the morning of the day of my wedding, Dad and I went for a run. I wanted "dirty" hair to better hold up my updo, and I figured I'd spend our three miles asking him for some marital advice, too. By then, he and my mom had made it through thirty-two years (and counting), four kids, two cross-country moves, and fourteen dogs and cats. Surely he'd done something right as a working partner and dad.

You know what he told me to do, this giver father of mine? Be selfish. Look out for number one. Put on my own oxygen mask before attending to my fellow passengers, even if they're my husband or my children, or my parents.

Dad actually spelled it out in a very premeditated order. He'd been thinking about this conversation for a while, it seemed. I present to you:

JAY R. SMITH'S ORDER OF LIFE PRIORITIES

Take care of your **country,** after you
take care of your **community,** after you
take care of your **friends,** after you
take care of your **extended family,** after you
take care of your **work,** after you
take care of your **children,** after you
take care of your **partner,** after you
take care of **yourself.**

Kind of radical, right? As we jogged along, I caught my breath long enough to argue a little bit. Why should your partner come before your children? ("So you are unified in your parenting, and so your children feel secure in that," Dad explained.) And why should your job come before your extended family—i.e., him, future Grandpa? ("Because your mom and I raised you to work, and by working you're making us proud. Also because your work will pay you, and with that money you will help support your husband and your kids.") It's not lost on me how lucky I am to have such a wise father, and—in true keeping with the list above—if I told him so, he would surely credit his partnership with my mother.

But it's honestly a little frustrating to have the Dalai Lama for a dad because here's the thing: *Life isn't always like that.* You can't just automatically prioritize your own self-care over everyone else's needs. And that is never more apparent than when you try like hell to "take care of number one" after having a baby and going back to work.

Here's what your first Saturday morning after your first week back at work might look like:

You are underslept (significantly underslept), and it occurs to you really for the very first time that you may never ever sleep in on a weekend again. Because the **baby** doesn't know that it's Saturday. You would like coffee, but should you have coffee? Will that affect your baby's morning nap if you nurse her after coffee? Before you can Google the answer, your **husband** emerges from the bedroom dressed in—are those workout clothes? Is he actually going for a run? Because no one ran the sterilizer last night, and the bottles from daycare yesterday are all still dirty and smelling like an expensive French cheese that you ate on your honeymoon. Oh, your honeymoon. When you had sex. Which is also something you used to like to do on Saturday mornings. But no thinking about sex, because then your **mother** calls to find out "how the sleeping is going," and your **friend** texts to find out if she can borrow the maternity dress that you wore to your **cousin**'s wedding (still need to send a gift! whoops!)—and BTW, don't forget to support Jane's run for tree-planting in the **community.** Checking the text, you also see that you missed a calendar notification for a **work** meeting that's been bumped smack into your pumping time on Tuesday, which was already jammed because it's Election Day and you'd planned to vote for the leadership of your **country.**

Something like that.

And you're supposed to take care of yourself *first*?! Does Starbucks deliver?

"I was really, really shocked when I first had my daughter how guilty I felt whenever I did things that were just entirely for me and not for her," says Eva Amurri Martino, actress and Happily Eva After blogger. "I was mourning the loss of being the multifaceted woman I was before. Like those pieces of my life just were gone." I relate, and that's one of the reasons that adjusting to the second baby was so much easier for me than the first. I knew that that mourning was only temporary. But back then, the first time around, it took me hundreds of deep breaths and several months of working motherhood to figure out the magic of my dad's list: It applied in the *long* term—not every hour, or even every week, but more like every six months-ish. Now I reassess seasonally: Have I taken care of my health? Has work usurped kids? Have I made my partner feel valued? Sure, I will have a rocky week when I'm on deadline for work. Or the kids will get sick and need every drop of patience I've got, sparing none for my sister or my spouse. Out-of-whack actually is the norm when you look at your life in tiny bites. But with a longer-term view, you can assess your attempts at prioritization (I will never call it "balance") more clearly. It's reassuring to see that you actually are doing "it all."

As for putting yourself first? I don't know any working mother alive who could color code her calendar and see that she'd given herself the most time. It's not about quantity. It's about satisfaction. This chapter will help you take happy advantage of what precious little personal time you have, so you can:

- find space to breathe
- take pleasure in your mornings, nights, and weekends with your family
- make work interruptions less annoying, and
- live a life that makes you ultimately better at your job.

Which leads us to . . .

A solution to the dreaded dilemma of "me-time"

I'm sorry to say, my survey data was downright dismal in this area. As I mentioned in Chapter 6, 79 percent of women reported that during their first three months back at work, they spent one hour or less per week doing something for themselves. Per week! Not

per day. Per week. One hour to take a walk alone or call a friend
or—gasp, horrors—read a magazine. ("That's definitely what gets
pushed aside in my life," says Rhode Island marine biologist Koty
Sharp. "Career Koty can function, and Mom Koty is doing really
well. But it's an effort to make sure I've saved time for Koty Koty,
too.") Before I got too depressed about this state of affairs, I dug
deeper into my stats and did some handy and enlightening cross
tabulation.

First, out of curiosity, I ran the math to check and see how
much worse the numbers would be for women who had more
demanding babies, babies with health problems. Surely they had
even less time to take for themselves. My assumption was dead
wrong: The percentage was the same! Of moms with sick babies,
almost the exact same percentage—78 percent—reported spending
one hour or less on themselves per week. Logical conclusion: This
extreme paucity of time spent on ourselves isn't due *only* to the
babies' needs. Sick babies have more needs: more appointments,
more pressure for mom to keep her health insurance, perhaps more
physical needs. And yet, their mothers weren't any less likely to
spend time on themselves. Interesting. Is this "no me-time" thing
something we do to serve our own minds and our own guilt, but
not necessarily our babies? Do we think it's our duty to neglect
ourselves?

Next, I looked at "me-time" versus the confidence women
reported in caring for their babies. (I'd asked what age their babies
were—from minute one to more than three months—when they
started feeling truly confident caring for them.) I discovered surprisingly little correlation. Mothers who spent less than one hour
per week on themselves started feeling confident with baby care
after about a month, on average. Mothers who spent one, two,
three, four, and five hours on themselves per week started feeling
confident at about a month, too. A month is just how long it takes,
it seems. The takeaway: Stealing time from yourself to care for
baby doesn't make you a better mom.

Finally, on a hunch, I cross tabbed the "me-time" numbers with those that reported whether or not women said they had a Working Mom Mentor (WMM) to look up to. Bingo. This was slightly more significant. Women who had a WMM were 6 percent more likely to spend one hour or more on themselves per week. They'd seen someone go through the transition successfully, and they confidently and optimistically granted themselves that extra little bit of self-care. Half the women I surveyed didn't have a WMM at all. Please, I implore you, let this book be your mentor. Its pages are full of mentors—women who've made it through, with lessons won the hard way and shared. And there was not a single happy, successful woman I talked to who didn't preach the gospel when it came to self-care.

But. (There's always a but with me.)

These women who preached self-care? They were realistic. Not one of them suggested that newly back-to-work moms schedule a luxurious weekly massage—or even spend time truly alone. Most of the women I spoke to said that they zoomed home at the end of their workdays to, yes, do the evening parenting rush. They woke up Saturday morning happy to hold their babies and not have to go to work. Their "off time" was rarely truly "off," and scheduling in "me-time" felt like a bit of a burden—one more thing they just weren't getting to.

The answer? Let's expand our definition of "me-time." It encompasses a lot.

Traditionally, of course, me-time is time spent alone, in your own skin, because it refreshes you to do something just for yourself. This kind of me-time is definitely worth the investment and forethought. "That return-on-investment matrix of what makes something worthwhile from a business perspective might get turned upside down from a personal perspective," says young-adult novelist (and former actress) Emmy Laybourne. "Because I think there are times when the investment of me paying a sitter $30 so I can get out and go to a yoga class is not very tangible, but it replenishes me. You have to figure out what those activities are for you and invest in them."

This kind of traditional me-time also keeps you from resenting your child—always a plus. "Someone was describing to me recently how her mother would say to her, as an adult, 'You don't know what I gave up for you,'" says Jennifer Justice, the entertainment lawyer and Superfly exec. "And it's like, you don't want to hear that. You didn't ask to be born. Don't tell us what you gave up. How is that good for anybody? I *never* wanted to do that to my kids." As a single mom of twins, JJ came around quickly to the idea that she needed a few hours of caregiver help on the weekends so she could carve out me-time. "I wasn't doing anything for myself before, and now I can go to a friend's birthday party and come back and walk the dog, too. It's huge."

But, me-time is also: time spent doing the things that make you feel happiest, and most like yourself—and that may include caring for other people. For example: It might bring you absolute joy to buy sweet little clothing for your baby girl on a sunny day. Is that shopping a chore just because it was a to-do and because your baby is with you in the carriage and because it robbed you of a napping opportunity on a Sunday afternoon off of work? No way. Or, let's say you have some volunteer work you love to do. I say: That qualifies as self-care. So does sex. Yes, your husband likes it, but if you do, too, that counts as me-time. And appreciating these not-technically-alone moments for the happiness they give you keeps you from feeling cheated and resentful. No one likes a martyr—least of all herself.

Some women's totally satisfying me-time looks a lot like . . . well, it looks a lot like work. When I ask Hilary Herrmann, a public school instructional coach coordinator in Fort Collins, Colorado, what she does for herself, she ponders that for a minute. "I think running errands counts," she says, "oh, and I started a once-a-month book club, and, oh,"—here she sounds genuinely excited—"I went back to school." School? That counts as downtime? "It's a way for me to be passionate and engage in some of the issues I'm not able to solve given the confines of my job," she says. "It energizes me, actually."

However you choose to define your me-time, get in the habit early on in your baby's life. The payoff as they grow is significant—and not just for your own sanity. "I think showing my children that I set aside time that is just for me is very important," says single mom of two Sarah Serafin, a medical transcriptionist. "It models the importance of self-care to them, and it teaches them that Mom isn't just Mom. She's a person, a special, unique person just like they are, who deserves this time."

The morning rush and the evening sprint—solved

Dark confession: A couple of weeks before I went back to work the first time, I lurked around a particularly candid (read: lurid, ridiculous) mommy board online where women shared advice and chit-chat on everything from MIL (mother-in-law) madness, to SAHM (stay-at-home-mom) frustrations, to baby nipple confusion (and DHs—dear husbands—who went to strip clubs and suffered their own form of nipple confusion, too). This new world of mom talk was eye-opening. I watched from afar but never posted anything myself until I couldn't stand the one burning question in my brain one more second: *How in holy hell were my mornings going to work?* On leave, I barely had my act together and my teeth brushed by 11:00 a.m., and yet, overnight, I was going to become capable of launching both the baby and my (best, work-ready) self for the day by eight o'clock? *What?* The WOHMs (work-outside-the-home moms) on the board had decent advice that boiled down to this:

- Ask your nanny to come earlier than you think you need her.
- Shower at night.

- Prep your pump supplies, outfit, daycare bag the night before.
- Try not to worry—you'll figure it out!!!!!!!! ;(

Those tips were helpful, truly (less helpful were the weirdos who asked me why I had a baby if I was only going to abandon him for ten hours a day—and thus, I promptly left the mommy message board world). But the bigger piece of advice I ended up learning, on my own, the hard way was:

- choose the couple of morning baby-care things you most enjoy—and outsource the rest.

This applied for evening baby care, too. I had assumed that mornings would be the messy part and that coming home would be a blissful end-of-day reunion with my little boo. The cuddles were sweet—but bath time, the three feedings (two for him, one for me and my husband), the calls and emails from the office, the emergency baby Tylenol drugstore run for teething, the diaper changes, the spit-up changes, the crib sheet changes, and let us not forget the pile of thank-you notes unwritten: So much to handle in that short evening window. A Pew survey found that 40 percent of working mothers say they always feel rushed. *Always.* This is no joke. Kim, a pediatrician and neuroscientist, told me that during the first few months back at work she started wearing only shoes that slipped on and off. "That way I didn't waste time taking them off when I walked in the door at the end of the day," Kim explains. The few seconds of unlacing before she could wash up and hold her baby were just that annoying to her. Hilary, the educational coordinator, says that before she had children, she used to come home from work so fried that she could hardly talk to her husband for an hour—"It was just, hand me a glass of wine and let me cook." That was pre-kids. "Then after having a baby, I was like, 'Oh my gosh, I haven't seen you all day and you're only going to be awake for two more hours, and I have to feed you, and clean out the pump parts, and make dinner, and make sure I have milk-free clothes for tomorrow," she says. More things to do. On less sleep and less energy.

"The biggest area of guilt for the working mothers I work with is feeling like they don't have enough time with their kids," says Rachel Cedar, founder of You Plus 2 Parenting, a counseling service for new moms of two. "And when they do get home, it's that time of day that's so full of transitions—dinner, bed, bath—that you immediately feel overwhelmed and not your best self, and it's not how you want to spend your time." The most important thing for your own happiness, says Cedar, "is really establishing a connection with your child in the time that you do have." Here's how you do that each evening:

Mentally shed work (see "Secret Weapon: Your Commute" later in this chapter and step five on page 166 for advice on how to make that emotional and logistical transition). And yes, that means putting your phone away, insists Samantha Boardman, MD, psychiatrist and founder of the blog Positive Prescription. "Technology distances us," she says. "The time that you do spend with your baby, really *be with* your baby, not in some half-there place."

Assess where your baby is in his or her routine so you don't inadvertently disrupt it.

Actively do only the handful of manageable baby-care tasks that give you the most satisfaction. The idea: If you're enjoying them, your baby will feel that connection you crave.

In my survey, I asked women to rank ten baby tasks according to how much they enjoyed them. Of course you should optimize the ones that bring *you* the most satisfaction, but here's how the ranking panned out overall:

1) dressing the baby (71 percent ranked this in their top three)
2) bathing the baby (59 percent ranked this in their top three)
3) getting the baby up from nap or night sleep
4) tummy time with baby

5) putting baby down to sleep

6) diapering baby

7) organizing the baby gear, gifts, nursery

8) attending pediatrician visits

9) doing the baby's laundry

10) writing thank-you notes for baby gifts (55 percent ranked this dead last!)

I related to number one; I loved dressing my babies and was able to shift their morning schedules and mine around to get in that one simple little pleasure daily. It gave me a palpable sense of comfort to sit at my desk and picture my son strolling around the neighborhood, without me, but dressed in tiny overalls that I'd chosen for him myself. In order to have that, I gave up doing his morning bath and made that an end-of-afternoon activity that he did with our nanny. I wish I had done more of that conscious shifting of duties, and I urge you to—and no judgment about what duties you do and don't like.

Hayley, a lawyer in Cleveland who adopted three babies within three years, outsources her kids' meals entirely to their daycare, which stays open late. "It drives my mother crazy that we don't have dinner with our kids, but it just didn't work. We would get home, they'd be starved, and I would still have to cook. They'd end up fighting and overtired. Now that we let them eat at daycare, when we get home at the end of the day it can just be playtime." Another hidden bonus of this plan is the stories she gets at the end of the day when the teachers make the kid hand-off. They're not swarmed by the earlier 5:00 p.m. rush, so they have time to talk. "One day I walked in and they were all laughing because my oldest, who's three, had led the dinnertime discussion among the kids to debate which teacher had the biggest boobies," says Hayley. "I was like, Of course he did. That's Finley."

After having her twin boys, Monica started arriving at her job forty-five minutes later, at 9:30, to give herself more time with them in the morning—time in which they do . . . well, not much, actually! "I made that change when I realized it was too hard to leave them in the bouncers while I got myself ready. Now my husband gets the boys up and leaves at seven, and I don't even start getting myself ready until eight, when our nanny comes. That hour is a good hour. I don't change them. I don't feed them breakfast. We just have a really nice life at home in the mornings." Monica says her most vivid memories of her own dad, a surgeon, were of him picking her up after she'd fallen asleep waiting up late at night to see him. "I saw him never, ever, ever," she says. "And so it's really important that my kids see me—even if it's time spent just hanging out."

"I have given over a lot of the domestic stuff," says Andrea Olshan, the real estate CEO. "But certain things matter to me and I've held on to those. Someone once said to me, 'I can't give it all up because then I don't feel human.' I appreciate that. So I go to the grocery store myself on the weekends, always. I pick out their clothes at night, even when I know I'm going to be traveling on business so it's a little piece of Mommy that's there. So they can see that I care. I think it matters to them to hear that 'Mommy made this chicken,' even if I'm at a board meeting while they're eating it. I can't guarantee that I'll be able to be at dinner, but I'm a morning person, so we have breakfast together. It's about doing what you *can* do. You have to give up control over the other stuff."

And please, no guilt allowed over the things you beg out of. "You're actually not supposed to know how to do all of this," says Cedar. "Grant yourself that grace!" While you're at it, rope in your partner morning and evening if you're lucky enough to have one who's around. Important distinction: You are not asking him to help, like he's your assistant. You are asking him to be your partner in caring for all members of the family, yourself included. There may be things (especially lactational things) that he can't do for you. Fine, suggests Cedar, then have him take care of you. "Just think about where you are struggling the most—like, 'I'm not eating breakfast in the morning, and that's making me cranky while I'm feeding the baby; can you please bring me a bagel?' A bagel can make a huge difference." I think I'm going to see if someone on Etsy can put that on a bumper sticker for me: A bagel can make a huge difference.

On the pressure to spend your off-time "bonding" (a sneaky little argument that will earn you a cocktail)

You know that sweet way that you can lie down on your back with your knees bent and perch your baby on your lap facing you? I have a picture of myself doing this with my newborn baby brother Tyler when I was fifteen years old, and that became my visual for what bonding with my own baby would be one day: knees up, staring soulfully into each other's eyes. Don't get me wrong, it's dreamy when it happens, but I realize now that Tyler and I were able to enjoy all that knees-up time because (duh) we had a mom taking care of us doing all the mom things. All I had to do was my homework. Expectations adjusted, I learned with my own babies that you can get in some good eye gazing while changing a diaper, or when baby is in the car seat perched atop a shopping cart in line at the drugstore while you buy contact lens solution. Infants aren't so choosy about candlelight and roses. They just like to connect.

Not convinced? Here's some quick math: In my survey, women reported spending an average of fifty-six minutes each workday morning with their babies. Of that time, fifty minutes were spent caring for the baby (additionally, mothers spent twenty-seven minutes getting themselves ready without the baby). That means that women spent a whopping *six minutes* each morning simply "enjoying" the baby. And on average, these same women (73 percent) were fully in love with their babies by age two weeks. You'd better believe some of that bonding time was happening at the changing pad.

A recent study of babies' cortisol levels at night backs me up. Researchers measured the effects of mothers' emotional availability during routine baby-care tasks on infants' stress hormone levels and found a very cool correlation: Three-month-old infants whose moms were more emotionally available during typical bedtime tasks had lower stress reactivity and developed earlier circadian patterning (aka, they slept better) than infants whose mothers didn't use these quotidian duties as opportunities to bond. (This is also, by the way, yet another argument for longer paid maternity leave: It's beneficial to have Mom home for bedtime during these early months.)

So: You're off the hook. Knees-up bonding time isn't so crucial as long as you approach the more routine stuff lovingly—which, of course you do.

Here's where the promise of cocktails comes in!

Let's shift any concerns you have about spending your "off" time bonding right over to a whole different (and perhaps more beneficial) bonding outlet: friends.

Four factors significantly predict women's adjustment to motherhood, research suggests: "Feeling unconditionally loved, feeling comforted when in distress, authenticity in relationships, and satisfaction with friendships." Sure, a quality marriage can provide these things as well, but friends were key. Specifically mom friends made right after childbirth. This particular brand of friendship improves new mothers' mental health, increases their sense of self-efficacy, and provides ongoing "reassurance that their babies are developing normally." I'm sure none of this shocks you. Friends are good. Friends who are there for you during stressful times in your career and marriage are even better.

But honestly, who has the time?!

(You do, remember, because you just got permission to quit scheduling in bonding time with your baby.)

But what if you already have more friends than you have time for?

Those friends, the true ones who just happen to not have a newborn right when you do, will sit tight and hang on. My three closest friends when I had Will were (a) just recovering from a miscarriage, (b) trying to figure out whether or not to get engaged, and (c) overseas photographing a war zone. I'll love them forever, but they weren't necessarily the best sources for nipple-shield advice.

So, here's what you're looking for in these new friendships: Similar political beliefs and educational background and likeminded taste in books, restaurants, vacation spots, and iPhone cases. Just kidding. None of that matters at all. Here's the *only* thing that you need to have in common with the women who will quickly become your lifeline: a baby, about the same age as yours. That's it.

Tech industry director and sales team leader Stephanie was still fairly new to town and new to her position at work when she had her daughter—and much of her pregnancy had been spent in emergency mode dealing with breast cancer treatment and a maternity leave that included a mastectomy. If anyone didn't have time to make new friends, it was Stephanie. But if anyone needed friends, it was also Stephanie. At the suggestion of a neighbor, she joined a local mothers' club in the Bay Area. "It just bonds you one thousand percent," she says. "I was surprised by the diversity of the mothers in the group who I befriended; you have to be openminded. It forces you to meet and understand people you normally wouldn't. You have this one major thing in common, and that is enough. It expands your world."

Pediatricians' offices often have new parent discussion groups. Check your local breastfeeding supply shop or baby store. Go to a postnatal yoga class. Or just search on Facebook with the name of your town or neighborhood and "moms." Chances are, a group exists. "I call it 'tall person time,'" says Sarah Serafin, who works from home. "It's just so helpful to surround yourself with people who are used to wet pants, runny noses, and reasoning with short people who speak broken English."

This is not a time to be shy. As a second-time mom, Rachel Cedar was comfortable enough to stand up at a mommy-and-baby class and essentially ask for friends. "I told people to come up to me afterward if they were interested, and I was flooded," she says.

"That little playgroup that resulted went on for about a year and then people started to slowly drift apart or move away, but for that specific moment in time, it was so great."

This was my own experience as well. In my fog of postpartum, I remember walking down Second Avenue a couple of blocks from my apartment and taking a flyer from someone who was handing them out—it must have been a moment of weakness or sleep deprivation, because everyone in New York City knows: *You never take the flyer.* But clutching the paper in my hand the next day, I walked into a dingy sports bar where the new mothers' group the flyer advertised was meeting in the back, eating limp salads. Never had a restaurant experience been better for me. I walked out of there with three new friends, also on maternity leave with baby boys. Back at work, Marni, Allison, Tara, and I reserved one night a month to pump a bottle, leave the babies, and go out. The husbands dealt, because the other husbands dealt, and peer pressure can be a useful thing! We talked in gory detail about the stuff no one else in my life particularly wanted to hear about (the best laundry spray for poop stain removal, the pain of sex after stitches), and they opened my eyes to the work environments and maternity leave policies of three fields that were different from my own. See? All that time I thought I was drinking wine, I was actually developing my career.

"You expand your network professionally," with these slightly inorganic friendships, says Stephanie. "Everyone's navigating the transition together, as you figure out childcare options, and how to balance everything. It's just really critical." Sure enough, Tara once hooked me up with her company's recruiter. I interviewed Allison for a story I wrote for a magazine earlier this year. Marni connected me to new sources in Florida for the survey for this book even after she eventually moved away.

A P.S. here: Some women find time with their single friends to be an enormously helpful escape from all things baby. If *not* talking about diapers is exactly what you need now, just go in knowing that these people—like all people—will complain about being "busy" and you will have to smile and nod and remember blissfully how that word used to mean something different to you, too.

(But also: doing nothing *can* count as something)

I'm dead set against scheduled bonding with your baby. But what about those wonderful found moments of doing truly nothing together? Pinch yourself so you remember them and appreciate them.

Some of police officer Cristyn Zett's most treasured memories from her son's infancy were just these moments. Gavin, who has Down syndrome, had to be woken up in the night to eat as he was recovering from heart surgery. Cristyn and her husband timed it so his feeding coincided with his mom's return from her late-night work shift. "I was in the vice unit at the time, in prostitution, gambling, bars, so my work was from six at night until two in the morning," she recalls. "I'd come home, and two to three-thirty in the morning was just mine and Gavin's time. I was tired, but it was just us. No phones ringing, no one coming in and out, none of the grind of baby stuff like tummy time. Just Mommy and Gavin time. I have to say that was actually my favorite part of going back to work."

Secret weapon: your commute

My survey respondents said that after having a baby, their commute was 49 percent more stressful. Is it any wonder? Time is more precious than it's ever been, and minutes spent wasted in traffic or on a stalled train are maddening. You aren't at work to do work. You aren't at home to do home. You're just stuck there, between your two lives.

But actually, there's the magic. For years, I carried around a poem that my friend KaRyn wrote for me in college after I revealed that I loved time on airplanes because of this very in-between-ness. It was just a little sentiment I'd revealed in passing, but she'd elevated it to lovely stanzas that I kept with me in my wallet to remind me of the beauty of being someplace unreachable. You're neither here, nor there. You're just in transition. Of course, these days, most of us are pretty reachable as we commute, but that opens up the possibilities for how you can best use this found time. You can . . .

USE IT TO WORK. This one is obvious, and it's likely something you did even before having a baby. Several mothers told me that they use their car time for conference calls, scheduling them at the end of the afternoon, so they can leave the office a bit early but keep working the full day. Sarah M., who works at a museum developing its children's programming, saves up her research and planning to-dos each day, doing Pinterest craft searches—one of the most fun parts of her job—on her train ride home to the burbs. A couple of other interviewees told me that they have a "commute" folder in their email to answer messages that can wait 'til the end of the day. (If you're driving, a dictation app is helpful!)

USE IT FOR SELF-CARE. Therapist Sarah Best encourages many of her patients to figure out how to use their commute to do a little self-care. "Many of the women I work with are living with a postpartum mood or anxiety disorder, but anyone can benefit," Best says. "They're working all day and parenting all night long, and maybe not sleeping well yet. So these twenty or forty-five minutes can be so useful for self-soothing." Best tells her patients to think of their five senses and come up with some plan to please at least one of them. "Maybe that's listening to a podcast, or having a really delicious snack that also gives you some nutrition. Or applying some fancy hand cream you love the smell of." This is not just about indulging yourself; it's about tricking your nervous system into chilling out. Best unpacks the science better than I could: "The sympathetic nervous system is 'fight or flight'—that's the stress. Its counterpart, the parasympathetic nervous system, we call 'feed and breed,' so pleasure is how we counteract stress," she explains. Cool, right? "If you find yourself calmed by the intro to the *Serial* podcast, you hear those first chords and you're like, Ahhhhhh, that's a way to get the parasympathetic nervous system going so the stress part of the system cannot fire with as much passion."

USE IT AS FRIEND TIME. Sarah M. also uses her commute as friend catch-up time, especially with other mothers who she knows are hard to pin down in person. "Some of my friends have just had babies and are home; another is a stay-at-home mom; another works but gets home an hour before I do. I know it's a time I can reach all of them. It's not the same as seeing them in person, but it's nice to have that connection."

USE IT FOR EXERCISE. Admittedly, this isn't possible for most moms, so if you're lucky enough to live within walking distance of your job, use that benefit. When Rachel Cedar lived in New York, she would even triple multitask: "I'd ask my sitter to bring the baby to my office on her way home, and then he and I would do what I called a stroller dinner," she says. "I would walk home, feeding the baby a bottle along the way. You have to be creative. I'd get exercise; he'd get extra Mommy time."

USE IT TO TRANSITION INTO HOME MODE. Your commute can be the transportation equivalent of changing into comfy pants. "When you get home, your brain has to unpack before you can truly *be* there," says Stephanie. "Otherwise I'll be singing a song to Caroline but be thinking, 'Oh gosh, I owe this person these three things before I go to bed.'" It's a complicated tap dance, and to avoid falling on her face, Stephanie has learned to actually schedule in transition time, whether she's returning home from a normal day or a longer work trip. "You are really at your best when you have had ten minutes to just gather your thoughts. Then you're focused."

One last note on commuting: Figure out how to de-schlep your schlep, because the less you have to carry, the less stress you carry too, it seems. Some moms buy two pumps or rent a locker at the gym ("Make the investment and the time—it's motivating," urges Rachel Cedar). Others use their car trunks as a secondary closet for a change of shoes, extra diapers for daycare, or dress-up event accessories. Or snacks. I say always have snacks.

Some extremely brief thoughts about your vacation time

If you are lucky enough to have vacation time (and/or if you were prescient enough to save yourself some post–maternity leave—current preggies, take note!), I have two words to say:

Take it.

Your time "off" for parental leave was not vacation. If you treat it as such by forgoing future *actual* paid time off, you may unwittingly denigrate the meaning of parental leave for those who follow you.

Take it.

And how to keep your weekend sacred(ish)

Crazy, revolutionary thought: Time away from work makes you better at your job. Jessica DeGroot, the founder and president of the ThirdPath Institute, counsels individuals, couples, and workplaces on how to have what she calls an "integrated career path" that marries home and work in a way that's beneficial all around. "We've worked with a whole bunch of leaders who've followed this path—male and female leaders who really moved ahead in their careers and also made time for their lives," DeGroot explains. "And what we learned is that there's a skill set that all of these individuals are using. Not only does it allow them to work in a way that they have time for life. It actually *improves* how they're getting their work done." It's a strong case for taking a real weekend off. But, look, everyone's got a boss or clients. And sometimes they need you. Here's how to do the Saturday and Sunday shuffle.

BE AVAILABLE BUT NOT *ALWAYS* AVAILABLE. As a professor and executive coach in Atlanta, Laura Morgan Roberts, PhD, teaches her clients the importance of image management. And as a mom of two in a travel-heavy, high-visibility job, she takes her own advice on the weekends. "Sometimes we think that managing your image means, 'Oh, I have to be responsive and reply to an email immediately because I don't want anyone to think I'm not committed,'" Roberts explains. "But an impulsive, immediate response is not always going to be the one that best demonstrates leadership abilities." Barring any emergency, it's actually better, says Roberts, to make people wait six or twelve hours so you can think first. One client she was advising was tempted to engage in a back-and-forth debate with the boss over the weekend. She told that client to cool it and collect his thoughts and then reply—later. "Remember, what we put in writing, even over email or text, is on the record. If you want senior executives to pay attention, take the time later to format your response. It can even be an attached Word document that requires being opened." That sends the signal that you've put in real thought. And if something's important enough to interrupt your time off, it should look like it.

TAKE A SCHEDULED "WORK BREAK." My beloved father-in-law David coined this term to describe how he worked in his early post-divorce years, while still managing to parent three young sons. On the days he had custody, he would shuttle them around to school and sports, ducking into his at-home office for a couple of hours at a time whenever he could.

If you have a job that requires you to get a chunk of work done on the weekends—or if it'll simply make your week more manageable, schedule a work break. In my experience, weekends only get ruined when you're constantly distracted. As best you can, plan a window (I recommend Saturday morning so you can get it out of the way), and use it with full concentration. Weekends don't have to be forty-eight straight hours of family time, says Rachel Cedar: "It's so amusing and fun to be together as a little family on the weekend, but it's important for women to understand that it's okay to ask your partner to take over." (Or a sitter if your partner is working or you're on your own.) Make that "work break" part of your weekend routine from the beginning, she suggests, and "you and your partner will see the value in that—the value is, you don't spend the whole weekend freaking out."

LET THE BACKGROUND MUSIC OF WORK INSPIRE YOU. Professor Roberts may not reply to work emails in real time—but she does read them and start thinking as she takes her kids to birthday parties, or drives to Friday-night dinner out. Because she knows she's got time scheduled to address whatever's come up, work is like background music, just humming along distantly. In DeGroot's experience, that processing time leads to higher-quality results. When you take breaks, DeGroot explains, "your brain is percolating. Without even trying to, you come back afterward and there's that brilliant answer to that problem."

What if your version of percolation/background music sounds more like a teakettle's shrieking? (Apologies for the over-metaphorication.) Time your email checks to give yourself the most control. This might require being more disciplined about toggling between two accounts—one for work, one for personal life. But if you craft a system for yourself—checking once per day at the beginning of nap time, or on Sunday evening when the markets open in Japan—you'll quickly stop feeling the guilt of avoidance. Your next check-in is scheduled.

And until then? Live your life! Be in the world, mother your child, and interact with the very customers you serve in your job. And know in your heart: Your "off" time makes you better in your career.

CHAPTER TWELVE

❧

Eighteen life-changing conversations

How to Initiate Them, and Exactly What to Say

Raise your hand if you love confrontation. Great, hi. Now, keep your hand up if you also love confrontation while sleep deprived. Awesome, thanks. You guys don't need this chapter.

Now that those two women are gone, can the millions of us left be honest? These conversations around employment and parenting are heart-wrenching and hard, even for women who negotiate for a living. I talked to business school professors and Hollywood talent managers and big-city lawyers—people who argue professionally!—who weren't sure how to advocate for themselves when they needed things like flextime or a place to pump. One woman I interviewed is an auctioneer, who talks a mile a minute selling precious art, but admits that she still sometimes has a hard time finding her voice with her mom when she disagrees with her advice. Sometimes you just need someone to give you the words (and a pep talk).

So first, here's that pep talk to motivate you to deal with your new work dilemmas and needs in a productive and empowering way. Then, with help from women who've been there, I'll spell out the specific words and strategies that'll get you through those conversations—and a big armful of sticky personal-life situations, too. (Did I mention my marriage came with two mothers-in-law? Hi, Neddy and Grammy Bo, love you!)

Why it's so darn important that new working moms ask for what they need (otherwise known as: your pep talk)

Don't even think about chickening out. Let me convince you so you can convince them. Here are seven compelling reasons you should initiate these conversations. (Besides the obvious: so you get what you want!)

THE SOONER YOU ASK, THE BETTER YOU'LL DO. Want to change job duties? Work different hours? You may not know what you want or need until you're back at work, and that's fine. But for anything you do anticipate in advance, don't wait! Asking early makes your request even more likely to get a yes. With enough notice, your employer can use your appeal as an opportunity to train some up-and-comer to do the very duty you're dreading, says Marcy Axelrad, Global Senior Director of Talent Operations at the online furniture and decor giant Wayfair. "I coach a lot of our women to start having those conversations around the four- or five-month mark of pregnancy, as soon as you're comfortable talking about the pregnancy," says Axelrad. "There are a lot of ongoing conversations at Wayfair that take place with employees about the different areas they want to explore and take on." That way if someone who's having a baby wants to travel less, HR has already identified which employees are looking to travel more. And the transition feels beneficial all around. The up-and-comer isn't going to feel dumped on. It's well planned, Axelrad explains: "It's not 'Hey, Marcy, Susan doesn't want to do this anymore;' it's 'Hey, Marcy, I know you've expressed an interest in developing more client relationships. We're going to be shifting some things around. If you're still interested, let's give it a try.'"

YOUR REQUEST MAY ACTUALLY *IMPROVE THE COMPANY.* Says Lindsey Pollak, Millennial workplace expert at The Hartford insurance company: "If you as an individual can put your request in the context of cultural change—that it's not just me wanting something, that this is the way the workplace is changing, that these policies are going to be important moving forward, I can be an example of why we are a good employer for Millennials—all of that builds toward a broader story." Nobody wants to be an exception to the rule, explains Pollak: "They want to be part of a larger movement, and when you put yourself in that context it's a lot easier for people to understand you're not getting special treatment because you're having a precious child." Your company may just not know what it needs yet!

FOR THE RECORD, YOU ARE N-O-T ASKING FOR A BLEEPING "ACCOM-MODATION." You guys already know how I feel about the term "mommy guilt" (see page 39). My other least favorite word is "accommodation." And the experts share my pet peeve. "If you feel like you're asking for a concession, the company's going to feel that way too," says Axelrad. "Often, these conversations are approached in a negative way, as a conflict, or as an accommodation, versus, here's my business proposal of what's going to work for both of us, and I'd love to take you through it. It's positive. How you put yourself out there makes a *huge* difference."

At the ThirdPath Institute in Philadelphia, founder and president Jessica DeGroot uses a different term entirely: "We call it a 'work redesign,' looking at your work to say, How could I do this work very effectively in a new way?" explains DeGroot. "You're not asking for a favor. You're saying here is a logical solution." She's seen it work again and again, even among her clients who are stuck in what she calls a "work-first culture" (isn't her vocab great?). "Uniformly, what all of our successful cases did was get really clear in their request that they weren't asking to work poorly, they were asking to work differently." Got that? Breathe it in. You are not being accommodated. You are providing a mutual solution.

IGNORANCE IS IN NO WAY BLISS. "We found in The Hartford's research that Millennials tend to know less than other generations about what their benefits actually are," says Pollak. "Reading the fine print arms you with information for negotiation, perhaps with a member of an older generation who may also not know what's available." This kind of research comes into play again and again in the successful conversations described below. Bosses want to be able to say yes. They want to keep you. Give them the backup that they'll need to cite to their own boss when they pass the request up the ladder.

ASK FOR THINGS THE RIGHT WAY, AND YOU'LL PROVE HOW VALU-ABLE YOU ARE. That research I mention above? It shows you've got chops. If you can negotiate with your boss in an informed and cool way, she'll know you're able to do that with your clients and customers, too.

OUR COUNTRY IS ABSURD ON THESE ISSUES, AND IT'S NOT YOUR FAULT. I talked to psychiatrist Christin Drake, MD, about how anxious many women get about having these conversations, and I found her perspective truly comforting and inspiring: "It is a unique situation of the American working mother that we have to ad hoc negotiate these things for ourselves," she says. "We're left to our own devices in terms of this planning but also, more important, in terms of the judgments we make about ourselves in the process. Recognizing that can quiet the noise in your mind a bit as you go into those meetings. Your new working motherhood is full of benefits to your workplace—that's recognized everywhere else in the world. We are assets, not liabilities. Feel that. And negotiate with that in mind."

AND ALSO, NO PRESSURE, BUT WE'RE ALL DEPENDING ON YOU. "Parental leave benefits are going to have to be driven not by policy but by individuals and a culture of individual companies," says start-up culture analytics expert Corey McAveeney of CultureAmp. Damn straight. A whopping 97 percent of Millennials want flexibility in their work hours and their time-off options, so know that you've got an army of expectant women coming up right behind you, begging you to lead the way. Says Wayfair's Axelrad: "Of course factors like team size matter, but as more and more companies see that they have a lot of really high-performing women trying different approaches—like physically being in the office three days a week—and that there's no negative impact to the company, more and more women will feel comfortable changing the culture." Someone just has to go first.

MAJOR P.S.: GET ALL WORK-RELATED MATERNITY AGREEMENTS IN WRITING. If you've spoken in person or on the phone, recap the conversation in an email to your supervisor to make sure you're clear on the details and ask for confirmation. Then save that email. Bosses leave. Reporting structures change. Companies get bought. You're going to want that backup.

Ten talks that will get you what you need at work

HOW TO ASK FOR A RAISE AT THIS AWKWARD MOMENT

The simple answer here is: Ask for it the exact same way you would any other time you deserved a change in compensation.

The more complicated answer is: Ask for it the exact same way you'd ask for it at any other deserving time . . . with the knowledge, in the back of your mind, that your employer may feel that he or she has already "accommodated" you this year.

Many women I spoke to felt a tremendous pressure to increase their earnings coming back to work. Some of the financial stress is practical (you have childcare to pay for), and some of it is emotional (you want to feel that working is worth it; and any inequity in compensation with your peers, or any overdue raise, is just really going to chap your hide now). Go ahead and talk about all that stress and swirl—with your partner, your family, your friends. But at work, focus entirely on performance.

"Asking for a raise is all business," says Deborah Grayson Rie-gel, MSW, PCC, Principal, the Boda Group, a leadership and team development firm, and founder of Talk Support, a communication coaching company. "Go in knowing that the least valid reason to ask for a raise is because you need more money, so take the personal out of it." And then dive right in. "Women undersell themselves, and I think organizations take advantage of that," Riegel says. Here's how to approach compensation like a pro:

GAME THE TIMING. You may feel mounting pressure with each paycheck, but "save your ask for when the time is right based on track record, and hopefully based on a previous conversation," says Riegel. What is your company's fiscal year? When are budgets most flush, and when is the pot dry? If you haven't discussed a bump in compensation previously, you may need to lay the groundwork now, with documentable goals, and then pick up the conversation again at an agreed-upon date.

ANTICIPATE THEIR POST-LEAVE HESITATION ... but then don't stoop to it. If you make a case entirely based on performance and deliverables, that frames the conversation and will make it more obviously wrong for your boss to lean on your leave as an excuse. But she or he may still go there. "If they say, 'But you were just on leave,' I would get curious and calmly ask what they mean by that," instructs Riegel. It's not rude, it's a dance that will progress the conversation in real terms. "Then if they talk about the cost of covering for you while you were out, you can say that what they're describing is the company's job to do—paying for a fill-in—not yours. It shouldn't come out of your compensation. It should really be a line item in their budget. It shouldn't be your burden that they have had to accommodate what they've legally had to do for you." This should steer the conversation back to performance.

FINALLY, MAKE YOUR CASE. Like I said, the advice here has nothing to do with your new status as a parent. How would you normally make a clear, calm, and informed case for a change in compensation that reflects your experience and contributions? That's exactly what you should do now.

HOW TO ADVOCATE TO CHANGE AN UNFAIR POLICY

When Holly, a lawyer in the Pacific Northwest (I've changed her name and identifying details), and her husband applied to adopt after years of infertility struggles, she was relieved to have found a path to motherhood and to be, as she calls it, "paper pregnant." Then she looked into her firm's maternity leave policy and was devastated to find out that while birth mothers received twelve weeks' paid leave, adoptive moms only got two. "It felt like a slap in the face," she says. "Not only can you not get pregnant, but you also don't count as a mom. I couldn't believe it." One partner told her she was essentially like a father since she wasn't giving birth. "I lost it, I was like, No I'm not. I freaked out, and then I decided to fight the policy," she says. (That partner should also look up the research on the importance of father/infant bonding. Just a side note. Anyway, back to Holly.)

Ever the lawyer, Holly started doing her research, calling around to every other similar law firm in town and getting copies of their (universally more generous) policies. She also reached out to the Dave Thomas Foundation, an adoption advocacy nonprofit, whose experts helped inform her argument but also were clear with her that her firm was within its rights. "Still," says Holly, "it just felt like discrimination, plain and simple, and that's what I told my firm, that I shouldn't be penalized just because I couldn't give birth." She spelled out her research to every colleague and superior who would listen and sent it by email to her associate class's adviser. He listened and moved it up the chain. Holly kept talking . . . and waiting. "It was a really fine line," she says, "making my case but still making it clear how much I loved working at the firm—that this was purely a policy issue. Sometimes I had to double back and explain so I didn't offend my colleagues."

Still, change didn't come quickly enough. With the months of her "paper pregnancy" ticking by, Holly decided to leave the firm she loved for a competitor that offered twelve weeks' paid leave. "I wasn't angry, more sad than anything else," she recalls. "Because I liked where I worked, I liked the people I worked with, I didn't want to have to leave, but I also wanted to be treated fairly."

At her new job, she kept in touch, cordially, with her old employer, and seven months later they called with an offer to hire her back, this time with the promise of six weeks' paid leave, a compromise. "I knew it was still not enough," says Holly. "We couldn't afford for me to take six additional unpaid weeks, but I took it as a sign of progress. I knew they were trying. So I went back."

Five months after that, Holly and her husband got another call: Baby Mack had been born. Premature, and with complications, he was in the NICU for weeks—weeks that Holly wisely and openly made work to her advantage. "I didn't want my six weeks of paid leave to start ticking until he was home," she says. "So I went to the hospital every day for morning rounds and then right to work. Days when he had tests and I wanted to be there with him, I worked from the hospital. I was still showing my connection to work, my dedication, and I think they saw that." Once home with baby Mack, she extended her leave a bit by working one day a week. "I didn't completely let go of work, ever, but I made my own model."

Sure enough, by the time Holly and her husband adopted their next child, the firm had changed the policy fully. "Now it's twelve weeks paid for all mothers," says Holly proudly. "Adoption is a life-changing, monumental event that happens so suddenly. You get the call: Come and get this baby, and you're a parent, just like that. With Mack we didn't have any supplies in the house; we hadn't wanted to get our hopes up. Then to have had only two weeks to be home with him and get settled into parenthood? That would have been crazy." And because she'd been honest, open, measured, informed—and then brave enough to act—her firm woke up. She'd made real change.

HOW TO ASK YOUR EMPLOYER TO RESCHEDULE SOMETHING FOR AFTER YOUR MATERNITY LEAVE

Cristyn, the Pittsburgh police lieutenant, has great advice here. She had originally planned to split her leave so she would come back to work after six weeks and then take the remainder of her time away for her son's impending heart surgery. "Then he got stuck in the NICU and the pediatric unit decided to move up his surgery, so I decided to take all of the leave at once instead," she recalls. Seems reasonable, but her department had supervisor training scheduled right in the middle of that time. Her boss, who didn't know when the department would be able to offer that training again, tried to convince her to come in for a few days. "It wasn't malicious," says Cristyn. "It was just kind of thoughtless. Maybe the guy just had never dealt with what it's like when they're going to cut your baby's chest open. I wanted to worry about absolutely nothing other than my baby in that moment." Surely there was some work-around the city could come up with—and to inspire her boss to get creative, Cristyn found just the right words. "I said, if you make me come back and anything bad happens in the surgery, I will never be able to face myself." The implication: She wouldn't be able to face her boss or the job either. It worked. They rescheduled.

HOW TO ASK FOR FLEXTIME

"Hit a wall, find a work-around. That's an expression I use a lot," says big-tech exec Stephanie. Before landing at her current company, where she helped launch some of its well-known women's initiatives, Stephanie worked at creative advertising agencies. As both an employee and manager there, she says, "I always found that a lot of life balance was just asking for stuff. So many people would be at their desks, frustrated that they couldn't get home, couldn't coach soccer or whatever their individual desire was, but it occurred to me that I could probably do both as long as my productivity wasn't compromised. I never worked for a company that wasn't willing to be flexible, provided you brought them the solution." Stephanie's current work hours allow her to attend her daughter's swim class on Friday mornings, coming in late, and staying late to make up the time. Her advice:

GIVE THEM CONTEXT. Remember that companies often won't offer flexible hours because they have no way of knowing what's important to you outside of the office. Obviously, you need an awareness of the environment and culture you work in before you start spelling out the personal details of the "why" of your request—and no need to air your dirty laundry—but be as open and clear as common sense allows. "I would feel uneasy simply saying to my boss, 'Hey, I'm going to come in at 10:00 a.m. on Fridays and then work 'til seven,' without any further details. It's much better for me to just be honest." In Stephanie's case, she revealed how much she values that swim class. "It signals to your manager what's important to you, and gives them a window into your life so they can help motivate you, too. Also, if what you serve up as a solution doesn't work for them, they will at least understand why you're asking, and you'll get to a better middle ground."

REMEMBER THEY ARE PAYING YOU TO DO YOUR JOB—YOU'VE GOT TO ACTUALLY DELIVER. And show them you know it! Says Stephanie: "Say, Okay, it's mission critical for me to be able to be the best employee for you if I can do x-y-z [whatever you're asking for], so here is what I need to be the most productive for the company. Then lay out your request and your solution."

ASK YOURSELF: WHAT'S IN IT FOR THEM? (Besides your eternal happiness.) "Think: What do I need to solve for and what do they need to solve for?" says Stephanie. Your goal is to anticipate their concerns but also go one step further and figure out, how can your request actually benefit them? It's a tricky question but one that practically guarantees you'll get to yes. Stephanie gives an example of a friend who works in consulting and took a salary cut to work a four-day week. That's fair, certainly, but to benefit her employer further, she took Thursday as her day off, rather than Friday, which is typically a travel day in consulting (with an already expected loss of productivity). This friend works from home on Fridays, offering her employer essentially more productive hours. (And here's a big P.S. from me to add a little research kindling to your fire: Flextime and a compressed workweek have been shown "to help employees experience greater enrichment from work to home," to increase job satisfaction, and to lower turnover intentions.)

HOW TO ASK FOR A DIFFERENT SHIFT
IF YOU'RE AN HOURLY WORKER

The same strategies above apply here, just in a more straightforward manner, says Wayfair's talent executive Marcy Axelrad. "The way we approach things for our professional roles might not work in the same way for people who are factory workers or who work in customer service," she says, referencing the company's well-known flexibility. It's harder to take work home or to work in a way that's not equitable with your peers if your skill set is the exact same as theirs. But the basic tenets of the ask aren't very different at all. "For these kinds of workers," says Axelrad, "I think it's similar: 'Hey, I need to change this shift. I can't work from 7:00 a.m. to 5:00 p.m. anymore. The shift that I need is 8:00 a.m. to 6:00 p.m., and how can we make that happen? Who should I be talking to? I want to stay here, and I've performed really well, so I know there's value in keeping me. So what can I do to change my shift?'"

HOW TO ASK TO GO PART-TIME
WHEN THAT'S UNCOMMON WHERE YOU WORK

This advice comes from Karen, a senior brand manager at Energizer in Connecticut, who was very conflicted about going back to work after having the first of her three sons. Talking herself into the plan was helpful as she prepared to approach her employer with the request, and then magically, her company actually gave her just the right words. Here's her story:

Karen was fortunate to have a six-month maternity leave,

"but I spent probably the first four and a half months with this gut-wrenching feeling every time I thought about going back to work," she says. "I was like, Okay, I need to crunch the numbers and see what kind of salary I really need to make. Maybe I can't quit, but I can go part-time."

Karen also had a hunch that her department was evolving culturally. She knew of one other person in the company who had gone temporarily part-time to care for a sick family member. Still, she thought her own part-time request would be, in her words, a long shot. Until: She went back mid–maternity leave for one day of a three-day workshop her team was doing. "The theme was 'play to win,'" she recalls, "and it was all about how you should only feel stress about the things in your life you can control and change— the rest you just have to let go. So, knowing that the company was giving us this training, I said to myself, Let's see if they'll put their money where their mouth is."

Karen scheduled a call with her boss, but only after doing three things to prep: (1) She researched the company's part-time policy. "It was very deep in the corporate website, hard to find, but allegedly, part-time is allowed," she says. (2) Karen talked herself through the worst-case scenario. "I thought, Okay, if they tell me no, what will I do? I will go back full-time but continue to look for other flexible options. And if they assume that I'm on my way out in the meantime, well, at least we're all on the same page." (3) She thought hard about who her strongest relationship was with in management. That was who she'd approach.

Finally, the ask: Toward the end of her leave, Karen emailed her boss asking her for a time to talk. On the phone she said: "I'm coming back, and I love the company, but I'm wondering if there are any options to go part-time? I've looked online and found our policy, but of course I wanted to talk to you personally." She also referenced how inspired she was by the workshop she'd attended. Her boss wanted to run it up the ladder and scheduled another call, where they worked out the financial details. Karen would work three days at a 60 percent salary, which felt like a real victory given the existing culture. "My advice is, don't expect them to give you the world if you're not willing to give it back and haven't already proven that," she says. "I was a high performer; they knew that I was committed."

In reality, she says, she wound up doing a lot of work at night, so, after her second son, she adjusted to a four-day week at 80 percent salary to make things more equitable. "There are days when I wake up upset to have passed up potential promotion opportunities to have kept this schedule—I've proven that I can do my full-time job in four days. But ultimately, the financial and title sacrifices are worth it to me to have time with my kids."

HOW TO ASK TO WORK FROM HOME
(AT LEAST SOME OF THE TIME)

First of all, be sure it's really what you want.

Working from home is a great option if you want to save yourself commuting time, or schedule a pediatrician appointment at lunchtime, or have some quiet time to concentrate on cranking out work without being pulled into meetings.

Working from home is not a great option if you envision using that time to save on childcare and be with your baby. A newborn may nap enough to give you eight hours of work time. A six-month-old doesn't. And if your productivity, deliverables, and availability slip because you're at home with your kid, you're not setting a great precedent for your own future requests—or anyone else's.

Okay, lecture over.

Still want to ask to work from home? Jennifer Dorian, General Manager of Turner Classic Movies, has both asked for and granted flexibility at various moments in her career. She says, "I would start the conversation like this: 'Hey, I know we've worked together for a while, and I hope you have a high level of trust in my work ethic and my quality of work. I wanted to talk to you about using my energy in the best way possible and also adapting to some of the things I need to do at home. So here's the schedule that I would propose, if you think it works for you. And I'm pretty sure I can get everything done because we'll still have good communication, and I'll still be available, and I'll really be using this time at home to focus on my assignments." Be aware, also, Jennifer says, that your ideal vision of this flexibility may change over time, and you can be honest about that—same goes for your employer, of course. "I would be really honest about your needs. I wouldn't play games, or ask for more than you want in the hope that they'll negotiate down," she says. You're asking for something that requires trust so you should demonstrate that you're being honest from that first conversation. If you sense hesitation on their part, reassure them that they aren't committing forever. "You could always ask, 'Can we just try this for three weeks, or a quarter, and then reevaluate?'" she suggests. By then you'll have proven your dependability, and if your own needs have changed again, you'll have another opportunity to open up the conversation.

HOW TO NEGOTIATE ANOTHER JOB OFFER
WHILE ON LEAVE

Carefully. Honestly. This may sound like the holy grail of maternity leave circumstances, but in our LinkedIn lives, it's not at all uncommon for women to be approached while out with their newborns. I talked to a handful who all, ultimately, decided to stay at their current companies—but not without using the offer as leverage for better employment terms. Their collective (and off-the-record) advice:

DO NOT FEEL GUILTY FOR BRINGING THIS UP WHILE ON LEAVE. Your leave is a family need, a federal right, and a corporate benefit.

THAT SAID, ACKNOWLEDGE THAT THE TIMING ISN'T IDEAL but that you wanted to be open and have this conversation as soon as possible.

DON'T BLUFF. You must actually be willing to take the other job if you're going to engage in negotiations with your current employer. If the other job isn't appealing, just let it be a little new-mom ego boost, and say no thank you.

THINK LONG AND HARD about what life will look like starting at a new employer with a new baby. There may be a benefit here: You can negotiate things like flextime from the get-go. But the drawbacks are real. It's almost impossible to suss out corporate culture from the outside, and don't underestimate the value of the relationships you've spent time fostering in your old job.

TO THAT END, DO NOT BURN BRIDGES. If you're taking a new job, see if they will cover the remainder of your leave time.

If you do decide to stay on with your current employer, you have a real opportunity to make positive change for yourself. Leah (not her real name), an executive at a huge international brand, shared this story:

"I was definitely thinking about three things while I was on my maternity leave: One, do I start my own company? Two, do I just leave altogether and take time off? Or three, do I take on another job entirely, something I'm really passionate about?

"Then, I got approached by number three, a lifestyle company that I use myself all the time—my friends and I love it. We are their customer. It was a big job in terms of title, and I knew that they'd done their research on me. Still, I wanted to talk to my current employer. I purposefully didn't let the other offer get to the point of a dollar figure. They'd made it clear that they wanted me and the ball was in my court, and I felt like, while I wanted to engage my current employer, I didn't want to be like, 'Here's the offer, give me a counteroffer.' That just didn't feel right. So instead, I made a meeting with my HR rep and my CEO, and said, 'The reason this other offer is appealing is because I can tell that the role I'm in today is not going to stimulate me tomorrow. I'd like to grow.' As it turned out, they were already trying to hire for a more senior creative role. They were going to hire from the outside, but when I came to them, they offered me the job to keep me. Of course, I had just told my husband that this would be our year of quiet: no more pregnancies, no moves, no new job. But this was an opportunity to take on something huge at a young age, from inside a company that clearly values me. It was daunting and thrilling. I accepted."

HOW TO REQUEST A LESS TERRIBLE PUMPING SPACE

The population of pumping-unhappily women I talked to was divided in two: those who had good spaces available that they couldn't use (think: moms who had to walk across testosterone-laden trading floors to get to the lactation suite, or moms whose spaces lacked tech like Wi-Fi that would have made work possible); and there were those whose workplaces simply had no space—and seemingly no resources for one. The best advice for both situations is one and the same: Come up with your own solution and ask for it. But how?

First, understand the boss's perspective. "We have a mom right now who is very upset with us because we haven't been able to give her a good, private, pumping space because we are simply overrun," one nonprofit director told me. "We don't have a private space for anything. We have four people in a one-person office. We lack resources, so how can I give up a space for pumping? I've tried to foster a mom-supportive environment, so right now we have, on a schedule, someone leave their office for her three times a day. But if she needs to pump off schedule, it's hard to accommodate."

Even in a supportive environment, this may be what you're up against: A stressed-out, overtaxed boss who is out of ideas—and out of time to come up with new ones. That's where you come in.

Of course you can and should make your boss aware of the law if there is no space for you, or if you're being forced to pump in the bathroom: Section 4207 of the Affordable Care Act covers your rights (and even companies that have fewer than fifty employees are obligated to comply unless they can prove that it would be an "undue hardship"). One added complication: Only employees who qualify as nonexempt under the FLSA (Fair Labor Standards Act) are covered. So if you're management, and not paid hourly, federal law might not be on your side.

But show that you've done a more personal kind of research, too: "It comes down to knowing your employer," says Rachel Jacobson, who is the in-house labor and employment lawyer at Winthrop University Hospital in Mineola, New York. "Chances are, you're returning to a place where you've worked for a significant amount of time. So you know the physical logistics of the location," as well as, I'll add, everyone's comfort (or lack thereof) with the different privacy options. "As an employer, I find it difficult to say no when someone comes to me with the answer. You may not have the entire solution worked out, but take your best ideas, and say, 'This job is important to me. This office is important to me. Here's what I'm thinking for how I can get this done and make it work for all of us," says Jacobson.

In lactation Shangri-la, you'd get a beautifully appointed room with Fiji water and Jonathan Adler furniture just down the hall from your desk. Barring that, here are some at least functional ideas women I talked to suggested:

- a supply closet, with a light, a laptop, and a privacy sign
- a slightly later start time so the first pump can happen at home
- a tension-rod curtain installed to cover an office's glass walls
- a temporary bamboo screen, unfurled across a cubicle's open side, with music playing for sound privacy

HOW TO REQUEST (MORE) TIME OFF
TO TREAT A POSTPARTUM MOOD DISORDER

It can happen: You're getting toward the end of your leave, and the postpartum anxiety that's plagued you recently hasn't yet dissipated. Or, you're already back at work, and postpartum depression hits for the first time. What if you've already taken your full FMLA twelve weeks? Can you take more time away? Short answer: yes. "A leave from work because of postpartum depression or anxiety is not the same thing as maternity leave," says Dr. Christin Drake, who has advised patients on how to ask their employers for more leave time. "If your symptoms make it impossible to work for a time, this should be treated as a separate illness, and should be covered by the Americans with Disabilities Act."

Here are your brass-tacks step-by-step directions for getting the time you need. (For the record, I'm going to let these experts use the word "accommodation" as many times here as they darn well please.)

UNDERSTAND YOUR RIGHTS. "The ADA requires that if you have a disability—and PPD or PPA certainly qualify in my opinion—the employer has to provide you with a 'reasonable accommodation,' if that accommodation would ultimately enable you to perform your job," says employment lawyer Rachel Jacobson. "And one recognized reasonable accommodation is a leave of absence."

STRATEGIZE WITH YOUR DOCTOR. "Before going to your employer, talk to your doctor about when she thinks you'll be able to come back to work, because the law won't require an employer to give an indefinite leave," says Jacobson. "I would also ask your doctor if there are other sorts of accommodations that would make it possible for you to ease your way back into work. For example, maybe your PPD is worse in the morning, leaving your child and running out the door, but you could get to work by 11:00 a.m. Or maybe you could work from home temporarily. Or work a different shift. Come up with a solution you and your practitioner feel is feasible. You know your job and what it requires, so you can think realistically about this from your employer's standpoint, too."

APPROACH THE CONVERSATION INTERACTIVELY. "The way the law works, when you make that request for an accommodation, the employer either has to give it to you, or they have to engage in what is called an 'interactive process,'" says Jacobson. "So you and your employer go back and forth, evaluating your limitations, the job's requirements, and how they can get you to the point where your disability needs are met, but your job responsibilities are also met. Once you open the door, your employer is *legally required* to have a conversation with you. And if I have a note from a doctor stating that an employee needs sixteen weeks off, as the employer I either get to say, 'Giving you that sixteen weeks is unreasonable,' or I simply have to grant it. And it's very difficult to say, 'Well, I already gave you twelve, how can I not give you four more?'"

KEEP YOUR FUTURE—BEYOND PPD—IN MIND. In these conversations, resist the urge to prove how bad you're feeling, because that automatically puts you on the defensive. "You need to be firm," says Wendy N. Davis, PhD, from Postpartum Support International. "Express your need in a way that makes you feel empowered. You want to use the words 'temporary' and 'treatable,' as in, 'This is a temporary and treatable condition. The best advice I've been given is that it would be wise to treat it now so I can be fully equipped when I come back.'" That way, says Dr. Davis, you've both reassured and educated your workplace—and helped prevent any awkwardness when you come back. It's okay to share the symptoms with them, if they need to understand how PPD/PPA would impact your work—lack of memory, inability to concentrate, increased emotional lability, crying jags, panic attacks—but to avoid a career hangover once you're well, you must stress how this is all transitory, urges Dr. Davis.

And eight more talks for your personal life

HOW TO BAIL OUT OF A BIG FAMILY OBLIGATION

A six-week-old baby. A mom about to go back to work. A terminally ill family matriarch across the country. Not a good combination, says Sydney (not her real name), who found herself in the awkward position of being begged to bring her newborn for one last goodbye to her husband's grandma. The trip would have been a lot under any circumstances, but the baby hadn't gotten his vaccines yet, and this was all happening in February, prime cold and flu season. "My husband's mother understood, thankfully," says Sydney. "But there was a ton of pressure coming from the rest of his family, especially his aunt—emails, phone calls, guilt trips, just pleading with us to come."

Sydney's solution: "First I talked to my husband. I said, I'm not allowing this guilt to come into our home. Your aunt cannot put it on us that her mother will somehow get well if she holds this newborn. She is out of line." Her husband got it. But to spare him from being the bad guy, she then went a route that I have employed myself with great flair ever since middle school gym class: the doctor's note. "Our pediatrician was more than willing," says Sydney. "She said that she wouldn't stop us from traveling if it's what we wanted to do—she'd give us a big list of precautions—but she also told us all the reasons why she advised against the trip, primarily, if he caught the flu, he'd end up hospitalized out of town, far from home." That was all she needed to hear. Sydney crafted a kind but firm email to the aunt: "I said that although we really wanted to come, our doctor cautioned us against it. People are just much more willing to listen to a 'professional opinion.' I sent the email to take some of the heat off of my husband. And of course he went himself and we did FaceTime to make sure that we were a presence there with the family."

HOW TO TELL YOUR FRIENDS AND FAMILY THAT YOU HAVE POSTPARTUM ISSUES WITHOUT FREAKING THEM OUT

The stigma of a mood disorder can be as painful as the illness itself. If your friends and family don't know a lot about PPD and PPA, they may worry about your safety or—harder to swallow—the baby's, especially with the added pressure of your return to work. Postpartum Support International's Dr. Davis offers this advice:

"Say something to the effect of 'I realize that I had/have postpartum depression/anxiety. And I've learned so much about it. One out of seven women experiences this. And I've learned that it's temporary and treatable. Also, the idea that mothers with postpartum issues are less connected with their babies comes from the media and is a mistruth. I've learned that most women who have postpartum depression/anxiety are actually overconnected with their babies, not the other way around.'" This kind of statement shows that you are in control and aware. "It also shows that you trust yourself," says Dr. Davis. "And you're educating people! Pass on that awareness and knowledge and spread the word."

HOW TO GET YOUR MOM TO GIVE YOU (A BIT) LESS ADVICE

Let me start with this: I interviewed a couple of motherless mothers, and they would have been delighted to have an overbearing mom telling them that their baby needed thicker socks on.

That perspective check aside, grandma drama is a really common issue for new mothers. You're trying your best not to take your frustration out on your partner or your baby, or your boss. So who becomes your annoyer numero uno? Mom. And whose advice do you need (and hate needing)? Mom's. "It's a relationship that is totally activated," says Dr. Elizabeth Auchincloss, Vice Chair of Education, Psychiatry, at Weill Cornell, with a knowing laugh. "If you have any issues—your mother is crazy, or difficult, or not there for whatever reason, that's always activated right then."

Your mother has more experience parenting—in fact, research has shown that Grandma is the number one source of advice and support to new moms.

But you know more about your specific baby right now.

And you both know that mothering is something you're best off learning for yourself.

Yet she can hardly help herself. So how do you get her to back off just enough? "When I figure that one out, I will let you know," says Deborah Grayson Riegel, the communication coach, also with a laugh (this is one of those laugh-a-minute interview questions, it seems). She pauses and then dives in with this plan:

Step 1: "I think you first have to ask yourself what is bothering you so much about her advice. Is it the amount, the tone, or the quality?" That can inform your response and give you a little clearheaded distance, says Riegel.

Step 2: "Then ask yourself: What is the most generous interpretation of what she is saying, instead of defaulting to the opposite," says Riegel. Most of the time, you'll uncover pretty positive motivations for her overzealousness. "You have to firmly believe that she intends the criticism to be additive, to help. She loves her grandbabies, she loves you, and wants to be included." I'll add: She may be a bit wistful, too, wanting a do-over of her own early motherhood, or wanting to save you the pain of getting something wrong.

Step 3: "Then, based on your most generous interpretation, ask yourself: Which of those things are you willing to give to her, and which are you not?" continues Riegel. "So, maybe that's saying to yourself, okay, I'm willing to give her the opportunity to be helpful to me, but I need to define what's helpful. Or if she's suggesting something that's simply a no in your book—she's saying you should be breastfeeding when you've made the decision not to, tell her that's off the table, and then move on to something else that's not. If you can somehow honor the underlying need she has to have an impact in a way that reduces your own stress, everyone wins."

What if, like another woman I talked to (let's call her Anya), you have a relative whose suggestions are almost all "off the table" things due to a simple chasm of value differences? Food, bedtimes, naps, clothes, all of it? "I finally had a broader conversation with my mother-in-law, and it worked," says Anya. "I told her: 'The choices we make in our house and the way I raise my children are not a reflection of or a judgment on you and how you raised yours. Your children are wonderful. I love them. Your son is my favorite person in the world. The choices that he and I make together are what we think is best for our children. This is not about you.'"

HOW TO ASK YOUR PARTNER FOR A SHIFT IN WORK ROLES

Do you want to work less? Do you want your partner to work less so you can work more? Or do you both want to contribute equally to the family income and the household? Big questions, but they all start with smaller conversations, says Jessica DeGroot of the Third Path Institute, who has dedicated her career to helping couples redesign their work lives to create time for family and community. This kind of negotiation is her bread and butter.

"Hopefully, long before anyone takes parental leave, you and your partner have had a conversation where you start to imagine your roles and what life looks like with a baby . . . and later on when you have a toddler, or a grade schooler," says DeGroot, who likes to cite Stephen R. Covey's message from his classic book, *The 7 Habits of Highly Effective People:* "Begin with the end in mind." DeGroot tells her clients to look into the future and ask each other: "What would a really satisfying life look like? What kind of work do we want to be doing? What do we want our afternoons to look like, or our weekends? Are we all eating dinner together? How much income do we really need? How clean does our house really need to be?" And she's seen the payoff of these conversations again and again. "What's fun now is with so much history working with so many couples, what I've learned from them is that the sky's the limit when couples start thinking about it jointly," she says. "Whatever 'it' is."

HOW TO ASK A RELATIVE
NOT TO ENCROACH ON YOUR BABY TIME

Nobody likes a baby hog. But working moms *really* don't like a baby hog, even a well-meaning one. One high-level executive I spoke to who asked to be anonymous (for obvious in-law reasons!) found herself immensely frustrated that her mother-in-law would come visit almost every evening right around the time when she herself got home from work. "This was my only forty-five minutes a day with the boys between work and bedtime," says Brooke (let's call her Brooke). "It got worse as they got older and she'd make comments like, 'Oh, Mommy's home now . . . I guess everybody only wants Mommy now that Mommy's home.'" That was the line in the sand for Brooke because now the kids were being brought into the bad dynamic. "Finally, I just decided to be really honest with her instead of passive-aggressive. I just said, 'I would like to find another time for you to come visit with the kids when I'm not around. It's too hard for me and for them to feel torn between us. I understand that you're trying to be involved and help. But I am not a stay-at-home mom. When I'm home I want to really be with them.'"

Two big points of information on this one:

- Brooke didn't ask her husband to fight her battles for her— but she did talk this through with him before addressing his mother.
- Consistency is important. Though she probably wouldn't have been as annoyed to have her own mom around at the witching hour, she has the same rule for all the grandparents. That way, it comes across as policy, not as something personal.

These days, it's not *all* peachy—Grandma is rarely around when Mom is—but she's happy, Brooke's happy, and the kids get special time with each of them.

HOW TO TELL YOUR GIRLFRIENDS TO HANG ON, YOU'LL BRB

If you've had a few months of leave, maybe by the end of it you've found time for girl time. Then you head back to work where the poopy diaper hits the fan and you suddenly (temporarily) stop returning all but the very tightest circle of invitations, calls, and even texts. What the hell, think your friends. Where'd she go?

To avoid hurt feelings, and ensure that your extended girl pack will stick things out, do a little preemptive damage control, says Riegel. "Prepare them," she says. "Tell your friends that you might disappear for a bit but that you hope they don't interpret this the wrong way—you care and need their friendship. Then put a date on the calendar for three months out so they know that you're serious about maintaining the friendship and that this is purely circumstantial."

Another great suggestion: "If you have a very close friend who relies on you, give her a safe word," says Riegel. It's silly but effective. "You might want to say, if you're having an emergency and things are going off the rails and you need me, use this word." (Just try not to make your husband jealous, okay?)

HOW TO CALM DOWN FRIENDS AND FAMILY
WHO OBJECT WHEN YOU PRIORITIZE YOUR CAREER

Oh, do I relate to this one. When Will was born, Ben was just through his first year of residency (pay rate: $11/hour—I did the math), and I can't tell you how many relatives on both sides asked me: "Are you going back to work?" Really? *Really?!* Take it from me: Getting huffy is not a helpful response. One ambitious executive I talked to—I'll call her Emily here—had a much better strategy:

Emily is an executive for a big multinational brand. Just a week or two after she was back from her maternity leave with her daughter, her mentor, a global-level executive, approached her and asked if she'd consider moving to the Japan office. "I didn't speak Japanese and had a brand-new baby, but back when I'd started at the company I'd checked the box saying that I'd be interested in working in Asia," says Emily. "You only get these opportunities so often. My husband, Charles, was incredibly supportive—moving abroad had always been one of our life goals, but we never thought it'd happen. We were leaning toward doing it."

Then she started telling her friends and family. "Everyone was like, You guys are *crazy*," Emily says. One girlfriend asked her if she secretly spoke Japanese. Her colleagues warned that she would end up divorced. "Everyone was worried about the risk of having him leave his job and care for our baby until he found new employment," she says.

But Emily's conversation with her mom was the hardest. "My mom said she would never come visit us if we moved. She threatened never to speak to me again. This was a woman who worked my whole childhood, and even she was objecting. I was hysterical crying." After that, Emily went home and told her husband, "Screw it, we're not doing this." His heroic response: "You've worked too hard to throw away this opportunity. Our baby is the perfect age. Snap out of it." She did. They were going for it.

At that point, decision made, Emily and Charles decided to go dark. "I hate to say that, but we stopped talking about it with people for a while. We realized that all the outside influence was making the decision confusing, and at the core of our little family's happiness, we wanted to do this." With that distance, Emily was able to see the big picture—and that everyone's objections were simply emotional and based in love.

"After a good long cry, I called my mom back and said, 'Mom, you are a working mom. You should understand the importance of having your own identity, and being the best and wanting the best and going for it. You never let anyone stop you. You raised me to be independent. I know you don't really want me to take a backseat.'" Emily also explained that Charles was 100 percent on board, saying, "I know you're really upset. Here's what this career move will do for us as a family. This is a 'we' decision and we've made it together." That legitimized it—to her mom and all her friends as she talked to them one by one.

Charles and Emily spent two years in Japan before she was offered an even bigger internal move back to New York, where she still had all of her wonderful old friends. And as for her time in Japan? I'll give you one guess who was the first person on the plane to come visit. Her mom.

RELATED: HOW TO SHUSH ANY WORKING-MOM JUDGER

You're *using formula*?! Your child is *in daycare*?! Your husband *didn't take a paternity leave*?! You're traveling *so soon*?! You put your baby to bed late *just so you can see her*?! People tend to speak at you in a lot of italics. Honestly, shame on them. Deborah Grayson Riegel offers three strategies I wish I'd had back when I needed them. Luckily people still judge you when your kids are older, too, so I'll employ them now.

> **Acknowledge their interest by saying:** "I so appreciate that you're thinking about what's best for our family. I know you love us. Here's what we think is best."
> **Legitimize their cultural cluelessness by saying:** "As you can see, this is a topic and debate that so many people are having right now. Here's the choice we're making."
> **Deflect their attention by asking:** "What did you do? It's always so interesting to hear how people come to a very personal decision like this. Say, would you like a deviled egg?"

All of these conversations get easier the more you have them (i.e., the more you don't avoid them). So ask for what you need— whether that's something concrete, or just compassion. Yes, you'll help yourself and your baby, but you'll also educate those around you. Let that help make you brave.

Afterword

By some ridiculous trick of the subconscious, this book took me exactly forty weeks to write. Just like pregnancy, the process was a life-changing, career-altering transition for me.

I remember so clearly being pregnant with Will and then with Teddy and looking in the mirror each morning trying to assess: What's changed? How big is he? Do I look pregnant-pregnant yet? Is anyone at work able to tell that I've fastened the button on my pants with a hair elastic? Nine months is a long time to get used to the idea of becoming a mother. It's not a gentle transition, what with the vomiting and lack of alcohol and sushi, but it feels, or at least it did to me, like the right amount of time. Early euphoria turns to disbelief—is that heartbeat still in there?; then just as fear and panic set in, you start to get a belly and feel little kicks, and people treat you kindly.

By month six—or, as it turns out, about page 200, if you're writing a book—you realize: This is happening. It's really happening.

This book is not a baby, obviously. I'm currently trying hard, in our Saturday night dinners with friends, not to refer to it as my third child. A book can't even begin to compare to that joy. But writing it has changed my life, my marriage, my mothering, and, yes, my career. I am so grateful.

These forty weeks have also shown me that something else is *really happening:* Our country is changing. Thank God. Opening my daily "parental leave" Google alerts as I wrote was like unwrapping a candy every morning:

Politicians announced not just family-friendly philosophies but actual paid-leave proposals, with dollars and figures.

Female executives penned heartfelt, personal blog posts sharing intimate details of their family lives, for the sake of being whole-self leaders.

Male executives did, too.

TV shows referenced all those new-working-mom feelings. And when one hit show found its star pregnant (congrats, Zooey Deschanel!), they wrote in a maternity leave for her—six episodes starred a fill-in character.

Companies posted countless "maternity leave fill-in" job offerings, proof that budgets are adapting.

New York became the fifth (and, by far, most generous) state to pass paid leave legislation. It's for moms *and* dads, and will be fully up and running by 2021.

And the private-sector policy changes! Wow. It's been a publicity arms race from Wall Street to Silicon Valley as companies strive to outdo one another. Twitter now gives its employees TaskRabbit gift cards so they can outsource kid-related errands. Facebook reimburses surrogacy and sperm-donation costs. Several companies, including IBM and Zillow, will ship breastmilk home for babies of mothers who are traveling on business.

Overall, the percentage of large American companies offering paid parental leave nearly *doubled* in 2015. As one of his last hurrahs, President Barack Obama worked to give all federal workers six weeks of paid leave. All branches of the military will now grant mothers twelve weeks of paid leave (which actually dialed back the eighteen weeks the Marines and the Navy had just started to offer, mumble, mumble . . . but still).

This is happening. It's really happening.

Of course, the vast majority of Americans don't have access to anything close to Google's eighteen weeks of paid maternity leave. But when YouTube CEO Susan Wojcicki announced the impact of that leave, I cheered for us all: The increase from twelve to eighteen weeks reduced the rate at which new mothers at Google quit by 50 percent. Wojcicki—fresh off of her *fifth* maternity leave at the company, by the way—was purposefully sending a two-fold message to other companies with that announcement: (a) Longer paid leave is good for business, and (b) even sainted Google didn't assume it had everything right. The world changes, people's needs change, and businesses—run by other human beings, parents, daughters, sons—must constantly course correct.

Your job is to surf this sea change. Make it through your own transition back to work, and stick with your career in whatever way you can. Set an example for the not-yet-parents around you. Course correct your own office culture so that even two or three years from now things can be easier with your next baby if you have one. Become the boss if that sounds good to you and make those cultural changes official.

And if all that sounds like too much to think about right this second, that's okay, too. Because the Fifth Trimester is just a season. And you'll get to the next one, and then the next.

Nine months after returning to work with my first son, my own Fifth Trimester was long past. On the Ferris wheel of home-work-home highs and lows, I didn't spend a lot of time thinking about whether I'd made the right choices. I just made them and tried to relish the thrill of the ride. Still, sometimes, at home in the evening, I'd fret over what was happening at the office, still lit up and buzzing. And at work, I'd catch myself daydreaming about what milestone my sweet boy was up to without me.

The memories of my time with Will from back then, maybe because those hours were so precious, are sharp in their colors and their emotions.

Like the night I came home, shed my work bag and shoes, and found my shirtless baby in his high chair enjoying his predinner before our real one.

"Hi, my big boy," I squealed, looking at his carrot-streaked face.

Right then, tossing his hands in the air over his head, he said his first word, which was so perfect I still can't believe it. William Davis Brody looked right at me, arms up, and yelled:

"Touchdown!"

Resources

CHILDCARE

The NICHD Study of Early Child Care and Youth Development
nichd.nih.gov/publications/pubs/documents/seccyd_06.pdf

Daycare Resources
Child Care Resources, Inc.   childcareresourcesinc.org
National Association for Early
        Learning Leaders   earlylearningleaders.org
National Association for the Education
        of Young Children   www.naeyc.org
National Child Care Association   www.nccanet.org

In-home Daycare Resources
National Association for Family
        Child Care   nafcc.org

Caregiver Agencies
The Association of Premier
        Nanny Agencies   theapna.org
Care   care.com
Babysitters Registry   babysittersregistry.com
International Nanny Association   nanny.org
Nannies4Hire   nannies4hire.com
Sittercity   sittercity.com

Additionally, many colleges and universities have babysitter job boards.

Au Pair Agencies
Agent Au Pair   agentaupair.com
American Cultural Exchange   goaupair.com
American Institute for Foreign Study   aupairinamerica.com
American Professional Exchange   proaupair.com
AuPairCare   aupaircare.com
Au Pair Foundation   aupairfoundation.org
Au Pair International   aupairint.com
Cultural Care Au Pair   culturalcare.com
Cultural Homestay International   chinet.org/au-pair
EurAuPair Intercultural Child Care
        Programs   euraupair.com
Expert Group International Inc.   expertaupair.com
InterExchange   aupairusa.org
The International Au Pair Exchange   tiape.org
USAuPair   USAupair.com

Support for Stay-at-Home Dads
City Dads Group   citydadsgroup.com/nyc
National At-Home Dad Network   athomedad.org

Support for Grandparent Caregivers
Foundation for Grandparenting   grandparenting.org
Generations United   gu.org
Grandparents' Guide for Family
        Nurturing & Safety   extension.psu.edu/youth/
                                               intergenerational/curricula-and
                                               -activities/handouts/grandparents
                                               -guide
Legacy3   legacyproject.org

CAREER DEVELOPMENT

For a comparison of company benefits   fairygodboss.com
                                           listyourleave.com
For flexible freelance employment options apresgroup.com
                                           flexcelnetwork.com
                                           inkwellteam.com
                                           pathforward.org
                                           saywerk.com
                                           thesecondshift.com
For freelance benefits   freelancersunion.org

BREASTFEEDING AND PUMPING

Supplies and Pump Rentals
Ameda   ameda.com
Medela   medela.com
The Upper Breast Side   upperbreastside.com
Yummy Mummy   yummymummystore.com

Milk Donation
The Human Milk Banking Association
     of North America   hmbana.org

Advice
For pumping and nursing questions   kellymom.com
For medication while breastfeeding infantrisk.com
For lactation consultants   ilca.org
                                    lalecheleague.org

For how-to videos on hand
     expressing   Jane Morton, MD, on youtube.com

RELATIONSHIPS

Bringing Baby Home workshops   gottman.com/couples/parenting

MENTAL HEALTH SUPPORT

Postpartum Progress   postpartumprogress.com
Postpartum Support International   postpartum.net
Seleni Institute   seleni.org

POLICY AND ADVOCACY

American Women   americanwomen.org
A Better Balance   abetterbalance.org
Boston College Center for Work &
     Family   bc.edu/centers/cwf
Center for Parental Leave Leadership cplleadership.com
Families and Work Institute   familiesandwork.org
It's Working Project   itsworkingproject.com
Lean In   leanin.org
National Partnership for Women &
     Families   nationalpartnership.org
The ThirdPath Institute   thirdpath.org
The Working Parent Support   workingparentsupportcoalition
     Coalition, Clinton Global   .launchrock.com
     Initiative

Acknowledgments

Know this: I gush, and I make no apologies for it. I'm basically forty-two weeks pregnantly huge with gratitude.

Researching and writing this book has been one of the joys of my life so far—made possible by a childhood rich in love, a career steeped in generous mentorship, and friendships and a marriage so supportive that I wish the English language had more words for "phew" and "thank you."

So first, to my parents, Susan and Jay Smith: Thank you for your shining example. Thank you for the dinnertime conversations that made me look beyond my own nose to the rest of the world, and for letting me know that my voice counted, and that I'd better do something good with it. Thank you for my education, without which I would not have found my love of writing and editing—or my husband. And thank you for reading and responding to this entire manuscript so lovingly and so quickly (for the record, seventy-two hours for Dad, thirty-six for Mom). And—not unrelated—thank you for never, ever retiring from parenting.

I fell in l-o-v-e love with my agent Stefanie Lieberman from minute one. Stef, thank you for being my champion and my friend, proving that the best professional relationships are personal, too. (At Janklow and Nesbit, thank you, Molly Steinblatt and Michael Steger, too.)

And my brilliant editor at Doubleday, Melissa Danaczko . . . I am so lucky to have been in your strong and gentle hands. Thank you for your unwavering passion for this project, for your generally far-smarter-than-me intelligence (much appreciated), for the nicest revision notes I've ever received, and for being my one-woman focus group with baby Adelyn. Margo Shickmanter, for the record, I think you need to write a book on how to be the world's best maternity leave fill-in. Thank you so much for your careful, thoughtful shepherding. And thank you also to Maria Carella, Todd Doughty, Ellen Feldman, Lauren Hesse, Emily Mahon, Claire Bradley Ong, and Nicole Pedersen. And to Matt Chase for his precisely perfect cover art.

At Arnall Golden Gregory, LLP, thank you to Anuj Desai, Frank White, and Matt Wilson.

This book had been simmering inside me unacted-on for many months, but the actual leap of doing it happened during an enormously transitional year in my career. My old magazine colleagues did more than stay in touch—they became true friends and incredibly generous buyers of lunch and connectors of contacts. And my newfound book publishing friends gave me a warm and welcome sense of belonging right from our first whispered hellos at the library.

Special thank-yous to Elisabeth Egan, who shared the perfect advice, names, commiseration, and encouragement at just the right time. This book could not have happened without you. Wendy Naugle, thank you for being the work wife (and friend) dream marriages are made of. Erin Zammett Ruddy, thank you for being my work sibling. And thank you to my editing mentors over the years: Alison Brower and Jill Herzig, I felt your pen strokes and margin notes at every paragraph. And Cindi Leive, thank you for my forever-inspiring *Glamour* years.

To my library ladies—Leigh Abramson, Cristina Alger, and Elyssa Friedland—thank you for practicing the communicative property of discipline, for being my sounding board, and for countless sandwiches on the front steps, rain or shine. Thank you to Sage Mehta for sharing her special workspace.

Speaking of libraries, thank you to the Hampton Library, the New York Society Library, the East Hampton Library, and the Thomas J.

Watson Library at the Metropolitan Museum of Art, where most of these pages were written. I most certainly did not sneak in any coffee.

To the moms and dads who took the time to share their experiences in surveys and interviews, dredging up fifth-trimester memories good and bad for the sake of making things easier for all of us: You are the best kind of people out there. Thank you.

I owe an enormous debt of gratitude to the people who loved my children—and schlepped them all over New York—while I was sitting on my tush writing. Jean Ramnauth, thank you for the hug you gave me on my way out the door when Will was three months old. I felt it for all seven years you were with our family. Nairoby Otero, I didn't realize when we hired a "big kid nanny" we were also getting a life coach. The wonder and joy (and patience) you show our boys works on the grown-ups, too. Thank you.

My girls: Liz O'Flanagan Walder, thank you for being ready to break kneecaps, or drive in for a hug, or both, at a moment's notice. Your steadfast friendship makes me a better mother, and I can't think of any better gift than that. Tara Todras-Whitehill, thank you for showing me by example how to be blunt, brave, and relentless. Renée Farster-Degenhart, thank you for sitting in my window freshman year. Thank you for opening my heart to new ways of seeing love and parenthood.

My moms: Ashley Baker Staats, Allison Beer, and Francesca Donner, this book is also dedicated to you. Thank you for supporting me and my family in one thousand ways through every twist and turn of this process. Ash, thank you for loving the telephone like it's 1997. Allison, thank you for always cutting straight through the bullshit. And Frantaco, thank you for being the cheerleader we all need.

I often say that my kids are lucky as heck to have six grandparents. But what I really mean is that *I'm* lucky. My in-laws are the best. David and Roberta Brody, and Nedra and Roger Richards, thank you for your boundless support. Mike and Dane, I love you fools. Hayley, thank goodness you came as part of the deal. Jason and Brad and Troy and Laura, you, too!

To my siblings, thank you for being Smiths with me. I wrote a book about Blair, my little sister, when I was in the second grade and she was a newborn. Sadly, *The Only Texan in the Family* never made it onto Amazon, but Aunt B, you were the first baby to inspire me to work hard at something. You still do. Brian, thank you for excellent advice, legal and otherwise, and for marrying wonderful Leah. Tyler, one of the happiest days of my life was holding brand-new baby you. I love you guys.

Listing your names hardly feels like enough, but all-caps THANK YOUs to these friends and colleagues for sharing contacts, advice, kindness, and talents: Ranya Barrett, Julia Beck, Debra Bednar, Shannon Bell, Emilia Benton, Michelle Bornstein, Jessica Borowick, Nancy Borowick, Allison Brown, Heather Cabot, Marissa Cohen, Christina Cool, Kelli Cooney, Christine Coppa, Dmitry Dragilev, LB Eisen, Lesley Enston, Audrey Glick, Julia Kaye Goodman, Shari Gottlieb, Amanda Grooms, Rachel Hayes, Steve Hindman, Jessica Jonas, Heather Ladov, Monica Lai, Jesse Lutz, Corey McAveeney, Noel Momsen, Kailyn Moore, Sophie Moura, Julie Penzner, Jennifer Peters, Leslie Robarge, Cindy Rosenthal, Genevieve Roth, Alexandra Rowley, Katie Sanders, Shari Schnall, Ellen Seidman, Sarah Serafin, Wendy Shanker, Randy Siegel, Rebecca Streicker-Calle, Lisa Sun and Project Gravitas, Tara Swanson, Mary Vertin, Jennie Wallace, Elisabeth Weed, Kara Weintraub, Beth Wilkinson, and Hayley Williams.

Now's the part in the speech where I start ugly-crying.

My boys, Will and Teddy, who make everything sparkle with newness and optimism: I love you times infinity. Will, you were just old enough as I wrote this book to understand why I wanted to do such meaningful work. Your pride is so precious to me. And Teddy, you were just young enough as I wrote this to remind me of the baby years, and the joy of coming home to huge hugs and snuggles.

And Ben, who told me to go for it: Whatever "it" may be, over the next (oh, let's say) six more decades, as long as you're holding my hand, that sounds good to me. Thank you so, so much. I love you.

Author Interviews

From February 2015 to February 2016, I interviewed more than one hundred working mothers, fathers, and other experts about the experience of going back to work after becoming a parent. Unless otherwise indicated in the notes, all quotes are from these interviews. Some of the interviews were conducted on background only. Others were conducted confidentially, and the names and identifying details of those sources have been changed or withheld by mutual agreement. Their pseudonyms have been marked in the author interview list with an asterisk. I am so grateful to everyone who contributed.

Leigh Abramson
Alaina
Aliza
Anya*
Elizabeth Auchincloss
Marcy Axelrad
Debra Bednar
Allison Beer
Scott Behson
Sarah Best
Samantha Boardman
Aaron Boodman

Michelle Bornstein
Brooke*
Allison Brown
Rachel Cedar
Chelsea Clinton
Dave Cohen
Amanda Cole
Sarah Davis
Wendy N. Davis
Jessica DeGroot
Francesca Donner
Jennifer Dorian

Sharon Dorram

Christin Drake

Mike Dunst

Ellen

Emily

Emily*

Emma*

Shira Epstein

Renée Farster-Degenhardt

Lydia Fenet

Katie Fiamingo

Robin Fredriksz

Hannah

Rachel Hayes

Lindsay Heller

Hilary Herrmann

Edward Ho

Holly*

Vivian Howard

Liisa Hunter

Rachel Jacobson

Kimberly Jaime

Janie*

Yasmine Delawari Johnson

Jennifer Justice

Marion Campbell Kammer

Amy Kawa

Cheryl Kramer Kaye

Katie Kelter

Kim

Heather Ladov

Laura Lando

Laura*

Emmy Laybourne

Oren Lazanski

Leah*

Karen Lesh

Josh Levs

Jules Leyser

Lila*

Liz

Nitzia Logothetis

Jen Lucky

Jesse Lutz

Sarah M.

Margot*

Eva Amurri Martino

Corey McAveeney

Chirlane McCray

Monica

Julie Murphy

Kimberly Shannon Murphy

Amy Earle Nadeau

Andrea Olshan

Lexi Petronis

Carolyn Pirak

Lindsey Pollak

Jessie Randall

Rekha

Deborah Grayson Riegel

Laura Morgan Roberts

Laurie Sandell

Matt Schneider

Sarah Serafin

Wendy Shanker

Koty Sharp

Alice Shillingsburg

Simone*

Amy Solomon

Lance Somerfeld

Eric Smith

Ashley Baker Staats

Stephanie

Tara Swanson

Sydney*

Terrence

Wendy Troxel

Jessica Weiser

Windsor Hanger Western

Hayley Williams

Tia Williams

Eileen Yam

Cristyn Zett

Notes

INTRODUCTION

xviii In Croatia, women get: International Labour Organization database; ilo
       .org.
xviii Here in the United States: Family and Medical Leave Act; http://www.dol
       .gov/whd/fmla/.
xviii The only countries: International Labour Organization database; ilo.org.
xviii Of the seventeen countries: Alison Earle, Zitha Mokomane, Jody Hey-
       mann, "International Perspectives on Work-Family Policies: Lessons from
       the World's Most Competitive Economies," *The Future of Children* 21, no. 2
       (Fall 2011): 191–210; http://www.ncbi.nlm.nih.gov/pubmed/22013634.
xix   More than half of mothers: Yeon K. Bai, Shahla M. Wunderlich, and Marni
       Weinstock, "Employers' Readiness for the Mother-Friendly Workplace:
       An Elicitation Study," *Maternal & Child Nutrition* 8, no. 4 (Oct. 2012):
       483–91; http://www.ncbi.nlm.nih.gov/pubmed/21978139.
xx   Even still, only 11 percent: U.S. Department of Labor; Bureau of Labor Sta-
       tistics, *National Compensation Survey: Employee Benefits in the United States,
       March 2012;* http://www.bls.gov/ncs/ebs/benefits/2012/ebbl0050.pdf.
xx   Globally, the report claims: "Maternomics," a report and short film, pro-
       duced for Vodafone by KPMG, the professional services firm, with data
       based on females with at least an intermediate-level education, employed
       in nonagricultural sectors. "Vodafone Pioneers Global Maternity Policy
       Across 30 Countries," Vodafone website, March 6, 2015.
xxi   For every month of parental leave: Elly-Ann Johansson, "The Effect of
       Own and Spousal Parental Leave on Earnings" (working paper, Insti-

tute for Labour Market Policy Evaluation, Swedish Ministry of Employment, Uppsala, Sweden, March 2010); http://www.econstor.eu/bit stream/10419/45782/1/623752174.pdf.

xxi   By 2010, 91 percent of businesses: Eileen Appelbaum and Ruth Milkman, *Leaves That Pay: Employer and Worker Experiences with Paid Family Leave in California* (Washington, D.C.: Center for Economic and Policy Research, 2011); http://cepr.net/documents/publications/paid-family-leave-1-2011 .pdf.

xxi   And get this: Amanda Kimball, "UC Davis Study of California Women Business Leaders," UC Davis Graduate School of Management, November 17, 2015; http://gsm.ucdavis.edu/sites/main/files/file-attachments/women execsummary11_16.pdf.

xxi   just under the national average: Matt Egan, "Still Missing: Female Business Leaders," *CNN Money* (March 25, 2015; http://money.cnn.com/ 2015/03/24/investing/female-ceo-pipeline-leadership/.

xxi   It's also worth noting: "Women in the Workplace: Research and Data," *FairyGodboss* (2016).

CHAPTER ONE. WHO'S TAKING CARE OF YOUR LITTLE PERSON?

3   Back in 2006: "NICHD Study of Early Child Care and Youth Development (SECCYD): Study Overview," Eunice Kennedy Shriver National Institute of Child Health and Human Development NIH, DHHS, website, last revised November 30, 2012; https://www.nichd.nih.gov/research/ supported/seccyd/Pages/overview.aspx.

4   a) potentially better for: "The Relation of Child Care to Cognitive and Language Development. National Institute of Child Health and Human Development Early Child Care Research Network," *Child Development* 71, no. 4 (July–August 2000): 960–80; http://www.ncbi.nlm.nih.gov/ pubmed/11016559.

4   b) potentially bad for their behavior: "Type of Child Care and Children's Development at 54 Months," NICHD Early Child Care Research Network, *Early Childhood Research Quarterly* 19, no. 2 (Second Quarter 2004): 203–30; http://www.sciencedirect.com/science/article/pii/ S0885200604000389.

4   c) potentially better academically: Ibid.

5   Yep, fifteen years: Eunice Kennedy Shriver National Institute of Child Health and Human Development, NIH, DHHS, *The NICHD Study of Early Child Care and Youth Development: Findings for Children Up to Age 4½ Years* (January 2006); https://www.nichd.nih.gov/publications/pubs/ documents/seccyd_06.pdf.

5   Maternal stress, unshockingly: Jordana K. Bayer et al., "Development of Children's Internalising and Externalising Problems from Infancy to Five Years of Age," *Australian & New Zealand Journal of Psychiatry* 46, no. 7 (July 2012): 659–68; http://www.ncbi.nlm.nih.gov/pubmed/22651982.

5   This one's obvious: Rada K. Dagher, Patricia M. McGovern, and Bryan E.

Dowd, "Maternity Leave Duration and Postpartum Mental and Physical Health: Implications for Leave Policies," *Journal of Health Politics, Policy and Law* 39, no. 2 (April 2014): 369–416; http://www.ncbi.nlm.nih.gov/pubmed/24305845.

13　Babies between the ages: Richard Bowlby, "Babies and Toddlers in Non-Parental Daycare Can Avoid Stress and Anxiety If They Develop a Lasting Secondary Attachment Bond with One Carer Who Is Consistently Accessible to Them," *Attachment & Human Development* 9, no. 4 (December 2007): 307–19; http://www.ncbi.nlm.nih.gov/pubmed/18049929.

21　Caregivers should practice: Eunice Kennedy Shriver National Institute of Child Health and Human Development, NIH, DHHS, *The NICHD Study of Early Child Care and Youth Development: Findings for Children Up to Age 4½ Years* (January 2006); https://www.nichd.nih.gov/publications/pubs/documents/seccyd_06.pdf.

21　In general, the report says: Ibid.

25　And nationally, the estimate: Gretchen Livingston, "Growing Number of Dads Home with the Kids," Pew Research Center Social & Demographic Trends, June 5, 2014; http://www.pewsocialtrends.org/2014/06/05/chapter-1-the-likelihood-of-being-a-stay-at-home-father/.

25　Neurologists have even studied: Eya Abraham et al., "Father's Brain Is Sensitive to Childcare Experiences," *PNAS* 111, no. 27 (July 2014): 9,792–97; http://www.ncbi.nlm.nih.gov/pubmed/24912146.

CHAPTER TWO. THE SECOND CUTTING OF THE CORD (THIS ONE YOU FEEL)

37　One study of new working moms: M. G. Killien, "The Role of Social Support in Facilitating Post-Partum Women's Return to Employment," *Journal of Obstetric, Gynecologic & Neonatal Nursing* 34, no. 5 (September 2005): 639–46; http://www.ncbi.nlm.nih.gov/pubmed/16227520.

CHAPTER THREE. GETTING THROUGH "I HAVE TO QUIT"

56　You may even know that: Kathleen L. McGinn, Mayra Ruiz Castro, and Elizabeth Long Lingo, "Mums the Word! Cross-National Relationship Between Maternal Employment and Gender Inequalities at Work and at Home" (Working Paper No. 15-094, Harvard Business School, June 2015; revised January 2016); http://www.hbs.edu/faculty/Publication%20Files/15-094_fd7498c4-a33c-45f2-9826-35012bcd87b9.pdf.

56　And that working mothers earn: At least married working mothers do. The so-called wage penalty still persists for unmarried mothers. Ipshita Pal and Jane Waldfogel, "The Family Gap in Pay: New Evidence for 1993 to 2013" (CPRC Working Paper No. 15-01, Columbia Population Research Center, Columbia University, January 2015); http://cupop.columbia.edu/publications/2015.

58　Simple but true: Maeve Wallace and Marie-Josèphe Saurel-Cubizolles, "Returning to Work One Year After Childbirth: Data from the Mother-

Child Cohort EDEN," *Maternal and Child Health Journal* 17, no. 8 (October 2013): 1,432–40; http://www.ncbi.nlm.nih.gov/pubmed/23054452.

60   But research has shown: Lisa Parcsi and Michael Curtin, "Experiences of Occupational Therapists Returning to Work After Maternity Leave," *Australian Occupational Therapy Journal* 60, no. 4 (August 2013): 252–59; http://www.ncbi.nlm.nih.gov/pubmed/23888975.

61   Also unsurprising: Bettina S. Weise and Johannes O. Ritter, "Timing Matters: Length of Leave and Working Mothers' Daily Reentry Regrets," *Developmental Psychology* 48, no. 6 (November 2012): 1,797–1,807; http://www.ncbi.nlm.nih.gov/pubmed/22103301.

62   Many companies have: Erich Stutzer, "Family-Friendliness in Business as a Key Issue for the Future," *GMS Gesellschaft für Medizinische Ausbildung* 29, no. 2 (April 2012); http://www.ncbi.nlm.nih.gov/pmc/articles/PMC3339704/figure/F6/.

62   Some motivation for you: C. Engelmann et al., "Career Perspectives of Hospital Health Workers After Maternity and Paternity Leave: Survey and Observational Study in Germany," *Deutsche Medizinische Wochenschrift* 140, no. 4 (February 2015): 28e–35; http://www.ncbi.nlm.nih.gov/pubmed/25686461.

CHAPTER FOUR. ON LOOKING HUMAN AGAIN (A NOBLE GOAL): PART 1

71   The phenomenon has been documented: Pauline Rose Clance and Suzanne Imes, "The Imposter Phenomenon in High Achieving Women: Dynamics and Therapeutic Intervention," *Psychotherapy: Theory, Research and Practice* 15, no. 3 (Fall 1978): 241–47; http://www.paulineroseclance.com/pdf/ip_high_achieving_women.pdf.

72   Recent research shows: Kristin J. Homan and Tracy L. Tylka, "Self-Compassion Moderates Body Comparison and Appearance Self-Worth's Inverse Relationships with Body Appreciation," *Body Image* 15, nos. 1–7 (September 2015); http://www.ncbi.nlm.nih.gov/pubmed/25978272.

74   One depressing survey: "Cetaphil Skin Confidence Report," Cetaphil Singapore website, April 2014; http://cetaphil.com.sg/skin-confidence/.

79   If you gaze in the mirror: Steven H. Dayan et al., "Quantifying the Impact Cosmetic Make-up Has on Age Perception and First Impression Projected," *Journal of Drugs in Dermatology* 14, no. 4 (April 2015): 366–74; http://www.ncbi.nlm.nih.gov/pubmed/25844610.

80   Another study out of Canada: Laura Hurd Clarke and Andrea Bundon, "From 'The Thing to Do' to 'Defying the Ravages of Age': Older Women Reflect on the Use of Lipstick," *Journal of Women & Aging* 21, no. 3 (2009): 198–212; http://www.ncbi.nlm.nih.gov/pubmed/20183145.

82   Instead, let me sum up: Jo-Ellan Dimitrius and Mark Mazzarella, *Put Your Best Foot Forward* (New York: Scribner, 2000); and Chris Serico, "What Does Your Hair Say About You?" Today.com, "Today Style," February 6, 2015; http://www.today.com/style/what-does-your-hair-say-about-you-message-your-style-t1226.

CHAPTER FIVE. ON LOOKING HUMAN AGAIN: PART 2

88   One recent synthesis: Emma L. Hodgkinson, Debbie M. Smith, and Anja Wittkowski, "Women's Experiences of Their Pregnancy and Postpartum Body Image: A Systematic Review and Meta-Synthesis," *BMC Pregnancy & Childbirth* 14, no. 330 (September 2014); http://www.ncbi.nlm.nih.gov/pubmed/25248649.

88   The *Today* show did: Rebecca Dube, "Survey: Do You Love Your Body?" Today.com, "Today Parents," February 6, 2013; http://www.today.com/parents/survey-do-you-love-your-body-1B8252227.

CHAPTER SIX. ON FEELING HUMAN AGAIN

106   The research itself: Pinka Chatterji and Sara Markowitz, "Family Leave After Childbirth and the Mental Health of New Mothers," *The Journal of Mental Health Policy and Economics* 15, no. 2 (June 2012): 61–75; http://www.ncbi.nlm.nih.gov/pubmed/22813939.

106   Another recent study pinpointed: Rada K. Dagher. Patricia M. McGovern, Bryan E. Dowd, "Maternity Leave Duration and Postpartum Mental and Physical Health; Implications for Leave Policies," *Journal of Health Politics, Policy and Law* 39, no. 2 (April 2014): 369–416; http://www.ncbi.nlm.nih.gov/pubmed/24305845.

106   And this is not some fleeting issue: Mauricio Avendano et al., "The Long-Run Effect of Maternity Leave Benefits on Mental Health: Evidence from European Countries," *Social Science & Medicine* 132 (May 2015): 45–53; http://www.ncbi.nlm.nih.gov/pubmed/25792339.

113   As I was editing: Albert L. Siu and the US Preventive Services Task Force, "US Preventive Services Task Force Recommendation Statement: Screening for Depression in Adults," *JAMA* 315, no. 4 (January 2016): 380–87; http://jama.jamanetwork.com/article.aspx?articleid=2484345.

113   And Dr. Davis told me: Anna Abramson and Dawn Rouse, "The Postpartum Brain," *Greater Good,* March 1, 2008.

120   Maternal postpartum sleep: Hawley E. Montgomery-Downs et al., "Normative Longitudinal Maternal Sleep: The First Four Postpartum Months," *American Journal of Obstetrics & Gynecology* 203, no. 5 (November 2010): 465.1e–465.7e. I love the impassioned and convincing argument in the "comments" section of this paper: "Finally, we submit that these data call for us to reconsider the duration of maternal leave policies in the United States where the Department of Labor, Family and Medical Leave Act . . . covers about half of private sector workers. These data suggest that maternal sleep is significantly impaired by sleep fragmentation through at least the third month postpartum. Considering the known impact of sleep disturbance on performance, requiring women to work outside the home and further curtailing their time for sleep may not be in the best interest of the woman, her family, or society." http://www.ncbi.nlm.nih.gov/pubmed/20719289.

120   Troxel has also studied: Wendy M. Troxel et al., *Sleep in the Military: Promoting Healthy Sleep Among U.S. Servicemembers* (Santa Monica, CA: RAND Corporation, 2015); http://www.rand.org/pubs/research_reports/RR739 .html.

121   This one comes straight from a study: Amanda L. McBean and Hawley E. Montgomery-Downs, "What Are Postpartum Women Doing While the Rest of the World Is Asleep?" *Journal of Sleep Research* 24, no. 3 (June 2015): 270–78; http://www.ncbi.nlm.nih.gov/pubmed/25431167.

126   A shocking percentage: Procter & Gamble, *P&G Changing Face of Motherhood Report 2012* (P&G Australia and New Zealand, 2012); https://www .pg.com/en_ANZ/downloads/sponser_of_mums.pdf.

133   The guilt you feel: Leonard Reinecke, Tilo Hartmann, and Allison Eden, "The Guilty Couch Potato: The Role of Ego Depletion in Reducing Recovery Through Media Use," *Journal of Communication* 64, no. 4 (August 2014): 569–89; http://onlinelibrary.wiley.com/doi/10.1111/jcom.12107/ abstract.

CHAPTER SEVEN. PUMPING DOESN'T HAVE TO SUCK

135   These include: lactation rooms: Safina Abdulloeva and Amy A. Eyler, "Policies on Workplace Lactation Support Within States and Organizations," *Journal of Women's Health* 22, no. 9 (September 2013): 769–74; http://www .ncbi.nlm.nih.gov/pubmed/23865789.

135   flexible scheduling, supportive bosses: Maryam Sattari et al., "Workplace Predictors of Duration of Breastfeeding Among Female Physicians," *The Journal of Pediatrics* 136, no. 6 (December 2013): 1,612–17; http://www .ncbi.nlm.nih.gov/pubmed/24011764.

135   and a sensitive work environment: Su-Ying Tsai, "Impact of a Breastfeeding-Friendly Workplace on an Employed Mother's Intention to Continue Breastfeeding After Returning to Work," *Breastfeeding Medicine* 8, no. 2 (April 2013): 210–16; http://www.ncbi.nlm.nih.gov/pubmed/23390987.

135   A supportive spouse or partner: Su-Ying Tsai, "Influence of Partner Support on an Employed Mother's Intention to Breastfeed After Returning to Work," *Breastfeeding Medicine* 9, no. 4 (May 2014); http://www.ncbi.nlm .nih.gov/pubmed/24650363.

144   And indeed a 2013 study: Yeon Bai and Shahla M. Wunderlich, "Lactation Accommodation in the Workplace and Duration of Exclusive Breastfeeding," *Journal of Midwifery & Women's Health* 58, no. 6 (November–December 2013): 690–96; http://www.ncbi.nlm.nih.gov/pubmed/24325729.

144   Workplaces of a certain size: "Fact Sheet #73: Break Time for Nursing Mothers Under the FLSA," United States Department of Labor, Wage and Hour Division, revised August 2013; http://www.dol.gov/whd/regs/ compliance/whdfs73.htm.

149   Technically, federal law: Ibid.

CHAPTER EIGHT. THE EASIEST WAY TO WIN AT REENTRY

159   As I write this: As defined by the Harvard Joint Center for Housing Studies.

159   or Millennials: As defined by the Pew Research Center.

159   and yes, there's some overlap: *The Atlantic* calls Generation Y a "fake, made-up thing." Philip Bump, "Here Is When Each Generation Begins and Ends, According to Facts," *The Atlantic* online, March 25, 2014; http://www.theatlantic.com/national/archive/2014/03/here-is-when-each -generation-begins-and-ends-according-to-facts/359589/.

163   But intra-office peace: "Generations at Work," The Hartford's *2013 Benefits for Tomorrow Study* and *2014 Benefits for Tomorrow Study* (Hartford, CT: Hartford Financial Services Group, Inc.); http://www.thehartford.com/ sites/thehartford/files/generations-at-work.pdf.

171   A study out of the Wake Forest School of Medicine: Joseph G. Grzywacz and Adam B. Butler, "The Impact of Job Characteristics on Work-to-Family Facilitation: Testing a Theory and Distinguishing a Construct," *Journal of Occupational Health Psychology* 10, no. 2 (April 2005): 97–109; http://www.ncbi.nlm.nih.gov/pubmed/15826221.

171   Another, similar study out of Germany: Heike Heidemeier and Bettina S. Weise, "Achievement Goals and Autonomy: How Person-Context Interactions Predict Effective Functioning and Well-Being During a Career Transition," *Journal of Occupational Health Psychology* 19, no. 1 (January 2014): 18–31; http://www.ncbi.nlm.nih.gov/pubmed/24447218.

171   A long, long time ago: Elizabeth Auchincloss, "Conflict Among Psychiatric Residents in Response to Pregnancy," *The American Journal of Psychiatry* 139, no. 6 (June 1982): 818–21; http://www.ncbi.nlm.nih.gov/ pubmed/7081499.

171   It's well known now: "Distribution of Medical School Graduates by Gender: Timeframe: 2015," the Henry J. Kaiser Family Foundation website; http:// kff.org/other/state-indicator/medical-school-graduates-by-gender/#table.

180   The number one workplace issue: "Millennial Mindset: The Hartford's Millennial Parenthood Survey," *The Hartford's 2015 Millennial Parenthood Survey* (Hartford, CT: Hartford Financial Services Group, Inc., 2015); http:// www.thehartford.com/sites/thehartford/files/millennial-parenthood.pdf.

CHAPTER NINE. THAT WHOLE 50/50 PARTNERSHIP THING

195   Plus, doing new things together: Arthur Aron et al., "Couples Shared Participation in Novel and Arousing Activities and Experienced Relationship Quality," *Journal of Personality and Social Psychology* 78, no. 2 (February 2000) 273–84; http://www.ncbi.nlm.nih.gov/pubmed/10707334.

206   Partner support has been shown to extend: Su-Ying Tsai, "Influence of Partner Support on an Employed Mother's Intention to Breastfeed After Returning to Work," *Breastfeeding Medicine* 9, no. 4 (May 2014): 222–30; http://www.ncbi.nlm.nih.gov/pubmed/24650363.

206   A whole slew of: Chih-Yuan S. Lee and William J. Doherty, "Marital Sat-

isfaction and Father Involvement During the Transition to Parenthood," *Fathering* 5, no. 2 (Spring 2007): 75–96; http://mensstudies.info/OJS/index.php/FATHERING/article/viewFile/260/pdf_76.

207   How you feel about yourself: Blair Paley et al., "Adult Attachment Stance and Spouses' Marital Perception During the Transition to Parenthood," *Attachment & Human Development* 4, no. 3 (December 2002); http://www.ncbi.nlm.nih.gov/pubmed/12537850.

211   In Sweden, where fathers: Asa Premberg, Anna-Lena Hellström, and Marie Berg, "Experiences of the First Year as Father," *Scandinavian Journal of Caring Sciences* 22, no. 1 (March 2008): 56–63; http://www.ncbi.nlm.nih.gov/pubmed/18269423.

CHAPTER TEN. WHAT IF YOU'RE YOUR OWN BOSS?

217   Between 1997 and 2015: *The 2015 State of Women-Owned Business Report* (American Express OPEN, 2015); http://www.womenable.com/content/userfiles/Amex_OPEN_State_of_WOBs_2015_Executive_Report_finalsm.pdf.

223   In the U.K.: "Maternity Allowance," Gov.uk website; https://www.gov.uk/maternity-allowance/what-youll-get.

223   a figure that would easily qualify: "Supplemental Nutrition Assistance Program (SNAP)," USDA Food and Nutrition Service website; http://www.fns.usda.gov/snap/eligibility#Income.

223   Even in Sweden: Dominique Anxo and Thomas Ericson, "Self-Employment and Parental Leave," *Small Business Economics* 45, no. 4 (December 2015): 751–70; http://link.springer.com/article/10.1007%2Fs11187-015-9669-6#page-2.

224   The state of California: "Self-Employed," State of California Employment Development Department website; http://www.edd.ca.gov/disability/Self-Employed.htm.

226   Lack of sleep (and dreaming, actually): L. Perogamvros et al., "Sleep and Dreaming Are for Important Matters," *Frontiers in Psychology* 4, no. 474 (July 2013); http://www.ncbi.nlm.nih.gov/pubmed/23898315.

CHAPTER ELEVEN. MASTER YOUR NEW TIME "OFF"

234   My dad's involvement: Linda Nielsen, "How Dads Affect Their Daughters into Adulthood," The Blog of the Institute for Family Studies, June 3, 2014; http://family-studies.org/how-dads-affect-their-daughters-into-adulthood/.

242   A Pew survey found: Kim Parker and Wendy Wang, "Modern Parenthood: Roles of Moms and Dads Converge as They Balance Work and Family," Pew Research Center website, Social and Demographic Trends, March 14, 2013; http://www.pewsocialtrends.org/2013/03/14/modern-parenthood-roles-of-moms-and-dads-converge-as-they-balance-work-and-family/.

246   A recent study of babies' cortisol levels: Lauren E. Philbrook et al., "Mater-

nal Emotional Availability at Bedtime and Infant Cortisol at 1 and 3 months," *Early Human Development* 90, no. 10 (October 2014): 595–605; http://www.ncbi.nlm.nih.gov/pubmed/25128871.

247   Four factors significantly predict: Suniya S. Luthar and Lucia Ciciolla, "Who Mothers Mommy? Factors That Contribute to Mothers' Well-Being," *Developmental Psychology* 51, no. 12 (December 2015): 1,812–23; http://www.ncbi.nlm.nih.gov/pubmed/26501725.

247   Sure, a quality marriage: Mary L. Nolan et al., "Making Friends at Antenatal Classes: A Qualitative Exploration of Friendship Across the Transition to Motherhood," *The Journal of Perinatal Education* 21, no. 3 (Summer 2012); http://www.ncbi.nlm.nih.gov/pubmed/23730129.

CHAPTER TWELVE. EIGHTEEN LIFE-CHANGING CONVERSATIONS

259   A whopping 97 percent: "Millennial Mindset," *The Hartford's 2015 Millennial Parenthood Survey* (Hartford, CT: Hartford Financial Services Group, Inc., 2015); http://www.thehartford.com/sites/thehartford/files/millennial-parenthood.pdf.

266   And here's a big P.S.: Laurel A. McNall, Aline D. Masuda, and Jessica L. Nicklin, "Flexible Work Arrangements, Job Satisfaction, and Turnover Intentions: The Mediating Role of Work-to-Family Enrichment," *The Journal of Psychology* 144, no. 1 (January–February 2010); http://www.ncbi.nlm.nih.gov/pubmed/20092070.

276   Your mother has more: Procter & Gamble, *P&G Changing Face of Motherhood Report 2012* (P&G Australia and New Zealand, 2012); https://www.pg.com/en_ANZ/downloads/sponser_of_mums.pdf.

AUTHOR INTERVIEWS

295   From February 2015 to February 2016: Chelsea Clinton's remarks come from a small roundtable discussion held in June 2016.

Index

ABOUT THE AUTHOR

Lauren Smith Brody is the founder of The Fifth Trimester movement, which helps businesses and new parents work together to create a more family-friendly workplace culture. A longtime leader in the women's magazine industry, Lauren was most recently the executive editor of *Glamour* magazine. Raised in Ohio, Texas, and Georgia, she now lives in New York City with her husband and two young sons.